I0896456

How Old Is the Hebrew Bible?

THE ANCHOR YALE BIBLE REFERENCE LIBRARY is a project of international and interfaith scope in which Protestant, Catholic, and Jewish scholars from many countries contribute individual volumes. The project is not sponsored by any ecclesiastical organization and is not intended to reflect any particular theological doctrine.

The series is committed to producing volumes in the tradition established half a century ago by the founders of the Anchor Bible, William Foxwell Albright and David Noel Freedman. It aims to present the best contemporary scholarship in a way that is accessible not only to scholars but also to the educated nonspecialist. It is committed to work of sound philological and historical scholarship, supplemented by insight from modern methods, such as sociological and literary criticism.

John J. Collins
General Editor

THE ANCHOR YALE BIBLE REFERENCE LIBRARY

How Old Is the Hebrew Bible?

A Linguistic, Textual, and Historical Study

RONALD HENDEL AND JAN JOOSTEN

YALE AYBRL

Yale UNIVERSITY PRESS

NEW HAVEN AND LONDON

"Anchor Yale Bible" and the Anchor Yale logo are registered trademarks of Yale University.

Copyright © 2018 by Yale University. All rights reserved. This book may not be reproduced, in whole or in part, including illustrations, in any form (beyond that copying permitted by Sections 107 and 108 of the U.S. Copyright Law and except by reviewers for the public press), without written permission from the publishers.

Yale University Press books may be purchased in quantity for educational, business, or promotional use. For information, please e-mail sales.press@yale.edu (U.S. office) or sales@yaleup.co.uk (U.K. office).

Set in Adobe Caslon type by Newgen.
Printed in the United States of America.

Library of Congress Control Number: 2018945720
ISBN 978-0-300-23488-6 (hardcover : alk. paper)

A catalogue record for this book is available from the British Library.

This paper meets the requirements of ANSI/NISO Z39.48-1992 (Permanence of Paper).

In memory of our friends and colleagues
Zipora and David Talshir

הַנֶּאֱהָבִים וְהַנְּעִימִם בְּחַיֵּיהֶם וּבְמוֹתָם לֹא נִפְרָדוּ

Disputes in religion depend on nothing except ignorance of grammar.

Non aliunde dissidia in religione pendent, quam ab ignoratione grammaticae.

—J. J. Scaliger

Contents

Preface
Or, Why Did We Write This Book?

The age of the Hebrew Bible is difficult to determine. It is a brittle text, fracturing under the slightest pressure. Any biblical book may turn out to contain strata and fragments composed at wholly different periods. Many books are projected into a distant past, written down on the basis of oral traditions and cultural memory that may span centuries, but the details about the events and characters reveal little about the age of the written account. The history of ideas (e.g., monotheism), institutions (e.g., the monarchy, sacrifice, festivals), or hidden power struggles (e.g., priestly rivalries or anti-Samaritan polemics) might give useful hints, if it weren't for the fact that most of these extratextual realities are known exclusively from the text that situates them in time. Even a relative dating based on the use of one text in another, or the response of one passage to an earlier one, is hard to achieve in the absence of clear criteria that help to decide in which direction the textual contact runs. Is Ezekiel the "father of the P source"? Or is he a priest indebted to priestly traditions of the type written down in the Pentateuch? Such debates may be interminable.

Many scholars argue that we should drop the whole issue and concentrate only on the final form of the text or its reception. Isn't the life of the Bible independent of its time of composition? Perhaps in many respects it is. But it is also shaped by its history, even as it shapes later history. Its central narrative relates to tribal, national, and cultural history from end to end. Its historylike narrative is neither a parable nor an atemporal myth. If we could only place it in its historical context, even approximately, we would understand its nuanced meanings better. But this means taking on the challenge of dating the texts.

In many cases the best evidence—sometimes, though not always, the only evidence—is language. Language evolves. Its sounds, semantics, and syntax change through time. This makes it possible, in theory, to determine, more or less, a chronology for individual writings. Dating texts by their language is a well-established practice in biblical studies as in many other fields. The procedures involved are complicated, and the results not always as precise as one could wish. There is leeway for discussion and debate. Yet, contrary to recent claims, dating Hebrew texts on the basis of their language is not impossible.

It is the conjunction of these two circumstances—the difficulty in dating biblical texts, and the opportunity granted by recent work in historical linguistics—that instilled in us the desire to write this book. Linguistic dating is not a new approach. Much of the historical-critical method as it developed in the nineteenth century is based on it, at least in part. But in recent times, as a result of the ever-growing necessity to specialize, the approach has fallen into disuse among biblical scholars, allowing it to be caricatured and prematurely rejected. The idea of this book is to reinscribe historical research on the Hebrew language where it belongs: at the heart of biblical studies. We aim to gather the fruits of recent research on Biblical Hebrew and to present them to the student and scholar in an accessible way. The book blends the functions of introduction, synthesis, and scholarly dialogue. We hope that it will instruct and inspire others to engage with this field of research.

It has been a rare pleasure to cowrite this book. We have discovered that two minds are better than one, especially when they are passionate about a common subject. The whole and the parts were jointly conceived, but each chapter has a primary author. Chapters 1, 2, 8, and appendix 2 are primarily Hendel's handiwork, and chapters 3–7 and appendix 1 are primarily Joosten's. Each of us reviewed and revised the other's contributions, so that we are both responsible for the whole.

It has also been a delight to pursue this project with visits on both sides of the pond, including memorable workshops at the University of California, Berkeley, and the Université de Strasbourg. We thank the France-Berkeley Fund for making this intercultural project possible. Our thanks also to many colleagues who participated in the workshops or otherwise helped us along the way: Steve Fassberg, Randy Garr, Noam Mizrahi, Na'ama Pat-El, Matthieu Richelle, Konrad Schmid, and Bill Schniedewind. We are grateful to the University of Oxford for providing a grant to cover the indexing, and to Vladimir Olivero for creating the indexes. Jodi

Beder deftly improved our prose. Finally, our thanks to each other's families for sharing meals, hikes, and guitar playing.

We know that agreement about basic issues is elusive in the current situation of biblical scholarship. Our goal is to think clearly about some complicated matters and to contribute to a multilayered understanding of the biblical text. We invite our readers—and our critics—to consider patiently the merits of our explanatory model, its consilience, simplicity, and scope.

Abbreviations

AB	Anchor Bible
ABH	Archaic Biblical Hebrew
ABRL	Anchor Bible Reference Library
AIL	Ancient Israel and Its Literature
AJSL	*American Journal of Semitic Languages and Literatures*
ANEM	Ancient Near East Monographs
AOAT	Alter Orient und Altes Testament
AOS	American Oriental Series
BA	*Biblical Archaeologist*
BASOR	*Bulletin of the American Schools of Oriental Research*
BDB	Brown, Francis, S. R. Driver, and Charles A. Briggs, *A Hebrew and English Lexicon of the Old Testament*
BETL	Bibliotheca Ephemeridum Theologicarum Lovaniensium
BHQ	Biblia Hebraica Quinta
Bib	*Biblica*
BN	*Biblische Notizen*
BO	*Bibliotheca Orientalis*
BZABR	Beihefte zur Zeitschrift für altorientalische und biblische Rechtsgeschichte
BZAW	Beihefte zur Zeitschrift für die alttestamentliche Wissenschaft
CAD	*The Assyrian Dictionary of the Oriental Institute of the University of Chicago.* Chicago: The Oriental Institute of the University of Chicago, 1956–2006.

CahRB	Cahiers de la Revue biblique
CBH	Classical Biblical Hebrew
CBQ	*Catholic Biblical Quarterly*
DDD	*Dictionary of Deities and Demons in the Bible.* Edited by Karel van der Toorn, Bob Becking, and Pieter W. van der Horst. Leiden: Brill 1995. 2nd ed. Grand Rapids, MI: Eerdmans, 1999.
DSD	*Dead Sea Discoveries*
ErIsr	*Eretz Israel*
FAT	Forschungen zum Alten Testament
FRLANT	Forschungen zur Religion und Literatur des Alten und Neuen Testaments
HALOT	*The Hebrew and Aramaic Lexicon of the Old Testament.* Ludwig Koehler, Walter Baumgartner, and Johann J. Stamm. Translated and edited under the supervision of Mervyn E. J. Richardson. 4 vols. Leiden: Brill, 1994–1999.
HdO	Handbuch der Orientalistik
HeBAI	*Hebrew Bible and Ancient Israel*
HS	*Hebrew Studies*
HSM	Harvard Semitic Monographs
HSS	Harvard Semitic Studies
HTR	*Harvard Theological Review*
IBHS	*An Introduction to Biblical Hebrew Syntax.* Bruce K. Waltke and Michael O'Connor. Winona Lake, IN: Eisenbrauns, 1990.
ICC	International Critical Commentary
IEJ	*Israel Exploration Journal*
IOS	Israel Oriental Studies
JANESCU	*Journal of the Ancient Near Eastern Society of Columbia University*
JAOS	*Journal of the American Oriental Society*
JBL	*Journal of Biblical Literature*
JBS	Jerusalem Biblical Studies
JCS	*Journal of Cuneiform Studies*

JHS	*Journal of Hebrew Scriptures*
JNES	*Journal of Near Eastern Studies*
JNSL	*Journal of Northwest Semitic Languages*
JQR	*Jewish Quarterly Review*
JSem	*Journal of Semitics*
JSJ	*Journal for the Study of Judaism in the Persian, Hellenistic, and Roman Periods*
JSNTSup	Journal for the Study of the New Testament Supplement Series
JSOT	*Journal for the Study of the Old Testament*
JSOTSup	Journal for the Study of the Old Testament Supplement Series
JSS	*Journal of Semitic Studies*
LBH	Late Biblical Hebrew
LHBOTS	The Library of Hebrew Bible/Old Testament Studies
NABU	*Nouvelles assyriologiques brèves et utilitaires*
OBO	Orbis Biblicus et Orientalis
Orient	*Orient: Report of the Society for Near Eastern Studies in Japan*
OTL	Old Testament Library
OtSt	*Oudtestamentische Studiën*
PLO	Porta Linguarum Orientalium
RB	*Revue biblique*
RBL	*Review of Biblical Literature*
RBS	Resources for Biblical Study
RevQ	*Revue de Qumran*
SBS	Stuttgarter Bibelstudien
SCS	Septuagint and Cognate Studies
SJOT	*Scandinavian Journal of the Old Testament*
SSLL	Studies in Semitic Languages and Linguistics
STDJ	Studies on the Texts of the Desert of Judah
TA	*Tel Aviv*
TBH	Transitional Biblical Hebrew

TCS	Text-Critical Studies
TLOT	*Theological Lexicon of the Old Testament*. Edited by Ernst Jenni, with assistance from Claus Westermann. Translated by Mark E. Biddle. 3 vols. Peabody, MA: Hendrickson, 1997.
TZ	*Theologische Zeitschrift*
VT	*Vetus Testamentum*
VTSup	Supplements to Vetus Testamentum
ZAH	*Zeitschrift für Althebraistik*
ZAW	*Zeitschrift für die alttestamentliche Wissenschaft*
ZDMG	*Zeitschrift der deutschen morgenländischen Gesellschaft*

How Old Is the Hebrew Bible?

1 All Things Change: Language and Method

The saying "everything flows" (πάντα ῥεῖ) is attributed to the Greek philosopher Heraclitus. His example is a flowing stream: "You cannot step into the same river twice" (δὶς ἐς τὸν αὐτὸν ποταμὸν οὐκ ἂν ἐμβαίης).[1] This claim may seem paradoxical: of course one can step into the same river twice. But it is never the same river, and it is never even the same foot. Their constituent matter—the watery and footy stuff—constantly changes. They seem to be stable over time, but they are really a chronological progression of physical states.

Languages and texts change too. Languages change over time and across speech communities. Texts change because scribes (and, more recently, typesetters) make mistakes and revisions. Biblical Hebrew and the Hebrew Bible look like stable entities, but they are not. Like rivers, they flow, but rather more slowly, over time. In this book, we elucidate some of the features of linguistic and textual change that allow us to discern different temporal states of the Hebrew Bible. This is a type of historical inquiry that has occasioned controversy and skepticism in recent years. Our aim is to show how this field of knowledge, when pursued with methodological rigor, is viable and illuminating. It allows us, within limits, to discern the ages of biblical literature.

Preliminary Sample: 2 Samuel 3:2–5

We begin with an example of the Hebrew Bible saying the same thing twice. A list of David's sons born at Hebron is presented in 2 Sam 3:2–5 and is slightly revised in 1 Chr 3:1–4. The Samuel passage exists in different forms in MT and 4QSam^{a}. In the versions of the genealogical list in Samuel (MT and 4Q) and Chronicles (MT), we can detect several temporal states of the language and text:

> 2 Sam 3:2 (MT)
> וַיִּוָּלְדוּ (*ketiv*: וילדו) לְדָוִד בָּנִים בְּחֶבְרוֹן
> And sons were born to David in Hebron.

This passage has a *ketiv-qere* variation in the first word: it is written וילדו but is read וַיִּוָּלְדוּ. The *qere* (written in the margin) has an extra letter, *waw*, that is not in the *ketiv*. This variation in consonants and vowels is the result of a linguistic change from the passive *qal* to the *niphal*. (The passive *qal*—in proto-Hebrew, **qutal*, **yuqtal*—was discovered by medieval Jewish grammarians and rediscovered by modern scholars.)[2] The consonants וילדו reflect the form **wayyul(ə)dū*, a converted imperfect *qal* passive of the root *yld*, "to be born." When the passive *qal* stem of this root became obsolete, the form was reinterpreted as a *niphal*, which had replaced the grammatical function of the passive *qal*. It was reanalyzed as **wayyiwwālədu*. The addition of the *waw* is necessary for the *niphal* form. The *qere* form is therefore a linguistic updating of an old, defunct verbal form.

Our identification of the form וילדו as originally a passive *qal* is confirmed by the repetition of this verb in the list's conclusion:

> 2 Sam 3:5 (MT)
> אֵלֶּה יֻלְּדוּ לְדָוִד בְּחֶבְרוֹן
> These were born to David in Hebron.

The perfect יֻלְּדוּ ("they were born") is vocalized as a *pual*. It is semantically equivalent to וילדו at the head of the list (2 Sam 3:2), where, as we have seen, it is vocalized as a *niphal*. But there are no verbs in Hebrew that are *niphal* in the imperfect and *pual* in the perfect. The perfect has been vocalized as a *pual* because it is impossible to vocalize it as a *niphal*, which would require an initial *nun*. The original passive *qal* vocalization of this form was probably **yul(ə)dû*, which was easily revocalized as a *pual*, *yull*^{e}*dû*. But there is a problem with the reanalysis of this form as a *pual*. The *piel* of the root *yld* means "to midwife," and the *pual* should therefore mean something like "to be midwifed." However, the verb here clearly has the *qal* meaning, "to be born."

H. L. Ginsberg described these revocalized passive *qal* forms as "Masoretically misconstrued" forms.[3] Strictly speaking, their vocalization is misconstrued. But more important for our purposes, they illustrate how the Hebrew language changed and how texts were modified to accommodate linguistic change. The MT of 2 Sam 3:3–5 embodies two different states of the language. The text was composed when the passive *qal* was a living form. The vocalization and variant spelling reflect a later period, when the passive *qal* was obsolete and had been replaced by the *niphal*, and the old form was sometimes reanalyzed as *pual*. We can identify two distinct language-states in this text, one overlaid on the other.

The Qumran text of this Samuel passage reflects the revised—and chronologically later—language-state:

> 2 Sam 3:2 (4QSam[a])
> ויולד לדויד בנים בחברון
> And sons were born to David in Hebron.

The form ויולד differs from the MT reading in two ways. It is singular rather than plural, which reflects the impersonal construction, וַיִּוָּלֶד־לוֹ ("and [sons] were born to him"). This variant of grammatical number (singular versus plural) is uninteresting for our purpose. More important, it has a *waw* as the third letter, as in the *qere* of MT. 4QSam[a] has the revised reading, with the verb construed as a *niphal*, indicated by this *waw*.[4] The writing of the form as a *niphal* reflects the state of the language after the demise of the passive *qal*.

The 4QSam[a] text has a second variant with diachronic implications: the spelling of "David." The short spelling דוד (see the MT passage) has been expanded to דויד. This is not a grammatical change but is purely graphemic. We know from Northwest Semitic inscriptions that the spelling of David without the internal *yod* is the older spelling: the ninth-century Aramaic inscription from Tel Dan writes "house of David" as ביתדוד. (the construct phrase lacks a word divider, as is often the case in inscriptions).[5] The same spelling of this phrase is probably found (partially restored: בת[ד]וד) in the Moabite Mesha stele, also from the ninth century.[6] The longer spelling, with the medial *yod* as an internal *mater lectionis*, is characteristic of later spelling practices, as reflected in Second Temple–period texts and inscriptions. The full spelling, דויד, is the predominant form in Chronicles, Ezra, Nehemiah, and other clearly Persian-period books. In both of these features—the defunct passive *qal* revised as a *niphal* and the long spelling of "David"—the 4QSam[a] passage shows how the language and text change over time.

The rewriting of the Samuel passage in Chronicles reflects the same language-state that we see in 4QSam[a]:

> 1 Chr 3:1 (MT)
> וְאֵלֶּה הָיוּ בְּנֵי דָוִיד אֲשֶׁר נוֹלַד־לוֹ בְּחֶבְרוֹן
> And these were the sons of David that were born to him in Hebron.

The Chronicler has replaced the old passive *qal* with a *niphal* perfect, נולד. There is no ambiguity about this form. The initial *nun* means that it is *niphal*, with no lingering trace of the passive *qal*. The word has been updated to the current state of the language. "David" is written in the long form, דויד, reflecting current spelling practice. The Chronicler's text is a window onto a state of the language that is later than the earliest stratum of the Samuel text in the MT *ketiv*. It updates the text to the contemporary language-state in the Persian period. The variants in the MT *qere*, 4QSam[a], and MT Chronicles independently attest this later language-state.

By a close examination of this brief passage, we can confirm that Heraclitus's adage applies to the language and text of the Hebrew Bible. They changed over time. The challenge is to ascertain what the changes are and how best to order them in a relative or absolute chronology. This is not a simple task, but it is a valuable one if we wish to learn something about the history of the biblical writings. There are scholars who contend that this task is impossible, for reasons that we address below. We hold that the task is both valuable and to a considerable degree achievable, as this example illustrates.

There remain, however, many gaps in our evidence and our knowledge. We have no native speakers or informants, only texts, which have their own scribal vicissitudes, as we can see in the relationship between MT and 4QSam[a] in this passage. To gain cogent and warranted knowledge, we must pay close attention to all the data that we have and not restrict our attention to MT. Because we are examining the succession of language-states, we must address every available body of textual data. This includes all the ancient versions of the Hebrew Bible, such as MT, the Qumran texts, the Samaritan Pentateuch, and the Septuagint, as well as epigraphic texts.

Having considered a sample of how Biblical Hebrew changed over time, let us consider the substantial resistance to historical linguistic inquiry in contemporary biblical scholarship. Then, in chapter 2, we turn to a fuller description of how Biblical Hebrew changed, focusing on the types and causes of linguistic change. This general outline will be elaborated and made more fine-grained in the chapters that follow.

Linguistic Change and Historical Method

The question we pose in this book is whether the historical linguistics of Biblical Hebrew is useful in determining the age of the biblical writings. Perhaps surprisingly, many scholars hold that it is not. A number of learned works on the literary history of the Hebrew Bible have appeared in recent years, but most ignore or dismiss the relevance of linguistic inquiry. These include the following scholarly syntheses, which are at the forefront of American and European scholarship: Joel Baden, *The Composition of the Pentateuch*; David Carr, *The Formation of the Hebrew Bible*; Reinhard Kratz, *The Composition of the Narrative Books of the Old Testament*; and Konrad Schmid, *The Old Testament: A Literary History*.[7] The only recent exception to this tendency is from Israeli scholarship: Alexander Rofé, in *Introduction to the Literature of the Hebrew Bible*, treats seriously the linguistic evidence.[8] What accounts for this lacuna in American and European scholarship?

We think the problem is twofold. The first is institutional. The historical linguistics of Biblical Hebrew is not taught in most graduate programs. This is an understandable result of the increased amount of both material and methods in the field, which forces scholars to specialize either in biblical exegesis or in Hebrew language. There is a substantial body of scholarship about Hebrew that is, as a consequence, inaccessible to most biblical scholars. One of the reasons we wrote this book is to bridge this gap.

The second problem has to do with critical method. This problem surfaces frequently in recent discussions of linguistic dating. Many studies have a standard of evidence and argument for linguistic matters that can be described as naïve positivism. According to the standard, any analysis that is not objectively proven true is excluded as subjective and unprovable. If a particular descriptive model has details that are susceptible to doubt, or if any of the data on which it is based can be accounted for by other possible means, then the whole model can be dismissed as mere guesswork. Anything less than certainty—including a lack of scholarly consensus—is taken to entail a lack of knowledge.

This standard of objectivity for linguistic arguments tends to make biblical scholars overly skeptical of well-warranted historical models for the linguistic history of Biblical Hebrew. This resistance to linguistic scholarship yields a deeply flawed approach to the history of biblical literature.

Let us consider the rationale given by one of the books mentioned earlier—David Carr's *Formation of the Hebrew Bible*—for setting aside the evidence of language in his inquiry. We cite Carr at length because unlike other scholars, he addresses this issue directly, and because his position is well informed. He writes:

> The language of biblical books is a much less stable and objective criterion for dating than it might first appear. To be sure, it is almost certainly not a coincidence that the biblical books most clearly datable to the fourth century or later (Daniel, Esther, Ezra-Nehemiah, 1–2 Chronicles) also feature an unusually large number of Persianisms, a concentration of Aramaisms (including loci where they cannot be explained as a literary trope), and other features characteristic of late biblical Hebrew. Moreover, it seems clear that the ability to write flawless (or virtually flawless) classical biblical Hebrew, though persisting in some quarters into the early Persian period (e.g., Haggai and Zechariah), became extremely rare in the Second Temple period.... Nevertheless ... [s]uch features in late biblical texts could be but late literary attestations of much earlier colloquial/dialectal Hebrew features, and their presence in the text in question also could be explained by the fluid transmission of a given text, especially if it is a relatively marginal text in the Hebrew corpus.... Given the fluid character of scribal transmission and the ways in which literary language was interpenetrated by various dialects of Hebrew across the stretch of Judean and Israelite history, linguistic features are only an approximate and precarious tool in the historical placement of Hebrew texts.[9]

Let us consider the steps of Carr's argument. He begins by granting that the most clearly datable late biblical books (Daniel, Esther, Ezra-Nehemiah, 1–2 Chronicles) have abundant features of LBH. He says that this correlation between linguistic features and other historical criteria, such as explicit references to the Persian Empire, is "almost certainly not a coincidence." But because other explanations are possible, he moves toward the conclusion that it still might be a coincidence.

The other possibilities are "much earlier colloquial/dialectal Hebrew features" that have been misconstrued by scholars as LBH features, and "the fluid transmission of a given text," which could have introduced LBH features. In other words, the features may not be late but dialectal, or they may be late but secondary scribal revisions. Carr does not consider whether one of these possibilities is more probable than the others in any instance, or whether one should even try to sort them out. It is sufficient to note that various possible explanations are thinkable to dispense with the study of linguistic history for the historical dating of biblical texts.

Notice the evaluative standards in this argument: because language is not "stable and objective," linguistic analysis is "an approximate and precarious tool." If a particular detail "could be explained" by other possibilities, such as local dialects or textual fluidity, then linguistic inquiry is moot. The "other possibilities" argument allows him to set aside evidence of language in toto. In the steps of his argument, Carr does not need to argue that any particular analysis of the linguistic data is wrong, only that it is not absolutely certain.

After dismissing the cogency of historical linguistic inquiry, Carr proceeds to his historical placement of biblical texts on other grounds, primarily the history of ideas and the associative links among texts. He dates most biblical texts to the exilic, Persian, and Hellenistic periods, with some having roots in the Neo-Assyrian period. There are some surprising exceptions. He argues that the Song of Songs may—in agreement with its superscription—be Solomonic. Following arguments advanced by Ian Young, he maintains that the possibilities of dialect and textual variation mean that "the linguistic profile of the Songs of Songs does not provide clear grounds for dating, either early or late."[10] The absence of "clear grounds" from language leads him to turn to what Benjamin Sommer calls "pseudohistoricist" criteria.[11] Carr argues that some passages in Hosea, Isaiah, and Proverbs are dependent on Song of Songs (rather than the reverse, or general dependence on tropes of the international genre of love poetry), and that the reference to Tirzah (6:4) was written when this city was the capital of the Northern Kingdom (rather than having been chosen by a later poet for its literary resonance because it means "pleasure, beauty"). As a consequence of these and other judgments, he argues for "a dating of some of its parts in or close to the tenth century."[12] This despite the density of the book's LBH features, which are uniformly distributed throughout the book, including Persian loanwords, Aramaisms, and late syntax.[13] The distinctive LBH profile of the book has no purchase in this approach.

The problems with the dismissal of the evidence of language are multiple. First, although textual change and dialect variation are important factors in the study of Biblical Hebrew (see chapters 3–4), they are not plausible causes for most or all instances of linguistic change. On the contrary, textual variation provides primary evidence for the linguistic history of Biblical Hebrew, as we have shown above in the example of 2 Sam 3:2–5. Textual variation is not an "other possibility" but is part of the historical record that requires explanation in the first place. Moreover, the appeal to textual fluidity is overstated. If textual transmission were completely fluid, then we would find no statistical differences among the texts: the features of Classical Biblical Hebrew (CBH), Transitional Biblical Hebrew (TBH), and Late Biblical Hebrew (LBH) features would be uniformly spread. But, as Carr grants for the clearly late books, this is not the case. There is clumping, density of distribution. Hence, when scholars claim that textual variation or dialects render historical linguistics fruitless, they are indulging in a logical and historical non sequitur. Textual variation and dialects include or entail linguistic change; they do not exclude it or render moot our ability to discern it.

Second, the possibility of other explanations does not eliminate the value of the most likely explanation.[14] The standard of objective certainty is not available in historical scholarship. We are dealing with the past, which can only be inferred, not directly known. The data with which we operate are necessarily incomplete, because most of the past has not been preserved. We are dealing with the traces of the past, not the past itself. As a result of the limits of historical evidence and inference, there is always a residue of uncertainty in any historical explanation. This is the condition of all historical scholarship.

The most likely explanation, one that is analytically warranted, is the best that we can achieve. We carefully study the evidence and try to make sense of the past. Certainty is not a relevant criterion, nor is the possibility of other explanations. Because our theories are always underdetermined by the data, and the data are incomplete, there is always the possibility of other explanations. Our task is to evaluate the possible explanations and determine which is the most probable.

The key methodological point is that historical knowledge is not objective but probabilistic. As Marc Bloch emphasized in his reflections on historical method, "the majority of the problems of historical criticism are really problems of probability."[15] Our task is to weigh probabilities and to determine which of the imagined possibilities is the most probable, the one most warranted by the (incomplete) data. Certainty and objectivity are false idols in historical criticism. Bloch's argument is worth quoting, as it addresses some of the recent objections to the use of linguistic evidence in Hebrew Bible scholarship (although he is referring to Latin texts):

> To what extent . . . are we justified in mouthing this glorious word "certainty"? . . . It is only for the sake of simplification that we sometimes speak

> of evidence rather than of probabilities. . . . It is not "impossible," in the absolute sense of the term, that the *Donation of Constantine* is authentic, or—according to the whim of some scholars—that the *Germania* of Tacitus is a forgery. Nor is it, in the same sense, "impossible" that a monkey might accidentally reconstruct either the *Donation* or the *Germania*, letter for letter, simply by striking the keys of a typewriter at random. . . . So far as it finds certainty only by estimating the probable and the improbable, historical criticism is like most other sciences of reality, except that it undoubtedly deals with a more subtle gradation of degrees.[16]

As Bloch observes, there are always other possible explanations. It is possible that any given document is a forgery, or authentic, or typed by monkeys. It is possible, as Carr maintains, that some or all of the Song of Songs was written in the tenth century BCE, perhaps by Solomon.[17] It is also possible, as the Copenhagen school maintains, that the Hebrew Bible was wholly written during the Hellenistic or Roman era.[18] But some of the possible explanations are more probable than the others. It is the task of the historian to discriminate among all the possibilities and to weigh carefully the "subtle gradation of degrees" of probability. A metaphysical certainty is beyond our means. In sum, the "other possibilities" argument and the standard of objective certainty are incommensurate with the procedures of historical research. The most probable approximations of the past are the best we can achieve, whether in historical linguistics, literary history, or other forms of historical inquiry. To expect more is to misconstrue the task.

A corollary to the "other possibilities" argument is the oft-heard objection that historical linguistic inquiry into Biblical Hebrew is "circular."[19] Like the other objections, this criticism is valid but misplaced. As philosophers tell us, all historical reasoning is circular, because we always start with entrenched rules and inferences, and we investigate the material traces of the past on the basis of those premises, which we then revise to accord with the evidence. In historical scholarship, we revise our inferences to fit the accepted rules, and we revise the rules to obtain reasonable inferences. As the philosopher Nelson Goodman observes: "This looks flagrantly circular. . . . But this circle is a virtuous one. The point is that rules and particular inferences alike are justified by being brought into agreement with each other. . . . The process of justification is the delicate one of making mutual adjustments between rules and accepted inferences; and in the agreement achieved lies the only justification needed for either."[20] This may seem paradoxical, but it is an apt analysis of how historical scholarship—and all inferential reasoning—works. It is important to recognize the scope and the limitations of historical scholarship, and to proceed with awareness of the nature of the task. As the textual critic A. E. Housman aptly cautioned, "We are thus working in a circle, that is a fact which there is no denying; but . . . the task of the critic is just this, to tread that circle deftly and warily."[21] Objectivity is not at hand; we must simply do the best we can, with circumspection and methodological tact.

Let us return to our initial question: is the evidence of language relevant for the study of the literary history of the Hebrew Bible? Since the Hebrew Bible consists solely of linguistic discourse, it would seem that the answer should be yes. To the extent that we can formulate well-warranted explanations of language change, these are clearly relevant for investigating the relative or absolute dates of biblical literature. There are many complications involved and many areas of expertise that are pertinent. Historical scholarship is a multifaceted task. It is not objective but inferential and probabilistic. It is always incomplete and corrigible. It involves conjecture, false leads, and contestable judgments.

Despite these limitations, the study of language is a necessary partner for the literary history of the Hebrew Bible. Its linguistic discourses contain evidence of their time of composition. As Bloch observes, "The style of Pascal belongs to him alone; but his grammar and the stock of his vocabulary belongs to his time."[22] The grammar and vocabulary of a work—even if complicated by the swerves of scribal transmission—are clues to its historical location.

Our study of these issues follows in the wake of many others. The first step was taken by the Dutch scholar Hugo Grotius, who in 1644 argued on linguistic grounds that Solomon could not have been the author of Ecclesiastes: "My proof of this is the many words which cannot be found anywhere else than in Daniel, Ezra, and the Aramaic translations."[23] This analysis has stood the test of time. The major breakthrough was Wilhelm Gesenius's *Geschichte der hebräischen Sprache und Schrift* (1815), in which he rightly states that "all known Near Eastern languages, which we can observe over a period of a thousand years, have undergone very obvious changes during that period."[24] Many scholars have made contributions to this field in the two centuries since.[25] In the next chapter we begin to chart the "very obvious changes" that span roughly a thousand years of Biblical Hebrew.

2 Kinds and Causes of Linguistic Change

All languages change over time. This is a curious fact, which anyone who has read old books knows to be true. For instance, when Shakespeare's Hamlet says, "When he himself might his quietus make / With a bare bodkin? Who would fardels bear . . . ?" we have no idea what he means. The words "quietus," "bodkin," and "fardel" have fallen out of English usage, and their meanings ("death," "dagger," and "burden") are obscure to us. When Ophelia replies, "How does your honor for this many a day?" we understand the words but not the idiom ("How have you been lately?"), which means we do not understand. Similarly, as we will see in chapter 7, there is evidence that well-educated Hebrew speakers in the fourth century BCE and later did not correctly understand some of the words and idioms in the Hebrew Bible. Many old words and constructions had dropped out of circulation or changed their meaning. Misunderstanding past states of the language is a perennial problem for speakers of any language. We might call it Heraclitus's curse.

Languages change for many reasons. As Lyle Campbell observes, a broad explanation "must include internal factors, external factors, the structure of the language as a whole and how different parts of the language interact with one another, the communicative and social functions of the language, the role of the individual, the role of society/the speech community, and more—that is, the complex interaction and competition among a large number of factors."[1] Among these many factors, we can point to two root causes, one having to do with linguistic competence and the other with linguistic performance: We learn language imperfectly, and our utterances are often ambiguous. These are mutually interacting conditions of language change. Let us explore these conditions further.

Each of us internalizes grammar slightly differently—we each speak our own idiolect, which creates the potential for creative misunderstanding. Mark Hale states this principle clearly: "Change takes place when the learner constructs a grammar that differs in some way from the input grammar(s) to which the learner is exposed."[2] Because our language acquisition skills are not perfect—although they are pretty good—there is always a gap between input and output. Because we can hear and understand differently, we are always producing new constructions of speech and grammar. We simplify forms and change them by analogy with other forms, and we create new forms and extend the meanings of old ones.

The potential ambiguity of utterances is a catalyst in this dialectic of change. Because some degree of ambiguity is always present in linguistic communication, there is a possibility that a speaker will misunderstand—or reanalyze—words and constructions. As Campbell observes, "Reanalysis depends on the possibility of more than one analysis of a given construction."[3] From the perspective of normative grammar, a reanalysis is always a misanalysis. But when, for sociolinguistic reasons, such changes are widely adopted, they become the new normal, and they supplement or displace the previous features.

A frequent type of reanalysis is the simplification of forms and structures. Simplification involves the reduction of nonessential contrasts. A modern example is the simplified spelling and grammar that proliferate on electronic media. Simplified speech takes fewer keystrokes. The same tendency to simplify occurs in spoken language. We will consider several examples of simplification of forms and constructions in Biblical Hebrew.

A countervailing tendency to the reduction of contrasts is the addition of new contrasts to increase expressivity. Sometimes these complications are therapeutic, curing problems caused by previous simplifications.[4] An example noted in chapter 1 is the graphic innovation of internal vowel letters (*matres lectionis*) to disambiguate the pronunciation of words (דוד → דויד, "David"). This graphic therapy partially cures the ambiguity of a consonantal alphabet. Simplification in one linguistic subsystem often triggers a compensatory complication in another subsystem. We will address later in this chapter several examples of complication or supplementation with the aim to increase expressivity.

An external cause of linguistic change is language contact (which we address more fully later). Speakers who are competent or fluent in more than one language transfer features of one to the other. Bilingualism and multilingualism trigger the reanalysis of native forms on the basis of similar features in the contact language. As we will see, loanwords and reanalysis of native forms are frequent consequences of language contact. This external mechanism of change, which reflects historical interactions with other language communities, has obvious implications for the history of a language. Familiar examples include the influx of French vocabulary into English after the Norman conquest, and the influx of American vocabulary into languages around the world today.

Because of these and other causes and mechanisms of change, language is incessantly in motion. Every language-state has old forms that are dying out and new forms that are taking root. Each synchronic state is a transitional slice in a sequence of diachronic change. This is simply to say that our grandparents speak a slightly different language from the one that we do, and our grandchildren will speak a slightly different language. The same conditions obtained for ancient Hebrew, including its spoken and literary forms. Change is a constant, although the pace of change is slower on the cultural periphery and in formal genres of speech and writing.

In this chapter, we address the kinds and mechanisms of language change during the history of Biblical Hebrew.[5] We address three major categories: phonological change, lexical and morphosyntactic change, and change due to language contact. All our examples involve diachronic change and have clear implications for the history of Biblical Hebrew. This map of the kinds and causes of change, though far from exhaustive, provides a panorama of the varieties of change during the biblical period. It is the broad backdrop against which we view linguistic changes in the following chapters.

Phonological Change

Sound change is a constant in language. The articulation of speech changes across dialects and over time. Sound changes radiate from one group to another in waves, which spread unevenly and may never reach the periphery. This is why the English spoken in rural Appalachia is closer in some features to Shakespeare's English than is the speech of modern Londoners.[6] There has been a greater pace of change in the center than in the periphery.

Some sound change is purely articulatory and does not change the underlying linguistic system. For instance, you might say "tomato" with long *a*, and I might say "tomato" with short *a*, but this difference of articulation does not change the meaning of the word, nor does it change the underlying system of phonemic contrasts. It may, however, indicate a difference of dialect and so have sociolinguistic significance. Other sound changes (e.g., phonemic mergers) do change the underlying structure. Some sound changes can have ripple effects across the phonological and morphosyntactic fields, where a simplification of sounds can motivate an array of compensatory complications. Below are two examples of phonological change in Hebrew.

Deletion of Final Short Vowels

In the earliest stage of Hebrew (proto-Hebrew), all final short vowels were lost. This is a conditioned change: $\breve{v} \rightarrow \emptyset$ / _# (meaning: "short vowel goes to zero in a word-final environment"). The deletion of final short vowels caused the collapse of the case system, motivating a compensatory expansion in the use of prepositions and the innovation (or expansion) of the direct object marker אֵת. The loss of final short vowels also caused the long prefix form (**yaqtulu*) and the short prefix form (**yaqtul*) to fall together in sound roots, motivating a reorganization of the verbal system. These are very early changes.[7]

We have occasional glimpses of the earlier phonological state in "frozen" archaisms, such as the case vowels that are sometimes preserved in personal names or in close juncture in construct chains:[8]

מְתוּשָׁאֵל ("Methushael," Gen 4:18) < **mutu* ("man")
שְׁמוּאֵל ("Samuel," e.g., 1 Sam 1:20) < **šimu* ("name")
בְּנוֹ בְעֹר ("son of Beor," Num 24:3,15) < **binu* ("son")
חַיְתוֹ־אֶרֶץ ("creatures of the earth," Gen 1:24) < **ḥayyatu* ("creature")[9]

Other than these rare and phonologically conditioned preservations of case endings, there are few phonological changes that have clear reflexes in the biblical text. One exception concerns changes in the articulation of sibilants.

Phonetic Changes of ס and שׂ

Samek and *sin* have a curious history. Although the details are murky, Egyptian transcriptions and other evidence indicate that in early Hebrew the phonetic realization of *samek* was something like [č] or [ʦ].[10] The Greeks borrowed *samek* as a grapheme for [ks], probably via Phoenician traders in the ninth to eighth centuries BCE, indicating that the old pronunciation was then still current.[11] Cognates indicate that the phonetic realization of *sin* was a voiceless lateral fricative [ɬ], pronounced like a breathy "lh."[12] Later the pronunciation of the two sibilants fell together and both were phonetically realized as [s]. This latter state is reflected in LBH and postbiblical Hebrew. The phonetic realization of a third sibilant, *shin*, was probably something like [š] in all phases of Hebrew.[13]

The older phonetic realization of *samek* is reflected in the shibboleth incident in Judges 12, where the odd form סִבֹּלֶת is used to indicate the Ephraimite pronunciation of *shin* in the word שִׁבֹּלֶת ("stalk of grain," "watercourse").[14] Because the Ephraimites (who lived west of the Jordan River) pronounced the *shin* differently than the Gileadites (who lived east of the Jordan), the word שִׁבֹּלֶת is presented as an effective test of the warring tribes' different dialects. The contrast is represented graphically in the text, with *samek* indicating the Ephraimites' flawed attempt to mimic the Gileadite pronunciation of the *shin* in שִׁבֹּלֶת. According to the story, if a soldier mispronounced this dialectal *shin*, the Gileadites would identify him as an Ephraimite and kill him. John Emerton aptly compared this situation to the use of the Dutch place-name Scheveningen as password to identify German spies during World War II.[15] In each case, a dialectal difference in the pronunciation of *shin* had deadly consequences. The *shibboleth* story hinges on phonetically contrasting realizations of the *shin* phoneme. This contrastive use of *samek* implies its earlier pronunciation, [č] or [ts], a sound that was close to but not quite the same as the Gileadite *shin*. This closeness of sounds is the key to understanding the acoustic test in the story.[16]

The older phonetic realization of *sin*, as a voiceless lateral fricative [ɬ], is indicated in Hebrew by the cognates of כַּשְׂדִּים ("Chaldeans") and בֹּשֶׂם ("balsam").[17] Hebrew *kaśdîm* corresponds to Akkadian *kaldu*. Richard Steiner plausibly infers that both words are independent renderings of a Chaldean ethnonym: "In that case, we have Hebrew *ś* and Akkadian *l* rendering the same Chaldean phone, suggesting that Hebrew *ś* had some feature in common with Akkadian *l*."[18] Because the Chaldeans became prominent only in the ninth-eighth centuries BCE, the *sin* of כַּשְׂדִּים probably reflects contemporary Hebrew phonology. The same phonetics of *sin* holds for the correspondence of Hebrew בֹּשֶׂם and Greek βάλσαμον ("balsam"). In this word, Semitic *sin* was represented in Greek with *ls*, also indicating the original pronunciation of *sin* as a lateral fricative.

This evidence indicates that the early pronunciation of *samek* and *sin* was current in the ninth-eighth centuries BCE and later. At some point their pronunciation fell together, and both were realized as [s]. This change is illustrated by the interchange of these two letters in words where the *samek-sin* distinction was originally a minimal contrastive pair. In some LBH texts, these distinctions become blurred:[19]

סכר ("to close") versus שׂכר ("to hire")
LBH: סֹכְרִים ("hire," "bribe," Ezra 4:5)

סכל ("to be foolish") versus שׂכל ("to be wise")
LBH: שִׂכְלוּת ("folly," Eccl 1:17)[20]

This phonetic merger seems to have been complete in most Hebrew dialects by the latter part of the Second Temple period. There are many *samek* and *sin* interchanges in the Qumran texts, including biblical texts.[21] In the following examples, the historical sibilant is *samek*, but in Qumran texts it interchanges with *sin*:

Ps 104:5 MT יסד, 4QPs[d] יוסד, 4QPs[l] ישד ("to found, establish")
Ps 119:20 MT גרסה, 4QPs[h] גרסה, 11QPs[a] גרשה ("be crushed")

Because sound changes radiate in waves, this phonetic merger did not happen everywhere at the same speed or in the same way. In the Samaritan dialect of the Second Temple period, *sin* merged with *shin*, and *samek* remained distinct. As a consequence there are no *samek-sin* interchanges in the Samaritan Pentateuch.[22]

Lexical and Morphosyntactic Change

In the lexical and morphosyntactic category of linguistic change we emphasize the mechanisms of simplification (reduction of contrasts), complication (expansion of contrasts), and systemic reanalysis. In each case the arrow of change is evident. The first three developments begin during the classical period and have implications for the relative chronology of the Pentateuchal sources. The other three developments begin in the postclassical period and illustrate the distinctive profile of LBH.

Simplification of Verbal Stems: Passive *qal* and *niphal*

In Northwest Semitic languages of the Late Bronze Age (Ugarit, Amarna Canaanite), three verbal stems semantically overlap in expressing the passive or reflexive of the *qal* stem: the passive *qal* (G–), the infixed *t* form (Gt), and the *niphal* (N).[23] The Iron Age Northwest Semitic languages reduce this redundancy in different ways. Old Aramaic preserves the passive *qal* and the Gt; Hebrew preserves the passive *qal* and the *niphal*; and Moabite may preserve only the Gt.[24] The semantic contrasts of these forms changed according to the new configurations.

As we observed in chapter 1, during the course of Biblical Hebrew this process of simplification continued, with the *niphal* taking the place of the passive *qal*. Old usages of the passive *qal* were reanalyzed in the reading tradition as *niphal*, *pual*, or *hophal*, depending on the consonants. Here are some examples from the root ילד ("bear," "be born"):[25]

> יֻלַּד־בֵּן ("a son was born," Gen 4:26), passive *qal*, reanalyzed as *pual*
> הַיּוֹם אֲשֶׁר יֻלַּדְתִּי בּוֹ ("the day on which I was born," Jer 20:14), passive *qal*, reanalyzed as *pual*
> הַנּוֹלַד־לוֹ ("who was born to him," Gen 21:3), *niphal*
> הִנֵּה־בֵן נוֹלָד ("behold, a son is born," 1 Kgs 13:2), *niphal*
> אֵל נוּלְּדוּ לְהָרָפָא ("these were born to the Raphah," 1 Chr 20:8), *nuphal*[26]

These cases of the passive of ילד illustrate the transition from passive *qal* to *niphal*. Notably, in the Pentateuch there is a contrasting distribution in J and P (the first passage above is J, the third is P).[27] J uses the passive *qal* of ילד exclusively.[28] In P we see the movement from passive *qal* to the *niphal* but not a clean break (e.g., the passive *qal* of נתן in Num 26:54). Some of P's genealogical lists—arguably drawn from source texts—use the passive *qal*.[29]

There are no cases of the passive *qal* of ילד in Hebrew inscriptions. However, a *niphal* of לקח in a sixth-century Hebrew inscription from Arad indicates that the transition from passive *qal* to *niphal* was occurring in some roots by this point.[30] This coheres with the biblical distribution. The passive *qal* occurs in TBH (e.g., passive *qal* of ילד in Ruth 4:17 and Job 5:7) but becomes obsolescent in LBH and is extinct in later phases of Hebrew.[31]

Simplification of First-Person Singular Pronoun: אָנֹכִי and אֲנִי

In older Northwest Semitic (Ugaritic) there are two first-person singular pronouns, a long form (written *ånk* for /ʾanākū/) and a short form (written *ån* for approximately /ʾanā̆/).[32] There is no obvious distinction of meaning between the two forms, but there is a distinctive distribution among genres. In nonliterary texts, only the long form appears; in literary texts, the two forms are interchangeable.

In the Iron Age Northwest Semitic languages, these two forms generally reduce to one. Old Aramaic preserves the short form, written אנה, while Phoenician and Moabite preserve the long form, written אנכ.[33] Only Hebrew, as far as we know, preserves both.[34] During the course of Biblical Hebrew, we can observe these two forms reducing to one, with the short form eventually becoming the sole form.[35] Rabbinic Hebrew knows only the short form.

In CBH, both forms, אָנֹכִי and אֲנִי, are used, usually interchangeably.[36] The main exception is Deuteronomy, which shows a marked preference for the long form, perhaps, as S. R. Driver suggests, "by rhythmical considerations" due to its "emph[atic] rhetorical style."[37] The P source, which has a mixture of classical and transitional features, has a nearly exclusive preference for the short form.[38] In TBH the short form becomes dominant and the long form mostly restricted to poetry. In LBH, the short form becomes virtually the sole usage, as it is in later phases of Hebrew. The following statistics illustrate this trajectory:[39]

		אָנֹכִי	אֲנִי
CBH	J and E	81	48
	Deuteronomy	55	2 (12:30; 29:5)
	Samuel	50	50
TBH	Jeremiah	37	54
	P and H	1 (Gen 23:4)[40]	130
	Ezekiel	1 (36:28)[41]	138
	Isaiah 40–66	17	67
	Lamentations	0	4
	Job	15	29
LBH	Chronicles	1 (17:1)[42]	30
	Ezra-Neh	1 (Neh 1:6)	17
	Esther	0	6
	Ecclesiastes	0	28
	Canticles	0	12
	Daniel	1 (10:11)	23

In Qumran Hebrew, the long form is used only in "rewritten Bible" texts that emulate Pentateuchal style, such as the Temple Scroll (11Q19) and 1QWords of Moses (1Q22).[43]

Although stylistic factors are part of the picture (e.g., Deuteronomy's parenetic style), there is a clear diachronic reduction from two pronouns to one. The process of simplification that had already occurred in the other Iron Age Northwest Semitic languages is readily apparent in the history of Biblical Hebrew.

Complication of Categories of Procreation: *Qal* and *hiphil*

In some CBH texts, the *qal* verb ילד ("bear," "beget") is used with male or female subjects.[44] The gender distinction is supplied by context, as in the following examples:

וְיָלְדוּ לָהֶם ("They [i.e., women] would bear children for them," Gen 6:4, J)
כּוּשׁ יָלַד אֶת־נִמְרֹד ("Cush begot Nimrod," Gen 10:8, J)
וּבְתוּאֵל יָלַד אֶת־רִבְקָה ("Bethuel begot Rebekah," Gen 22:23, J)
צוּר יְלָדְךָ ("the rock that begot you," Deut 32:18)
אֲנִי הַיּוֹם יְלִדְתִּיךָ ("I today have begotten you," Ps 2:3)
שְׁמַע לְאָבִיךָ זֶה יְלָדֶךָ ("heed your father who begot you," Prov 23:22)

In matters of procreation, some clarity may be desired. Hebrew speakers generated a new contrast that eliminates this gender ambiguity. The *qal* of ילד is restricted to the mother, who "bears," and the causative *hiphil* is used for the father, who "causes to bear." This is a rational way for the language to disaggregate the doubly agentive (causative) and singly agentive (transitive) gender roles in procreation. The *hiphil* is used for the male occasionally in CBH and regularly in TBH:

וַיּוֹלֶד גִּלְעָד אֶת־יִפְתָּח ("Gilead begot Jephthah," Judg 11:1)
אַחֲרֵי הוֹלִידוֹ אֶת־שֵׁת . . . וַיּוֹלֶד בָּנִים וּבָנוֹת ("After he begot Seth . . . he begot sons and daughters," Gen 5:4, P)[45]
כִּי־תוֹלִיד בָּנִים ("when you beget children," Deut 4:25)[46]
אֲשֶׁר תּוֹלִיד ("whom you will beget," 2 Kgs 20:18)
וְהוֹלִיד בֵּן ("if he begot a son," Ezek 18:10)
יִשַׁי הוֹלִיד אֶת־דָּוִד ("Jesse begot David," Ruth 4:22)

The *qal-hiphil* gender distinction continues in LBH (with one exception) and later phases of Hebrew.[47] This increase of distinctions roughly correlates with the shift of the passive *qal* of ילד to the *niphal*. Both changes in the morphosyntax of procreation are standard features in the P source.

Simplification of Plural Marker in Prefix Conjugations

In CBH, the second- and third-person feminine plural prefix conjugations are the same form, תִּקְטֹלְנָה. The corresponding masculine forms are תִּקְטְלוּ (2mpl) and יִקְטְלוּ (3mpl). During LBH this contrast of grammatical gender was simplified, with the masculine forms taking the place of the feminine. This reduction of contrasts is illustrated by the following:

> וַתָּבֹאנָה וַתִּדְלֶנָה וַתְּמַלֶּאנָה ("and they [3fpl] came, drew water, and filled [it]" Exod 2:16), CBH
> אַל־תִּקְרֶאנָה לִי ("Do not call [2fpl] me," Ruth 1:20), TBH
> אִם־תִּמְצְאוּ אֶת־דּוֹדִי מַה־תַּגִּידוּ לוֹ ("if you [2fpl] find my love, what will you say to him," Cant 5:8), LBH

In this verse the form תִּקְטְלוּ, now unmarked for gender, replaces the old feminine form תִּקְטֹלְנָה (twice). This is one of many late features in Song of Songs. As a result of this simplification of contrasts, the feminine plural form of the prefix conjugations becomes obsolete in LBH and disappears in later phases of Hebrew.[48]

Complication of Categories of Writing

In CBH and TBH סֵפֶר means any kind of written text, including letters, legal documents, and books (i.e., book-scrolls).[49] Here are some examples:

> וְאֶשְׁלְחָה סֵפֶר אֶל־מֶלֶךְ יִשְׂרָאֵל ("so that I may send a *letter* to the king of Israel," 2 Kgs 5:5)
> כְּדִבְרֵי הַסֵּפֶר הֶחָתוּם ("like the words of a sealed *book*," Isa 29:11, referring to a book-scroll tied with a cord and clay seal)
> סֵפֶר כְּרִיתוּת ("*certificate* of divorce," Deut 24:1,3)
> סֵפֶר הַמִּקְנָה ("*deed* of purchase," Jer 32:11)
> חיהוה אם נסה איש לקרא לי ספר לנצח ("As Yahweh lives, no one has ever tried to read a *letter* to me," Lachish 3.9–10, early sixth cent. BCE)[50]

As one can see, English has multiple designations corresponding to the semantic field of סֵפֶר.

In the Neo-Babylonian and Persian period, when Hebrew speakers were exposed to Aramaic as the language of administration and law, foreign words (from Aramaic, Akkadian, Persian) were borrowed into Hebrew to designate different categories of writing. The Aramaic loanword כְּתָב displaced סֵפֶר as any kind of written text, and the meaning of סֵפֶר was generally narrowed to "book-scroll."[51] The Akkadian loanword אִגֶּרֶת, also adopted from Aramaic, was used alongside כְּתָב for "letter." Other loanwords were used for short periods (e.g., נִשְׁתְּוָן, "letter," a Persian loanword, in Ezra 4:7; 7:11) but did not become naturalized in Hebrew. Here are some examples from TBH and LBH:

> בִכְתָב בֵּית־יִשְׂרָאֵל ("in the *register* of the house of Israel," Ezek 13:9)
> וַיֹּאמֶר חוּרָם מֶלֶךְ־צֹר בִּכְתָב ("Hiram, king of Tyre, said in a *letter*," 2 Chr 2:10)
> כִּכְתָבָהּ ("according to its *writing* [viz. script]" Esth 1:22)
> סֵפֶר מֹשֶׁה ("the *book* of Moses," Neh 13:1)
> אִגֶּרֶת הַפּוּרִים הַזֹּאת ("this *letter* about Purim," Esth 9:29)

As Avi Hurvitz observes, this complication of the lexicon reflects "the intensive impact of the rich Aramaic formulary in the sphere of writing-related terminology."[52] This example of linguistic complication through exposure to a prestige language introduces the larger issue of language contact, which we address in the section "Language Contact."

Systemic Reanalysis: Stative Verbs and Tense

The most global linguistic change in Biblical Hebrew was the restructuring of the verbal system that occurred in LBH. This semantic and syntactic reanalysis affected virtually all areas of the verbal system. This is not the place for a full treatment of this change,[53] but the following example of stative verbs and tense gives a sample of its extent. In CBH *qatal* has various present-tense functions, including the expression of present states. In LBH, because of a reanalysis of the temporal system, *qatal* evolves toward a preterite tense and most of its present tense functions are replaced by other forms and constructions.

Historically, the stative *qatal* descends from the predicate adjective. This is why there is no formal difference between the adjective and the uninflected (3ms) stative *qatal* in forms like *zāqēn* and *kābēd*. In Hebrew, as in older Northwest Semitic (Ugaritic), stative verbs are adjectival in meaning. As John Huehnergard observes, "For verbs with stative meaning (adjectival verbs, such as 'to be old,' 'to be great'), the suffix-conjugation does not have a specific tense value (cf. BH *zāqantî* 'I am old, have become old')."[54] In Hebrew, when Samuel says, וַאֲנִי זָקַנְתִּי וָשַׂבְתִּי ("As for me, I am old and gray," 1 Sam 12:2), the *qatal* stative verbs express the state of being old and gray, but the specific tense value (past or present) is supplied by context. If the context were marked as past, the utterance would mean "I *was* old and gray."

This temporal ambiguity of the *qatal* of stative verbs is reduced in LBH when *qatal* develops toward a preterite (simple past) tense. In compensation, the participle and long prefix conjugation (*yiqtol*), which also have (relative) present-tense functions in CBH, gradually replace the present use of the *qatal* of stative verbs.

John Cook has mapped the distribution of the different forms in Biblical Hebrew—*qatal*, participle, and *yiqtol*—that are used for ידע ("to know") in the present tense.[55] This is the most widely distributed stative verb in Biblical Hebrew.[56] As the graph in figure 1 shows, there is a clear trajectory from the dominance of the historically older form, *qatal*, to its replacement by the newer forms, the participle and *yiqtol*. As Cook observes, the diffusion of this innovation—caused by the decline of the present-tense uses of *qatal*—corresponds to the shape of an S curve. This is a typical shape for the diachronic diffusion of new linguistic features: "The diffusion of the new construction is gradual in the beginning, accelerates in the middle states, and slows again as it gains ascendancy at the close of the process. Thus, we fully expect to find old and new constructions side-by-side in the data, but we also expect to find an increasing frequency of the form in the shape of an S-curve."[57]

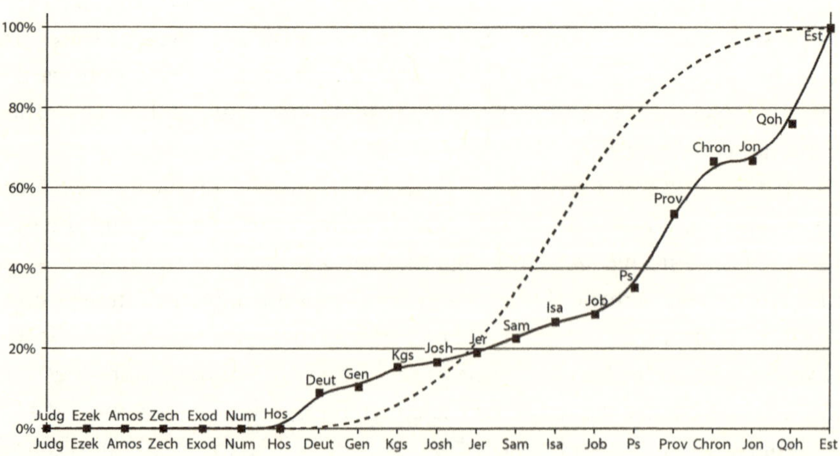

Figure 1. *Frequency of new constructions (participle and* yiqtol*) expressing a present state for* yd'

This map of the gradual replacement of the original construction is a sample of the large-scale change in the Hebrew verbal system that distinguishes LBH from CBH.[58]

Language Contact

As we have observed, one of the catalysts of language change is language contact. There are many motives and mechanisms for contact-induced change. Necessity and prestige are key factors.[59] Nowadays English is the prestige language for science and popular culture, and many English words populate world languages (e.g., email, keyboard, weekend), often to the disdain of local language purists. There is a need for such words, but there is also the factor of prestige, a desire to emulate the dominant culture. Necessity and prestige combine in the dissemination of English loanwords in the modern world.

Clusters of loanwords are diagnostic indicators for the historical phases of Biblical Hebrew. As we will see, a succession of foreign empires—Neo-Assyrian, Neo-Babylonian, and Persian—left their imprint on Hebrew vocabulary. As Mats Eskhult emphasizes, there is "a concurrence between the time factor and the borrowings, so that late words occur in those texts where they are, so to speak, supposed to be found."[60] The distribution of foreign loanwords provides an external control for the history of Hebrew.

The adoption of loanwords requires a degree of familiarity but does not require fluency in the foreign language. In her discussion of the mechanisms for contact-induced change, Sarah Thomason calls this condition *passive familiarity*, "when a speaker acquires a feature from a language that s/he understands (at least to some extent) but has never spoken actively."[61] This describes the likely contact situation for the loanwords from Philistine, Akkadian, Persian, and Greek listed in this chapter.

Sustained language contact produces more fundamental change. Thomason describes the contact mechanism for major changes in bilingual environments as *code alternation*, when "regular use of two languages in different situations might make deactivation of each one more difficult, so that bits of each language . . . leak into the other."[62] The intensive contact with Aramaic during the Persian period produced striking instances of such "leakage."[63] In the instances of syntactic interference presented below, speakers fluent in both languages reanalyzed features of Hebrew morphosyntax on the basis of similar features in Aramaic.

As Na'ama Pat-El observes, syntactic interference requires a longer period of language contact than the borrowing of loanwords: "Syntactic changes are possible in situations of prolonged close contact . . . unlike lexical changes, which may occur even with passing contact. Moreover, syntactic interference happens in a situation when the source language is considered dominant over the receiving language."[64] The prolonged close contact with Aramaic during the Persian period provides the backdrop for these syntactic changes.

During this era, Imperial Aramaic, with its admixture of Persian words, was the language of administration and law. It was used out of necessity by scribes, administrators, property owners, mercenaries, and craftspeople in the Judean community because it was the prestige language. As Frank Polak comments: "Because of administrative and social exigencies, the entire Judean community was affected by Aramaic. Real estate contracts, for instance, would be written in Aramaic, as they were in Elephantine and Samaria. Any complaint and judgment would have to be argued before the royal judges. Hence, Aramaic would be the preferred language of all persons doing business with the government, that is to say, probably the entire property-owning and professional part of the population, including even craftsmen. Thus Aramaic developed into the main language in administrative, legal, and commercial contexts (prestige language)."[65]

A degree of Aramaic literacy was necessary for many, and fluency was required for some, such as the governor Nehemiah and his associates. The use of Aramaic in administration was already in place by the late sixth century BCE, as David Vanderhooft has argued on the basis of the early Yehud seals, which are written in Aramaic.[66] During the Persian period Aramaic script began to displace the old Hebrew script not only for administrative, legal, and commercial use but also in the transmission of sacred texts. The old Hebrew script became a relic, to be revived in later times of national resurgence.[67] In the meantime, Aramaic was both the prestige language and the everyday script. As William Schniedewind emphasizes, "Although the province of Yehud was economically poor and demographically depopulated, we still find hundreds of inscriptions in Aramaic."[68] The regular use of both spoken and written Aramaic profoundly affected the lexicon and syntax of LBH.

In the following we address two types of contact-induced change in Biblical Hebrew: (1) loanwords from the domain of administration and commerce, indicating passive familiarity with different prestige languages at different periods, and (2) syntactic interference due to code alternation, resulting from the prolonged and intensive language contact with Aramaic in the Persian period and after. As we will see, the distribution of these changes has clear implications for the history of Biblical Hebrew.

Loanwords: Administrative and Commercial

We address loanwords in the semantic fields of administration and commerce because they closely track the history of international relations in the Levant during the biblical period. (We exclude loanwords that were borrowed in earlier Northwest Semitic, such as the Egyptian loanwords for writing materials and units of measure.)[69] The distribution and clustering of these loanwords illuminates the historical sequence of foreign prestige languages and underscores what Eskhult calls "a concurrence between the time factor and the borrowings."[70] The location of these loanwords consistently correlates with the diachronic distribution of other linguistic features, thus providing an external check and adding another layer to a "thick" analysis of the history of Biblical Hebrew.

Philistine

The word for Philistine ruler in Biblical Hebrew is סרן, found only in the plural, סְרָנִים and סַרְנֵי פְלִשְׁתִּים ("rulers of the Philistines"; Josh 13:3; Judg 3:3; 16:5–30; 1 Sam 5:8–11; 6:4–18; 7:7; 29:2–6; 1 Chr 12:20).[71] The Greek cognate τύραννος ("tyrant") and the Luvian *tarwanis* both designate rulers.[72] The initial *t* in these cognates indicate that the Hebrew *samek* has its older pronunciation as [ʦ] or [č] and not its later pronunciation as [s]. This word seems to be borrowed from the Philistine lexicon.[73]

Notably, in the seventh-century Ekron inscription (written in Phoenician), the Philistine king אכיש ("Achaean") calls himself שר עקרן ("ruler of Ekron"), using the Northwest Semitic word שַׂר ("prince, ruler).[74] In 1 Sam 29:2–6, the terms סַרְנֵי פְלִשְׁתִּים and שָׂרֵי פְלִשְׁתִּים are used interchangeably. As the Philistine king uses the Semitic word in a royal dedicatory inscription, it would seem that שַׂר was the prestige term at the time. The distribution of שַׂר and סרן is suggestive. As Assaf Yasur-Landau observes, "The use of these interchangeable terms is perhaps a question not only of Semitic/non-Semitic titles but also of chronology: *seranim* being an earlier term and *sarim* a later one."[75] In any case, this Philistine loanword in Samuel and elsewhere is a notable feature, indicating an historical situation of passive familiarity with the Philistine language.[76]

Akkadian

There are dozens of Akkadian loanwords in Hebrew, some mediated through Aramaic.[77] The administrative words mostly refer to foreigners, but some were nativized as Hebrew words (e.g., מֶכֶס, "tax"; סָרִיס, "official"; צִיר, "ambassador, messenger"). These words primarily appear in books that describe events from the Neo-Assyrian or Neo-Babylonian period, but some continued to be used in Persian administrative language (e.g., פֶּחָה, "governor"; סְגָנִים, "governors," "prefects"; שֵׁגַל, "queen"). Where the loanword has a sibilant, it is often possible to distinguish between Neo-Assyrian and Neo-Babylonian origins:

טִפְסַר (military official, Jer 51:27; Nah 3:17) < Neo-Assyrian *ṭupšarru*

מֶכֶס ("tax," Num 31:28–40; also מִכְסָה, "computation," Exod 12:4; Lev 27:23) < Neo-Babylonian *miksu*

סְגָנִים ("governors, prefects," e.g., Isa 41:25; Jer 51:23,28,57; Ezek 23:6,12,23; Ezra 9:2; Neh 2:16; 4:8,13; 5:7,17; 7:5; 12:40; 13:11; Aramaic in Dan 2:48)[78] < Neo-Assyrian via Imperial Aramaic סִגְנִין

סַמְגַּר ("an official," Jer 39:3)[79] < Neo-Babylonian *simmagir*

פֶּחָה ("governor," e.g., 1 Kgs 10:15; 20:24; 2 Kgs 18:24 = Isa 36:9; Jer 51:23,28,57; Ezek 23:6,12,23; Hag 1:1,14; 2:2,21; Mal 1:8; Ezra 8:36; 2 Chr 9:14; BA in Ezra 6:6) < Akkadian via Imperial Aramaic פֶּחָה

צִיר ("ambassador," Isa 18:2; 57:9; Jer 49:14; Obad 1; Prov 13:17; 25:13) < Neo-Assyrian *ṣīru*, perhaps via Aramaic

רַב־מָג ("a military official," Jer 39:3,13) < Neo-Assyrian *rab mugi* or Neo-Babylonian *rab mungu*

רַב־סָרִיס ("a high official" or "eunuch official," 2 Kgs 18:1; Jer 39:3,13; Dan 1:3,7–11,18) < Neo-Assyrian *rab ša rēši*

רַב־שָׁקֵה ("a high official," 2 Kgs 18:17,19,26–28; 37; 19:4,8; = Isa 36:2,4,11–13,22; 37:4,8) < Neo-Babylonian *rab šaqê*

שֵׁגַל ("queen," Ps 45:10; Neh 2:6) < Neo-Assyrian **sēkalli*

תַּרְתָּן ("field marshal," 2 Kgs 18:17; Isa 20:1) < Neo-Assyrian *tartannu*

As one can see from the distribution, these loanwords occur where they are expected, in texts that address events of the Neo-Assyrian or Neo-Babylonian period. Their borrowing indicates a historical situation of passive familiarity with Neo-Assyrian and Neo-Babylonian administrative language. With a few exceptions (e.g., words that continued to be used in the Persian administration, and the diction of Daniel, which emulates the Neo-Babylonian period), these texts reflect CBH or TBH and likely stem from the Neo-Assyrian and Neo-Babylonian eras.

Persian

There are sixteen words in Biblical Hebrew that are clearly Persian loanwords. Twelve of them are from the fields of administration and finance; all occur only in the LBH corpus.[80] As Aren Wilson-Wright observes, it is likely that most of these loanwords were borrowed in the period of intensified Persian administration after the mid-fifth century BCE, when the province of Yehud was fortified by the Persian military after the Egyptian revolt in 464–454 BCE.[81] (In contrast, the biblical works that stem from the early Persian period, like Haggai, First Zechariah, and Third Isaiah, do not contain Persian loanwords.) Many of these loanwords were mediated by Aramaic, but it is possible that some are direct borrowings from Persian. Only a few were nativized into Hebrew: גֶּנֶז ("treasury"), דָּת ("law"),[82] and פַּרְדֵּס ("garden"):

אֲחַשְׁדַּרְפָּן ("satrap," Esth 3:12; 8:9; 9:3; Ezra 8:36) < Old Persian *ḫšaçapāvan*
אֲחַשְׁתְּרָן ("royal," Esth 8:10,14) < OP *ḫšaça + ana*
אַפֶּדֶן ("palace," Dan 11:45) < OP *apadāna*
גִּזְבָּר ("treasurer," Ezra 1:8) < OP **ganzabara*
גֶּנֶז / גַּנְזַךְ ("treasury," 1 Chr 28:11; Esth 3:9; 4:7) < OP **ganza / *ganza + ka*
דָּת ("law," Ezra 8:36; Esth 1:8; etc.) < OP *dāta*
נִשְׁתְּוָן ("letter," Ezra 4:7; 7:11) < OP **ništāvan*
פַּרְדֵּס ("royal garden," Neh 2:8; Eccl 2:5; Cant 4:13) < OP *paradayadām*
פַּרְתְּמִים ("nobles," Esth 1:3; 6:9; Dan 1:3) < OP *fratama*
פִּתְגָם ("decree," Esth 1:20; Eccl 8:11) < OP **patigāma*
פַּתְשֶׁגֶן / פַּרְשֶׁגֶן ("copy," Esth 3:14; 4:8; 8:13) < OP **patičagnya-*
תִּרְשָׁתָא ("governor," Ezra 2:63; Neh 7:65,69; 8:9; 10:2) < OP **tršāta*

It is obvious that the use of Persian administrative and commercial loanwords derives from a period when Persian was the prestige language. The clustering of these words exclusively in books written in LBH corroborates the diachronic placement of LBH in this period.

Greek

There are only a few Greek loanwords in Biblical Hebrew, and a few in biblical Aramaic.[83] Two words for coins in Hebrew appear to be Greek loanwords, mediated by Greek traders and/or Aramaic:

אֲדַרְכֹּן ("daric," a gold coin, Ezra 8:27; 1 Chr 29:7)[84] < Greek δαρεικῶν
< OP **daru(i)yaka*, **zaruyaka*, "gold"

דַּרְכְּמוֹן ("drachma," a silver coin, Ezra 2:69; Neh 7:69–71)[85] < Greek δραχμή

The silver tetradrachm was the mostly widely circulated coin during the Persian period; the earliest examples from the province of Yehud date to the late sixth and early fifth centuries BCE.[86] Persian imperial coinage, including the gold daric, was introduced by Darius I around 500 BCE.[87] The mention of these coins is indicative of the time when these texts were written. The Chronicler's enumeration of David's temple fund in darics is a vivid anachronism, which illuminates the Chronicler's historical context.[88]

Syntactic Interference

After loanwords, the other major category of contact-induced change in Biblical Hebrew is syntactic interference, in which bilingual speakers reanalyzed features of Hebrew syntax by analogy with Aramaic. The two examples considered here are (1) לְ reanalyzed as a direct object marker by analogy with Aramaic לְ, and (2) the syntactic extension of אֲשֶׁר (later שֶׁ) by analogy with the Aramaic דִּי, including the innovation of new compound particles. These reanalyses are based on features that are innovations in Imperial Aramaic and therefore can be dated to the Persian period.

לְ AS DIRECT-OBJECT MARKER

The direct-object marker in Old Aramaic, אית or ות, was replaced in Imperial Aramaic by the preposition לְ, which previously marked the object for a restricted group of verbs.[89] In Hebrew, לְ also marks the object for a restricted group of verbs. By analogy with Imperial Aramaic לְ, the syntax of Hebrew לְ was reanalyzed to extend to other verbs. This syntactic reanalysis expanded in LBH, although לְ never wholly replaced אֵת. In the following example, using the common verb לקח ("take"), the first instance has the object marker אֵת and the following instances have לְ or a combination of both object markers:

וַיִּקַּח יוֹסֵף אֶת־שְׁנֵיהֶם אֶת־אֶפְרַיִם . . . וְאֶת־מְנַשֶּׁה ("Joseph took them both, Ephraim . . . and Manasseh," Gen 48:13)
וַיִּקַּח רַב־טַבָּחִים לְיִרְמְיָהוּ ("the head of the guard took Jeremiah," Jer 40:2)[90]
וַיִּקַּח אֶת־שָׂרֵי הַמֵּאוֹת לַעֲזַרְיָהוּ ("he took the heads of the hundreds, Azariah," 2 Chr 23:1)

As Na'ama Pat-El observes, this expansion of לְ as direct-object marker is related to the LBH expansion of אֵת to mark the nominative.[91]

EXTENSION OF אֲשֶׁר AND שֶׁ BY ANALOGY WITH דִּי, AND NEW COMPOUNDS

The Aramaic particle דִּי, known from Old Aramaic onward, has relative, causal, and conjunctive functions.[92] Its syntax overlaps with the Hebrew particles כִּי and אֲשֶׁר (and older זוּ, with which it is cognate). Bilingual speakers in the Persian period reanalyzed and extended the syntax of אֲשֶׁר by analogy with the syntax of Aramaic דִּי. This is most evident in places where אֲשֶׁר and שׁ are used instead of כִּי in causal and conjunctive clauses. In the following contrasts, the first instance has the older usage with כִּי:

יָדְעוּ כִּי־רְעֵבִים אֲנַחְנוּ ("they know *that* we are starving," 2 Kgs 7:12)
אֲנִי יָדַעְתִּי אֲשֶׁר עֲבָדֶיךָ יוֹדְעִים ("I know *that* your servants are knowledgeable," 2 Chr 2:7)

אָמֹר אָמַרְתִּי כִּי־שָׂנֹא שְׂנֵאתָהּ ("I thought *that* you must surely hate her," Judg 15:12)
וָאֹמְרָה אֲשֶׁר לֹא יִפְתָּחוּם ("I said *that* they must not open them," Neh 13:19)
אָמַרְתִּי שֶׁגַּם־זֶה הָבֶל ("I said *that* this too is vanity," Eccl 8:14)

In the wake of this reanalysis, new Hebrew compound particles with אֲשֶׁר and שֶׁ were created by analogy with Aramaic compound particles with דִּי. As Pat-El has shown, two Aramaic compounds with דִּי that were innovations in Imperial or early Middle Aramaic were the basis for several Hebrew calques (translational transfers).[93]

The new Aramaic compound בְּדִיל דִּ(י) ("because," "on account of") was built from בְּ + דִּי + לְ + דִּי. A limited variety of Hebrew compounds were created by analogy, built from בְּ + שֶׁ/אֲשֶׁר + לְ (+ שֶׁ/אֲשֶׁר):

בַּאֲשֶׁר לְ- ("because of," Jonah 1:8)
בְּשֶׁלְּ- ("on account of," Jonah 1:7,12)
בְּשֶׁל אֲשֶׁר ("on account of which," Eccl 8:17)
בְּשֶׁל שֶׁ- ("in order that," 4QMMT B12, C32 [= 4Q394 1.15; 4Q398 2.6])

The new Aramaic compound דִּ(י)לְמָה ("lest," "that not") was built from דִּי + לְמָה ("lest"). Two Hebrew compounds were created by analogy:

אֲשֶׁר לָמָּה ("lest," Dan 1:10)
שַׁלָּמָה ("lest," Cant 1:7)

The extension of אֲשֶׁר and the new compounds, the latter created by analogy with innovations in Imperial or Middle Aramaic, provide external support for the chronology of language change in Biblical Hebrew.

* * *

This partial sketch of the kinds and causes of change in Biblical Hebrew provides a backdrop for the chapters that follow. Before we begin to fill in the details about the diachronic phases of Hebrew—from classical to transitional to late—we turn to the linguistic and textual issues that complicate historical linguistic inquiry, including issues of dialects, literary style, and the textual condition of the Hebrew Bible.

3 How to Handle Linguistic Variation

Languages change over time, as we have illustrated in the previous chapters. Words fall from use and are replaced by different ones. Other words see their meaning change in various ways. Grammatical functions evolve over time, and new forms emerge.

The study of language change is based on the comparison of features that can be contrasted as early and late. Meaningful evidence of evolution can take many forms, but ideally we require a set of at least two contrasting phenomena, one early and one late. When item A in some texts corresponds in meaning or function to item B in other texts, the evidence may be indicative of language development. Some passages use the *qal* passive of ילד in the meaning "to be born," while other passages use the *niphal* in the same meaning. In the history of Hebrew, the internal passive is earlier than the *niphal*. All other things being equal, a passage with the *qal* passive may be considered earlier than a passage using the *niphal*. Many other instances of variation are understood well enough to interpret them in diachronic terms.

However, the path from diachronic linguistics to the dating of texts is not a straight one. The presence of linguistic features that are relatively early does not automatically establish that a text is early, nor does the presence of relatively late features necessarily show that a text is late.[1] A number of complicating factors must be taken into account. Notably, linguistic variation implies that earlier and later forms may occur side by side in a given text without diachronic implications. The present chapter looks first at linguistic variation as it manifests itself in Biblical Hebrew, then at the way the diachronic approach is able to handle it.

Sources of Synchronic Variation

Diachronic change is only one factor causing linguistic variation. All languages, at any point in time, exhibit a very wide range of variety. Dialectal differences between British and American usage are well known: "I am mad about my flat" may mean "I love my apartment" or "I am angry because of a flat tire," according to which side of the Atlantic one is on. Dialectal differences of this kind are frequent also between regional varieties of speech within countries where English is spoken. Another factor of variety is stylistic register: formal speech employs other words and forms than familiar discourse; a pastor may use different language in the pulpit than in the home; and poetry has its own repertoire of linguistic forms. In addition, variation may reflect sociolinguistic factors: a guild may develop professional jargon, and a religious sect may adopt a peculiar type of speech. Finally, some variation is hard to classify. Although "true" synonyms are generally agreed not to exist, it would take a courageous linguist to define the difference between "nonetheless" and "nevertheless" or between "among" and "amongst."

Many instances of synchronic variation can be illuminated by reference to language history. American English "gotten" is an older form than British English "got," and the second-person singular pronoun "thou," still used in the Yorkshire dialect, is an earlier form replaced by "you" in most other varieties of English. While "nonetheless" and "nevertheless" are nearly indistinguishable in contemporary English, their age sets them apart, the second word being much older than the first. Such cases show that earlier and later forms of expression are not always neatly distributed through time in the way one expects. Early and late forms coexist in the hodgepodge that is contemporary English.

In Biblical Hebrew, too, variation may be attributed to many different factors.[2] On the theoretical level, we can enumerate the following factors, other than diachronic development.

Dialects

Hebrew was spoken in different dialects in different localities, and some of the local diversity seems to appear in written texts.[3] A possible instance is the attestation of a number of *ketiv* forms of the 2fs perfect with a *–ty* suffix instead of the normal *–t* suffix, such as Jer 3:4, הֲלוֹא מֵעַתָּה קראתי [*qere*: קָרָאת] לִי אָבִי? ("Have you not recently called me 'My father'?"). The *ketiv* spelling with *yod* indicates a pronunciation with final *i* vowel (*qārāʾtî*), which may reflect a northern dialect. It corresponds to the reconstructed Proto-Semitic and may therefore be regarded as older. The final *i* vowel is also preserved in the Samaritan pronunciation (e.g., in Gen 18:15, צָחָקְתְּ, "you laughed," is pronounced *ṣā̊ʾiqti* in the Samaritan reading tradition). Exactly how this feature was distributed in ancient Hebrew speech is hard to say.[4]

Several scholars have attempted to identify dialectal elements in biblical texts that may have been composed in northern Israel.[5] Although the existence of such regionalism is highly plausible, the results of the approach often remain uncertain. For example, it is possible that the *hapax legomenon* וַיְזוֹרֵר ("and he sneezed," 2 Kgs 4:35) reflects a verb typical of Northern Hebrew.[6] The Judahite equivalent would be some form of the root עטש (cf. Job 41:10). But it is problematic to base dialectal distinctions on a single occurrence. Although much work has been done on this issue, many uncertainties remain.

Style Switching

In some texts, the author may have imitated foreign or dialectal traits for artistic effect.[7] Scholars have noted that direct speech situated in a foreign setting is at times colored by foreign expressions.[8] Several good examples of this feature may be found in the patriarchal narratives. For instance, Abraham instructs his servant to go and find a wife for his son: "You shall not take a wife for my son of the daughters of the Canaanites . . . but (כִּי) you shall go to my country . . . and take a wife for my son Isaac" (Gen 24:3–4). Abraham speaks good Hebrew, using the adversative particle כִּי. However, when his servant later quotes his master's words to Laban and his family, he instead uses the Aramaic-like אִם־לֹא (Gen 24:38).[9] This phenomenon, somewhat confusingly referred to as "style switching,"[10] may account for much of the linguistic strangeness of the dialogues in the book of Job.

Style switching is also sometimes invoked to explain the presence of rare words or forms in the speech of Israelite characters from various locales. Thus the Shunammite woman is represented as saying לֹא תַשְׁלֶה אֹתִי ("do not mislead me," 2 Kgs 4:28), using the verb שׁלה in a meaning that is otherwise unattested in the Hebrew Bible but is well known from Aramaic.[11] This usage may have been chosen to characterize the speech of northern Israelites. The standard language of the Hebrew Bible might have used the *hiphil* of נשׁא "to deceive" instead (see 2 Kgs 18:29).

Poetic Style

We are on firmer ground making a distinction between prosaic and poetic style. Several words (e.g., the verb אתה, "to come"), forms (e.g., third weak verbs preserving the original *yod*, יִשְׁלָיוּ, Ps 122:6), and syntactic constructions (e.g., asyndetic relative clauses) are in Biblical Hebrew wholly, or mostly, limited to poetic texts.[12] Many of the poetic features can be characterized as archaisms. Others may have been borrowed from regional dialects or foreign languages. Whatever their origin, they make up a poetic "dialect." Poets could draw from this idiomatic resource forms of expression that their audiences would understand but that would not normally be used in more ordinary types of communication.[13] Admittedly, the line between poetry and prose is hard to draw, and exalted prose can use words and forms that are otherwise found only in poetry (e.g., חַיְתוֹ־אֶרֶץ in Gen 1:24; the form חַיְתוֹ is otherwise limited to poetry: Zeph 2:14; Pss 50:10; 79:2; 104:11).

Register

The notion of register is important in chapter 5, where we compare Biblical Hebrew to inscriptional Hebrew. Unfortunately, within the biblical corpus the question of register is difficult to evaluate. Most of the biblical texts are literary in nature and therefore presumably belong to the literary register of Hebrew.[14] Samples of represented speech at times contain distinctive expressions that may reflect specific levels of spoken language:[15]

> Num 11:15
> וְאִם־כָּכָה אַתְּ־עֹשֶׂה לִּי הָרְגֵנִי נָא הָרֹג
> If this is the way you are going to treat me, put me to death at once.

Although this is Moses speaking to God, the content of the speech is more reminiscent of a family squabble than a formal liturgy. The enclitization of the pronoun with the following participle (אַתְּ־עֹשֶׂה), unique in the Hebrew Bible, may imitate a phenomenon occurring in natural speech. It is, however, difficult to attain certainty in this matter. Our sources of information are too scarce to say anything much about variations due to register.

Professional Jargon

The notion of professional language may be relevant to some priestly usages. For example, מִנְחָה is used to mean "grain offering" in Exodus, Leviticus, and Numbers.[16] The word usually means "gift" or "tribute." The specialized meaning probably reflects priestly terminology used in the Jerusalem temple. Admittedly, this special usage is attested in some nonpriestly texts as well.[17]

Literary Allusions

A special factor of variation affecting the Hebrew Bible is literary allusion. Many texts refer overtly or covertly to earlier texts or traditions, not all of which have survived. This may lead to the use of expressions that are otherwise unexpected. For example, in Deuteronomy the gentilic עִבְרִי ("Hebrew") is used only in the law on the release of slaves in Deut 15:2.[18] It almost certainly refers to Israelites, who are elsewhere in the book called בְּנֵי יִשְׂרָאֵל ("children of Israel").[19] The variation in this case results from the fact that Deut 15 rewrites an earlier legal text, a version of which is preserved in Exod 21:2.[20] In the language of Exodus, עִבְרִי is far more common. Similarly, Isa 27:1 uses language that is so strange in its biblical context and so close to a famous Ugaritic parallel that most scholars accept that the biblical writer is alluding to an existing story of divine combat:

Isa 27:1
On that day YHWH with his cruel and great and strong sword
will punish Leviathan the fleeing serpent (לִוְיָתָן נָחָשׁ בָּרִחַ),
Leviathan the twisting serpent (לִוְיָתָן נָחָשׁ עֲקַלָּתוֹן),
He will kill the dragon in the sea.

CAT 1.5 I 1 (Myth of Baal)
When you smote Lotan the fleeing serpent (*k tmḫṣ . ltn . bṯn . brḥ*),
When you put an end to the twisting serpent (*tkly . bṯn . ʿqltn*)

In this case, the intertextual reference creates variation in the language of the Hebrew Bible. The adjectives בָּרִחַ ("fleeing") and עֲקַלָּתוֹן ("twisting") might never have been in the corpus were it not for the use of this literary device in Isa 27:1.[21]

Other Possible Factors

Despite this wide spectrum of possible explanations, the source of variation in the Hebrew Bible remains uncertain in many instances. Scantiness of attestation makes it impossible to determine which factors are at play.

The words אָמָה and שִׁפְחָה both translate into English as "female slave" or "maidservant"; they are near synonyms. Scholars have tried to define exactly how they differ in terms of dialect, epoch, or type of discourse, but without much success.[22]

With a corpus like the Hebrew Bible, composed as it is of a relatively small set of texts whose date is a matter of discussion, the multiple sources of variation may be an obstacle for diachronic analysis. Any feature one would like to claim as belonging to a specific time may instead reflect a distinct dialect or register, or it may be due to literary allusion to an older text. If one naïvely followed the trail of linguistic features, one might attribute Ps 122 or Isa 27:1 to the Bronze Age! An interesting illustration of the dilemma is the use of the expression אִם־לֹא (Gen 24:38), mentioned earlier in the discussion of Gen 24. While Alexander Rofé lists this as an Aramaism indicating the postexilic date of the chapter, Gary Rendsburg replies that the usage is due to style switching and cannot therefore be used for dating purposes.[23]

The Way Out: The Contrast between LBH and CBH

Nondiachronic factors of variation complicate diachronic analysis. However, as we intimated at the end of chapter 1, they do not make an historical approach to Biblical Hebrew impossible. What makes diachronic study possible is that the linguistic data line up in an extraordinary way, particularly in prose texts. While most biblical prose represents the literary genre of historical (or "history-like") narrative, two subcorpora using distinct varieties of Hebrew clearly stand out.

Two Distinct Corpora

A small number of biblical books are dated to the Persian period or later by the events they recount: Esther, Ezra-Nehemiah, and Chronicles, whose genealogies extend at least to the fourth century BCE. These same books are written in a particular type of Hebrew. Notably, their lexicon contains many words borrowed from Aramaic and several words borrowed from Persian.[24] Manifestly, the language of these books reflects strong influence from the administrative language of the Persian period, Official or Imperial Aramaic. The same type of Hebrew, commonly referred to as Late Biblical Hebrew (LBH), is found in Daniel and Ecclesiastes.[25] The book of Daniel is situated in the sixth century but has since long been unmasked as a writing of the Hellenistic age because of its manifest allusions to the Maccabean wars. Ecclesiastes is fictively attributed to Solomon but is similarly recognized as one of the latest books of the Hebrew Bible.[26]

In contrast to these books, the prose of the Pentateuch and Former Prophets, referred to as Classical Biblical Hebrew (CBH), has relatively few Aramaic loanwords and practically no words of Persian origin.[27] The difference shows up with particular clarity in those cases where a word in the late books corresponds exactly to a different one in the earlier corpus: a "letter," אִגֶּרֶת in Ezra-Nehemiah and Chronicles, is referred to with the native Hebrew word סֵפֶר in Kings; and a "garden," פַּרְדֵּס in Nehemiah and Ecclesiastes, is called גַּן in Genesis and Kings. Such a constellation enables one to see the language evolve practically before one's eyes: new words of foreign extraction replace earlier indigenous words. Another type of clue occurs when a word turns up with different meanings in the two corpora. The noun חֵפֶץ means "desire" in Samuel and Kings, but "matter" or "thing" in Ecclesiastes. The second meaning derives from the first by way of a semantic process of generalization. This process is paralleled in Arabic: *šay'* ("thing") derives from *šâ'a* ("to desire"; compare *inšalla* ['in šâ'a llāh], "if God wills").

Diachronic Stages or Contemporary Dialects?

From the early nineteenth century onward, Hebraists have interpreted the differences between CBH and LBH in diachronic terms. The CBH corpus, Genesis to 2 Kings, was attributed primarily to the preexilic period, and the LBH corpus to the postexilic period. In recent times, some scholars have rejected this diachronic scheme and argue instead that the differences between CBH and LBH reflect distinct style forms, the former more conservative, the latter more open to foreign influences.[28] In light of our discussion of the synchronic factors of variation, this would seem to be a possible approach. In telling a story like Esther, set in the Persian period, an author might well have opted to incorporate a number of Aramaic and Persian words to provide some local color. He might refer to a written missive as אִגֶּרֶת because that is what letters were called in the Persian Empire. Another author, or perhaps even the same one, relating events of Israel's past—the monarchical period and before—might have tried to use a purer style of Hebrew, without foreign loanwords. On examination, however, this theoretical possibility turns out not to fit the data.

To begin with, such an explanation does not work well for Chronicles, which relates almost entirely to the monarchic period yet exhibits the same signs of lateness as the other LBH books. Second, and more specifically, the "stylistic" approach does not easily account for the many grammatical differences between the two corpora. As has become increasingly clear in recent times, the syntax of LBH is essentially different from that of CBH.[29] For instance, in CBH the infinitive absolute is used in binding commands, given by an hierarchical superior (e.g., Exod 20:8, זָכוֹר אֶת־יוֹם הַשַּׁבָּת לְקַדְּשׁוֹ, "Remember the Sabbath day to keep it holy"), but in LBH this usage is practically unattested.[30] Another example is the adverb הַרְבֵּה ("much"), which in LBH is nominalized and can be combined with prepositions (Neh 5:18, לְהַרְבֵּה), a combination that is never found in CBH.[31] These and other syntactic differences indicate that LBH is not a mere style but reflects a real state of the language. Although authors have a degree of control over the vocabulary they use in their work, this is less true of their use of syntax.[32] Late syntax cannot be attributed to stylistic choice as easily as late vocabulary. Also, while there would be an obvious motivation for using Aramaic or Persian terms in a writing referring to the Persian period, syntax doesn't as easily convey a foreign flavor.

Sample Passages

In addition to these considerations, the sheer density of features setting apart the two types of language makes it difficult to view them as mere style forms. The contrast between CBH and LBH is best illustrated by juxtaposing two extracts of biblical prose narrative, one from each corpus:

Gen 12:10–20

10 וַיְהִי רָעָב בָּאָרֶץ וַיֵּרֶד אַבְרָם מִצְרַיְמָה לָגוּר שָׁם כִּי־כָבֵד הָרָעָב בָּאָרֶץ׃ 11 וַיְהִי כַּאֲשֶׁר הִקְרִיב
לָבוֹא מִצְרָיְמָה וַיֹּאמֶר אֶל־שָׂרַי אִשְׁתּוֹ הִנֵּה־נָא יָדַעְתִּי כִּי אִשָּׁה יְפַת־מַרְאֶה אָתְּ׃ 12 וְהָיָה כִּי־יִרְאוּ
אֹתָךְ הַמִּצְרִים וְאָמְרוּ אִשְׁתּוֹ זֹאת וְהָרְגוּ אֹתִי וְאֹתָךְ יְחַיּוּ׃ 13 אִמְרִי־נָא אֲחֹתִי אָתְּ לְמַעַן יִיטַב־לִי
בַעֲבוּרֵךְ וְחָיְתָה נַפְשִׁי בִּגְלָלֵךְ׃ 14 וַיְהִי כְּבוֹא אַבְרָם מִצְרָיְמָה וַיִּרְאוּ הַמִּצְרִים אֶת־הָאִשָּׁה כִּי־יָפָה
הִוא מְאֹד׃ 15 וַיִּרְאוּ אֹתָהּ שָׂרֵי פַרְעֹה וַיְהַלְלוּ אֹתָהּ אֶל־פַּרְעֹה וַתֻּקַּח הָאִשָּׁה בֵּית פַּרְעֹה׃
16 וּלְאַבְרָם הֵיטִיב בַּעֲבוּרָהּ וַיְהִי־לוֹ צֹאן־וּבָקָר וַחֲמֹרִים וַעֲבָדִים וּשְׁפָחֹת וַאֲתֹנֹת וּגְמַלִּים׃
17 וַיְנַגַּע יְהוָה ׀ אֶת־פַּרְעֹה נְגָעִים גְּדֹלִים וְאֶת־בֵּיתוֹ עַל־דְּבַר שָׂרַי אֵשֶׁת אַבְרָם׃ 18 וַיִּקְרָא פַרְעֹה
לְאַבְרָם וַיֹּאמֶר מַה־זֹּאת עָשִׂיתָ לִּי לָמָּה לֹא־הִגַּדְתָּ לִּי כִּי אִשְׁתְּךָ הִוא׃ 19 לָמָה אָמַרְתָּ אֲחֹתִי הִוא
וָאֶקַּח אֹתָהּ לִי לְאִשָּׁה וְעַתָּה הִנֵּה אִשְׁתְּךָ קַח וָלֵךְ׃ 20 וַיְצַו עָלָיו פַּרְעֹה אֲנָשִׁים וַיְשַׁלְּחוּ אֹתוֹ
וְאֶת־אִשְׁתּוֹ וְאֶת־כָּל־אֲשֶׁר־לוֹ׃

> [10] Now there was a famine in the land. So Abram went down to Egypt to reside there as an alien, for the famine was severe in the land. [11] When he was about to enter Egypt, he said to his wife Sarai, "I know well that you are a woman beautiful in appearance; [12] and when the Egyptians see you, they will say, 'This is his wife'; then they will kill me, but they will let you live. [13] Say you are my sister, so that it may go well with me because of you, and that my life may be spared on your account." [14] When Abram entered Egypt the Egyptians saw that the woman was very beautiful. [15] When the officials of Pharaoh saw her, they praised her to Pharaoh. And the woman was taken into Pharaoh's house. [16] And for her sake he dealt well with Abram; and he had sheep, oxen, male donkeys, male and female slaves, female donkeys, and camels. [17] But YHWH afflicted Pharaoh and his house with great plagues because of Sarai, Abram's wife. [18] So Pharaoh called Abram, and said, "What is this you have done to me? Why did you not tell me that she was your wife? [19] Why did you say, 'She is my sister,' so that I took her for my wife? Now then, here is your wife, take her, and be gone."[20] And Pharaoh gave his men orders concerning him; and they set him on the way, with his wife and all that he had.

This beautiful piece of prose exhibits several expressions typical of CBH that are never found in the LBH corpus:

1. The syntagm הִנֵּה־נָא (v. 11) is attested twenty-two times in the CBH corpus and four times in the poetry of Job, but not once in LBH. These statistics are not accidental; they are symptomatic of wider-ranging developments. The modal particle נָא is vastly more frequent in CBH than in LBH.[33] Moreover, while in CBH it is syntactically flexible, being attached to verbs, particles, and even once to a noun in the vocative, in LBH its use is severely restricted: it occurs only immediately following a modal verbal form (imperative, jussive, cohortative).
2. Temporal כִּי (v. 12) is frequent in CBH but virtually absent from LBH.[34]
3. The passive *qal* (וַתֻּקַּח in v. 15) is a regular feature in CBH, but it is almost completely lacking from LBH. The passive *qal* of לקח is attested fifteen times in the Hebrew Bible: seven times in the CBH prose corpus and eight times in prophetic books and Job. There are no cases in LBH. The parallel to Gen 12:15 in the Esther story has the *niphal* instead of the passive *qal* (וַתִּלָּקַח, Esth 2:8):

Esth 4:1–8

1 וּמָרְדֳּכַי יָדַע אֶת־כָּל־אֲשֶׁר נַעֲשָׂה וַיִּקְרַע מָרְדֳּכַי אֶת־בְּגָדָיו וַיִּלְבַּשׁ שַׂק וָאֵפֶר וַיֵּצֵא בְּתוֹךְ הָעִיר
וַיִּזְעַק זְעָקָה גְדֹלָה וּמָרָה׃ 2 וַיָּבוֹא עַד לִפְנֵי שַׁעַר־הַמֶּלֶךְ כִּי אֵין לָבוֹא אֶל־שַׁעַר הַמֶּלֶךְ בִּלְבוּשׁ
שָׂק׃ 3 וּבְכָל־מְדִינָה וּמְדִינָה מְקוֹם אֲשֶׁר דְּבַר־הַמֶּלֶךְ וְדָתוֹ מַגִּיעַ אֵבֶל גָּדוֹל לַיְּהוּדִים וְצוֹם וּבְכִי
וּמִסְפֵּד שַׂק וָאֵפֶר יֻצַּע לָרַבִּים׃ 4 וַתָּבוֹאינָה נַעֲרוֹת אֶסְתֵּר וְסָרִיסֶיהָ וַיַּגִּידוּ לָהּ וַתִּתְחַלְחַל
הַמַּלְכָּה מְאֹד וַתִּשְׁלַח בְּגָדִים לְהַלְבִּישׁ אֶת־מָרְדֳּכַי וּלְהָסִיר שַׂקּוֹ מֵעָלָיו וְלֹא קִבֵּל׃ 5 וַתִּקְרָא
אֶסְתֵּר לַהֲתָךְ מִסָּרִיסֵי הַמֶּלֶךְ אֲשֶׁר הֶעֱמִיד לְפָנֶיהָ וַתְּצַוֵּהוּ עַל־מָרְדֳּכָי לָדַעַת מַה־זֶּה וְעַל־מַה־זֶּה׃
6 וַיֵּצֵא הֲתָךְ אֶל־מָרְדֳּכָי אֶל־רְחוֹב הָעִיר אֲשֶׁר לִפְנֵי שַׁעַר־הַמֶּלֶךְ׃ 7 וַיַּגֶּד־לוֹ מָרְדֳּכַי אֵת כָּל־אֲשֶׁר
קָרָהוּ וְאֵת ׀ פָּרָשַׁת הַכֶּסֶף אֲשֶׁר אָמַר הָמָן לִשְׁקוֹל עַל־גִּנְזֵי הַמֶּלֶךְ בַּיְּהוּדִים[35] לְאַבְּדָם׃ 8 וְאֶת־
פַּתְשֶׁגֶן כְּתָב־הַדָּת אֲשֶׁר־נִתַּן בְּשׁוּשָׁן לְהַשְׁמִידָם נָתַן לוֹ לְהַרְאוֹת אֶת־אֶסְתֵּר וּלְהַגִּיד לָהּ וּלְצַוּוֹת
עָלֶיהָ לָבוֹא אֶל־הַמֶּלֶךְ לְהִתְחַנֶּן־לוֹ וּלְבַקֵּשׁ מִלְּפָנָיו עַל־עַמָּהּ׃

1 When Mordecai learned all that had been done, Mordecai tore his clothes and put on sackcloth and ashes, and went through the city, wailing with a loud and bitter cry; 2 he went up to the entrance of the king's gate, for no one might enter the king's gate clothed with sackcloth. 3 In every province, wherever the king's command and his decree came, there was great mourning among the Jews, with fasting and weeping and lamenting, and most of them lay in sackcloth and ashes. 4 When Esther's maids and her eunuchs came and told her, the queen was deeply distressed; she sent garments to clothe Mordecai, so that he might take off his sackcloth; but he would not accept them. 5 Then Esther called for Hathach, one of the king's eunuchs, who had been appointed to attend her, and ordered him to go to Mordecai to learn what was happening and why. 6 Hathach went out to Mordecai in the open square of the city in front of the king's gate, 7 and Mordecai told him all that had happened to him, and the exact sum of money that Haman had promised to pay into the king's treasuries for the destruction of the Jews. 8 Mordecai also gave him a copy of the written decree issued in Susa for their destruction, that he might show it to Esther, explain it to her, and charge her to go to the king to make supplication to him and entreat him for her people.

Literarily, this prose passage is as fluid and capable as the previous one. But the language is essentially different. Several features typical of LBH, and completely absent from the CBH corpus, occur in this short passage:

1. There are three Persian loanwords: דָּת ("decree," vv. 3 and 8), גִּנְזֵי ("treasures," v. 7), and פַּתְשֶׁגֶן ("copy," v. 8). Each of these words occurs elsewhere in LBH: דָּת in Ezra 8:36; גנז, in the form גַּנְזַךְ, in 1 Chr 28:11; פַּתְשֶׁגֶן, in the slightly different form פַּרְשֶׁגֶן, in Ezra 7:11.[36] But none of them is found in CBH.[37]

2. Aramaic influence can be seen in the noun כְּתָב ("writing," v. 8), whose morphology marks it out as a loanword.[38] This word is found in Daniel, Ezra, Nehemiah, and Chronicles but never in CBH.[39] Also reflecting Aramaic is the noun פָּרָשָׁה ("precise amount," v. 7). Although this noun is attested only in the present verse, the nominal pattern it represents, *qaṭṭālā*, was imported from Aramaic.[40]
3. A phraseological feature limited to LBH is the combination of the prepositions עַד and לְ (v. 2).[41] It is found more than twenty times in Ezra and Chronicles but practically never in CBH.[42]
4. Several syntactic features of the passage are typical of LBH. אֵין + infinitive in a modal meaning, "none might enter" (v. 2) is attested eight times, in Esther, Ecclesiastes, Ezra, and Chronicles but never in CBH.[43] The use of the participle to express repeated action in a past time frame, "wherever the king's commandment and decree *would arrive*" (v. 3), is also rather frequent in LBH but extremely rare in CBH.[44]

As illustrated by these samples, the linguistic differences between CBH and LBH are extensive and profound. Hurvitz's recent *Concise Lexicon of Late Biblical Hebrew* lists eighty items characteristic of LBH for which CBH uses a different word.[45] To this number, many syntactic usages should be added.[46] The linguistic differences between the two corpora are also systemic: LBH features are typically attested in more than one of the LBH books, and similarly, CBH features are usually found throughout the CBH corpus. Moreover, generally speaking, the LBH features are typologically later than their CBH counterparts: Aramaic and Persian loanwords displace earlier Hebrew words; the internal passive recedes and external marking with prefixes takes over; the nonfinite forms—infinitives and participles—extend their functions to the detriment of the finite tenses.[47] Consequently, it is almost impossible to conceive of the two corpora in other than diachronic terms. A single diachronic contrast has little value in determining the date of written texts: an early feature might figure in a late text or a late feature in an early text for any number of reasons, as detailed previously. However, the systematic accumulation of relatively early features in the CBH corpus and relatively late features in the LBH corpus makes dialectal, stylistic, or literary explanations infeasible. The conclusion must be that CBH and LBH do indeed reflect successive stages in the development of the language. In fact, as it appears, the two corpora must have been produced at some temporal distance for their language to have grown so far apart. As Heinrich Graetz famously wrote, "Ezra could not have written a single complete verse of the Pentateuch."[48]

Some scholars have objected that the CBH-LBH contrast is based not on linguistics but on historical considerations.[49] In this view, the whole theory reflects circular reasoning and is therefore spurious. This objection is not completely unfounded. The LBH corpus was originally identified as a function of the books' references to the Persian period. Nevertheless, the circular argument has proved to be viable in this case. The prima facie evidence for the relative lateness of the LBH corpus accords with the linguistic facts: the language of the LBH corpus is thick with features that are identifiable as relatively late. Many of these features contrast with features of CBH that are on independent grounds identifiable as relatively early. Progress in the linguistic analysis of Hebrew has further clarified the contrast. The distinction between LBH and CBH was at first established on the basis of lexical evidence. But when at a later stage syntactic evidence emerged, it fully confirmed the picture.

The Criterion of Distribution

The existence of the two subcorpora provides the diachronic approach of Biblical Hebrew with a solid foundation. The notion of "late" Biblical Hebrew not only rests on typological considerations; it can be verified empirically. Let us look back for a moment to the first example in chapter 1: the contrast between *ketiv* and *qere* in 2 Sam 3:2. How do linguists know that the passive *qal* of ילד is early and the *niphal* late? They do so for two complementary reasons:

1. First, the passive *qal* in the meaning "to be born" is typologically earlier than the *niphal* in the same meaning. The *niphal* at first competed with the passive *qal* and in the end replaced it entirely. (Languages often replace forms that are less clearly marked—the passive *qal* is formally marked only by vowel pattern—with more clearly marked ones.) The passive *qal* is an archaic form that completely fell from use in the post-biblical period.
2. Second, although the passive *qal* of ילד is frequent in the CBH corpus, it is practically absent in LBH.[50]

Either reason might be counted as sufficient in deciding between early and late linguistic usage. In practice, many linguists have often used only one of the two approaches, as the material allows, sometimes to good effect. However, when the two approaches are combined, that is, when a word that is typologically later is also attested exclusively, or nearly so, in the LBH books, the claim for a diachronic explanation becomes nearly incontrovertible.

No one has insisted more on the importance of this corpus-based approach than Avi Hurvitz. Early in his career, Hurvitz developed a set of four criteria that need to be observed in historical research on Biblical Hebrew.[51] They have remained the bedrock of his method. The first of these criteria is that of "late biblical distribution." It requires that a word or expression can be regarded as representing LBH only if it is limited exclusively, or predominantly, to books of the LBH corpus.

The import of this principle is crucial. While typological considerations will often be valid in theory, they may not always lead to practical results. Some linguists have argued that the relative particle שֶׁ developed out of the relative particle אֲשֶׁר by a process of grammaticalization.[52] They may well be right, and if they are, there can be no doubt that אֲשֶׁר is an earlier form than שֶׁ. However, in a historical approach to the Hebrew language, this contrast can only be used with caution. Although שֶׁ is indeed found many times in the LBH corpus, שֶׁ/שַׁ is also attested several times in the CBH corpus.[53] A case like this does not show that the diachronic approach is built on sand, but only that diachronic development is one factor among others in language variation. Perhaps the later form שֶׁ came into vogue faster in some dialects than in others. Or perhaps the use of the shorter form had some literary effect. Whatever the explanation, the opposition between אֲשֶׁר and שֶׁ is not probative when it comes to tracing the internal chronology of Biblical Hebrew.

In contrast, where the distribution of a feature aligns neatly with the demarcation of the CBH and LBH corpora, it provides a firm basis for language-historical claims. Features attested exclusively in LBH, with a distinct counterpart in CBH, show concretely, within the limits of the available evidence, how the language evolved. The same can be said for features attested only in CBH but never in LBH.

The (Positive) Identification of CBH

From Wilhelm Gesenius to Avi Hurvitz, the diachronic study of Biblical Hebrew has been mostly a one-way street. A text with enough late features is regarded as LBH, while a text with no late features, or very few, is regarded as CBH. The rationale for this one-sided procedure, based solely on LBH features, is straightforward: because later authors know the CBH corpus (or at least part of it), and adopt much of its language, the presence of CBH features does not indicate that a text is early. Let us return for a moment to the contrast between CBH סֵפֶר and LBH אִגֶּרֶת, both meaning "letter." While all occurrences of the LBH word are in the LBH corpus, the CBH term is found throughout the Hebrew Bible.[54] The use of סֵפֶר as "letter" in Esther and Chronicles illustrates this principle: the authors of these books surely knew the word from studying earlier books like Samuel and Kings. What one ends up with is a method that positively identifies late language, but defines early language exclusively in negative terms.

Although this one-sided approach has a long history in the theory and practice of Hebrew language study, it does not accord with the facts. As we have illustrated, there are many usages that occur repeatedly in the CBH corpus but never in LBH. In some cases this distribution may be due to chance. However, when it can be shown that LBH employs a different feature in place of the CBH one, the absence in the late corpus must be judged to be significant. If additionally the disappearance of the feature can be explained from linguistic typology, the probative value is strengthened even more. Examples include the features enumerated above:

- the syntagm הִנֵּה־נָא
- temporal כִּי
- the passive *qal*

All three are frequent in CBH but practically absent from LBH, where other features take their place. Their eclipse makes sense in terms of the broader development of Hebrew over the first millennium BCE. Significantly, all three belong to the area of grammar, not vocabulary. This illustrates what we have emphasized: while it is relatively easy for a late author to adopt obsolete lexemes from old texts, it is more difficult to adopt obsolete grammar.[55]

Several other features, all of them from the realm of grammar, show up in a similar distribution. Without aiming for exhaustivity, the following features, typical of CBH but practically unattested in LBH, may be mentioned:

- infinitive absolute expressing a command[56]
- iterative *weqatal*[57]

- וַיְהִי followed by a circumstantial clause[58]
- ה *locale* following a noun in the construct state[59]
- the particles פֶּן ("lest"), טֶרֶם ("not yet"), לִקְרַאת ("toward"), לָכֵן ("therefore")

Some of these features continue from CBH into transitional Hebrew (see chapter 6). A few are found once or twice in parallel passages in Chronicles, where the author was merely copying from a source text. In Qumran Hebrew, where the effort to compose new texts in the language of scripture became more systematic, some of these features resurface. Nevertheless, in a global view, all of them distinctively characterize CBH. Many of them are also typologically early—note that none continue into Mishnaic Hebrew. Consequently, the identification of CBH need not proceed along negative lines only. Although positive markers are less abundant than for LBH, the ones that exist confirm the basic opposition between the two corpora.

Conclusions

The many kinds of linguistic variation complicate diachronic linguistics. For various reasons that cannot always be identified, relatively early features occasionally turn up in later texts, and late features in early texts. Nevertheless, CBH and LBH can clearly be recognized as distinct diachronic stages in the development of the Hebrew language. The differences between them are numerous and comprehensive, affecting both the vocabulary and the grammar. Moreover, CBH is without doubt the earlier variety and LBH the later one. They are not dialects, nor style forms, but *chronolects*. In fact, because language evolution is a slow process, a certain amount of time must have passed between the epochs during which the two corpora were composed.

CBH is found in Genesis through 2 Kings, LBH in Chronicles, Ezra-Nehemiah, Esther, Ecclesiastes, and Daniel. The clear implication of this division is that many biblical passages fall outside the CBH-LBH opposition. Some align globally with one of the two main phases: for example, Amos aligns almost entirely with CBH, while Psalm 103 aligns with LBH. Other passages reflect a transitional period situated between CBH and LBH, as we argue in more detail in chapter 6. Finally, a handful of poetic passages, such as Gen 49, Exod 15, Deut 32, and Judg 5, seem to reflect a phase prior to CBH.[60] This phase is referred to as Archaic Biblical Hebrew (ABH). The transitional and archaic phases are less well defined than the basic opposition between CBH and LBH: the texts representing them are mostly in poetry, and the corpora are relatively small, particularly for ABH. The bedrock of the diachronic approach to Hebrew is the relatively secure CBH-LBH contrast.

The distinction between CBH and LBH by itself does not yield more than a relative dating. In order to relate each chronolect to a definite period in history, other arguments must be brought into play. Chapters 5–8 examine data that tend to validate the attribution of CBH to the monarchic period and LBH to the Persian period. First, however, we need to take a closer look at an additional source of variation that affected the Hebrew Bible, namely textual alteration.

4 Textual History and Linguistic History

In the preceding chapter, we addressed the manifold factors of linguistic variation. Language is, in Roman Jakobson's term, a "dynamic synchrony," a system in an evolving equilibrium of past and incipient changes.[1] In such systems, earlier and later features mix in different proportions and do not necessarily match the progression of time. These and other factors of variation complicate the task of historical linguistics and make it more interesting. They do not make that task impossible.

A further source of variety relevant to Biblical Hebrew is textual history. The biblical texts have been preserved by scribal transmission stretching over many generations. Textual transmission, involving an orally mediated reading tradition as well as physical copying, gave rise to textual variation. Although the Masoretic tradition is more or less unified, non-Masoretic biblical manuscripts, mostly from the Dead Sea Scrolls, diverge from the MT in many details. The ancient versions, too, particularly the Septuagint, indicate the existence of variant Hebrew texts. Deciding which reading is the older one is a delicate and complicated affair. Even when no Hebrew variants are available, textual critics may question whether the received text corresponds to the original Hebrew version.

Textual variation interferes with diachronic linguistics. A famous example is the Hebrew text of the Blessing of Moses:

> Deut 33:2
> מִימִינוֹ אשדת (*qere*: אֵשׁ דָּת) לָמוֹ
> From his right hand went a fiery *law* for them. (KJV, reflecting the *qere*)
> At his right, a host of his own. (NRSV, after the *ketiv*)

The Hebrew word דָּת ("law"), as traditionally identified in this verse,[2] raises a question for the historical linguist.[3] The noun דָּת is otherwise attested only in the late books of Esther and Ezra.[4] This would be the only case of a Persian loanword in the Pentateuch. Yet the difficulty is superficial, for the text is problematic. The MT itself indicates that the reading דָּת is only one possibility, because it is the *qere*, the text as read. The *ketiv*, the text as written, has a different reading, אשדת.[5] The versions also indicate different readings. The Septuagint has ἐκ δεξιῶν αὐτοῦ ἄγγελοι μετ' αὐτοῦ ("at his right, *angels* with him") and the Peshitta has ܡܢ ܝܡܝܢܗ. ܝܗܒ ܠܗܘܢ ("from his right he *gave* to him"), neither of which seems to reflect the *qere*. The textual data are messy, but they suffice to raise doubts about the authenticity of the Masoretic *qere*. The *qere* may reflect a late midrashic interpretation of an earlier text that was at some point no longer understood. The expression אֵשׁ דָּת ("fire of the law") does not represent the earliest text of the verse, and as such does not provide a solid basis for historical linguistics.[6]

The present chapter evaluates the issue of textual variation and how it affects the diachronic approach to Biblical Hebrew.

The Masoretic Pointing

The MT is notoriously a layered text. One of its latest layers is the Masoretic pointing: the vocalization and accents. The pointing as it has come down to us was devised during the Middle Ages and cannot have been added to the text much before the ninth century. Consequently, some textual critics adopt an indifferent attitude toward the pointing, disregarding the cantillation completely and altering the vocalization at will. Hebraists are generally more appreciative.[7] The Tiberian vocalization included in the MT includes much phonological information that could not have been known in the Middle Ages unless it was transmitted via a reliable reading tradition spanning many centuries. The oral reading and the written transcription of the text went hand in hand for many centuries: biblical scribes would copy a text they knew intimately. Although the vowel signs are medieval, the oral sounds they encode are much older. There are, of course, variants of vocalization. Transcriptions in the Septuagint or in Origen's second column of the Hexapla, Babylonian or Palestinian pointing in early manuscripts, and the oral tradition of the Samaritan Pentateuch offer many alternative readings differing only in the vocalization. Such variation does not show that the Tiberian vocalization is spurious or arbitrary. The variants should be evaluated text-critically, just like variants in the consonantal text.[8]

In general, from a text-critical and linguistic perspective the Tiberian pointing of the received text is of excellent quality. Only occasionally can it be demonstrated to be secondary. A small number of exegetical variants are widely recognized, where the vocalization does not reflect the earliest text but a later interpretation:

> Isa 1:12
> כִּי תָבֹאוּ לֵרָאוֹת פָּנָי מִי־בִקֵּשׁ זֹאת מִיֶּדְכֶם
> When you come *to appear before me*, who has required this from your hand?

Literally, the Hebrew means "to be seen my face," which is syntactically awkward. Instead of the *niphal* לֵרָאוֹת, it seems the *qal* לִרְאוֹת was originally meant.[9] This was changed because it suggested too corporeal an image of God.[10] This example has some historical linguistic relevance because the elision of the *he* in *niphal* infinitives is not usual in Biblical Hebrew but becomes more common in the postbiblical period. As transmitted in the MT, the form does not fit the language of the book of Isaiah, but that of a later period.[11]

Other variants of vocalization have their origin in the evolution of the language itself. Where the consonantal text allowed it, postclassical or postbiblical grammar at times insinuated itself into the reading tradition:

> 1 Sam 3:7
> וּשְׁמוּאֵל טֶרֶם יָדַע אֶת־יְהוָה וְטֶרֶם יִגָּלֶה אֵלָיו דְּבַר־יְהוָה
> Now Samuel did not yet know YHWH, and the word of YHWH had not yet been revealed to him.

In Biblical Hebrew, the particle טֶרֶם is usually followed by the imperfect, even in past-tense contexts.[12] This makes the combination טֶרֶם יָדַע suspicious. As Samuel Driver writes in his *Notes on Samuel*, "The parallel יִגָּלֶה makes it probable that the narrator himself would have vocalized יֵדַע."[13] The change from imperfect to perfect reflects the influence of later Hebrew. In the Bible, טֶרֶם + perfect is attested only twice, but in Qumran Hebrew it is found eight times.[14]

Many other possible cases of secondary vocalizations have been pointed out in the literature.[15] As can be seen in the two foregoing examples, such changes in the vocabulary can hamper a diachronic approach. The examples also illustrate, however, that standard procedures of textual criticism often resolve the problem. Textual criticism and diachronic linguistics complement each other. The judicious combination of the two approaches paves the way to a correct understanding of the text.[16]

The Consonantal Text

The consonantal text of the Hebrew Bible is attested, fragmentarily, from the third century BCE onward. Thus, its material attestation goes back more than a millennium before that of the vowels and the cantillation. Nevertheless, it too has come down to us in varied forms. Manual copying leads to divergences, some of which may spread through a large part or all of the manuscript evidence. On which text, then, should historical linguists base their analysis? And if one cannot be certain that the available text conforms to the original writing, how can its language be used for dating purposes?

Textual corruption indeed constitutes a challenge to the diachronic approach. Where it does, however, textual criticism often comes to the aid of the historical linguist:

2 Sam 13:39
וַתְּכַל דָּוִד הַמֶּלֶךְ לָצֵאת אֶל־אַבְשָׁלוֹם
And King David completed [*sic*] to go out to Absalom.

The phrase דָּוִד הַמֶּלֶךְ in the MT, in this order, is unexpected in the book of Samuel.[17] This sequence is typical of LBH.[18] Everywhere else in Samuel and Kings, twenty-two times in all, we find the sequence הַמֶּלֶךְ דָּוִד. If an analysis were based on the MT only, one would have to conclude that this verse reflects LBH. However, when textual criticism is taken into account, the LBH expression in this MT verse is shown to be secondary.

The MT, with a feminine verb (תְּכַל) and a masculine subject, is hardly correct. Julius Wellhausen conjectured, on the basis of the Lucianic Greek, that instead of דָּוִד ("David"), רוּחַ ("spirit") was to be read:[19]

LXX[L]: καὶ ἐκόπασε τὸ πνεῦμα τοῦ βασιλέως Δαυιδ τοῦ ἐξελθεῖν ἐπὶ Αβεσσαλωμ
Retroversion: ותכל רוח המלך לצאת אל אבשלום
And the *spirit* of the king pined away after Absalom.

The graphic difference between דוד and רוח is small. Because רוּחַ is usually feminine, the emendation restores grammatical correctness to the verse. In addition, the verb כלה ("to come to an end") combines with רוּחַ in an idiomatic way attested elsewhere in the biblical corpus.[20] The conjectured reading has received confirmation from the Qumran scrolls:[21]

4QSam[a]: [ותכל רו]ח המלך ל צ[את אל אב]שלום

Wellhausen's emendation of the MT is now widely accepted among textual critics.[22] A number of conclusions can be drawn from these considerations:

- The corruption in the MT should probably be attributed to accident, not to conscious modernizing. Yet the corrupted text partly follows the grammar of LBH, with which a late scribe would have been familiar.
- The reading וַתְּכַל רוּחַ הַמֶּלֶךְ can be restored on the basis of normal text-critical procedures, without reference to historical linguistics. Yet notably, the restored reading is in accord with CBH grammar.

This example illustrates the way textual criticism and historical linguistics, far from conflicting, reinforce one another.

Let us consider another example where the MT and the Qumran text have divergent readings:

1 Sam 20:31
MT: כָל־הַיָּמִים אֲשֶׁר בֶּן־יִשַׁי חַי עַל־הָאֲדָמָה לֹא תִכּוֹן אַתָּה וּמַלְכוּתֶךָ
For as long as the son of Jesse is alive on the earth, *you and* your kingdom will not be established.
4QSam[b]: כל הימים אשר בן ישי חי על האדמה לא תכן את ממלכתך
For as long as the son of Jesse is alive on the earth, your kingdom will not be established.

In this case the secondary nature of the MT does not leap to the eye as it does in the preceding example. Most commentaries see no need to discuss the text. Nevertheless, the comparison of the MT with the text of 4QSam[b] exposes a problem. While the verb כון ("to establish") is used frequently in connection with kingship in Samuel-Kings, it never combines in those contexts with a personal pronoun (as here: אַתָּה, "you").[23] What is "established" is the rule or the kingdom, not the present or future king. Therefore, the clause תִכּוֹן אַתָּה וּמַלְכוּתֶךָ is somewhat anomalous. In contrast, the text of 4QSam[b] conforms to expectations. This text is also confirmed by the Old Greek reading, οὐχ ἑτοιμασθήσεται ἡ βασιλεία σου ("your kingdom will not be established"). Internal and external criteria make it likely that the non-Masoretic reading is the older one, whereas the MT reflects a scribal mistake. The process of corruption can be retraced with confidence: the *nota accusativi* את in the older text marked the subject of the *niphal* תִּכּוֹן. This type of syntax is entirely normal.[24] However, the *nota accusativi* is neither necessary nor frequent in this function. One understands, therefore, how את could be misread as the personal pronoun אתה ("you"). This change further led to the addition of a connecting *waw* between "you" and "your kingdom."

It is interesting to observe that the slight rewriting of the passage also led to the substitution of one word meaning "kingdom" for another. While the older form of the text preserved in 4QSam[b] reads ממלכה, the usual noun in CBH, the secondary form of the text transmitted in the MT has מַלְכוּת, a typical feature of LBH.[25]

The next example illustrates some fine points of textual variation and grammar:

> Deut 19:3
> MT: תָּכִין לְךָ הַדֶּרֶךְ
> You shall prepare yourself the way (and divide the borders of your land, which YHWH your God causes you to inherit, into three parts, that every manslayer may flee there).
> SP: תכן לך הדרך
> LXX: στόχασαί σοι τὴν ὁδόν
> Measure for yourself the way.

In this passage, the possibilities are more evenly balanced. The MT reading is plausible, "to prepare the way for the manslayer seeking asylum." But so is the reading of the Septuagint, "to measure the way." In the scenario of the Septuagint version, the territory will be divided into three parts as a function of the distance a manslayer would have to cover to get to a city of refuge. The consonantal text of the Samaritan Pentateuch confirms the Septuagint reading and reveals its Hebrew source text:[26] instead of MT's תָּכִין, an imperfect *hiphil* of כון, the translation reflects a form of the root תכן ("to measure"), probably the infinitive absolute, *qal* or *piel*. Most commentators and textual critics have been perfectly happy to adopt the MT, but the alternative reading arguably fits the context better.[27]

In linguistic perspective, the SP-LXX reading is in accord with normal CBH usage, but the MT reading is not. In CBH prose there are few instances of the long form of the imperfect in first position in the clause and none of the second-person imperfect in this position.[28] In CBH, the normal, nonjussive imperfect is almost entirely limited to nonfirst positions in the clause. The linguistic argument inclines one to prefer the non-Masoretic reading. Even if the textual argument is inconclusive by itself, linguistics and textual criticism can be shown to be compatible.

Picking Up the Slack: The Criterion of Accumulation

Although textual criticism often comes to the aid of historical linguistics, this is not always the case. The textual state of the Hebrew Bible is not such that one can identify, let alone restore, all the secondary alterations. As we noted earlier, some scribal mistakes happened early enough in the textual history to affect all attested witnesses. The text of the Hebrew Bible is to some extent uncertain. This does not imperil the diachronic approach, however. The comprehensive difference between the CBH and LBH corpora, documented in chapter 3, could hardly be the result of textual corruption.[29] Again, one of the methodological principles formulated by Hurvitz is helpful at this point.[30] To argue for a late date of a biblical text, an accumulation of late elements is required: "A text suspected of being of post-Classical provenance can be so classified only if it contains an abundance of late linguistic features."[31] As we saw in chapter 3, a short extract from the book of Esther exhibited at least seven late features. A text of any length written in LBH will show at least a handful of features.

Textual uncertainty does not negate the diachronic approach. In fact, its most immediate implication is that in dating a text on the basis of linguistic criteria, one should tolerate a small number of deviant features. It is well known, for example, that the Joseph story contains a small number of late linguistic features, notably the Aramaisms שַׁלִּיט ("governor, 42:6) and מָזוֹן ("food," 45:23).[32] Both of these are well-known Aramaic loanwords in Hebrew, whose other attestations are limited to the LBH corpus (see Eccl 10:5; 2 Chr 11:23). Nevertheless, the presence of these words does not indicate that the Joseph story was composed at a late date, or that it is contemporary with LBH literature. If the Joseph story were coeval with the LBH corpus, one would expect it to exhibit not two or three late elements but twenty or thirty. In fact, however, Gen 37–50 is written in brilliant CBH, with a number of features that are never found in LBH:

- "Fine linen" is שֵׁשׁ (Gen 41:42), not בוץ as in LBH.[33]
- The particle אֲבָל has an asseverative meaning (Gen 42:21), not an adversative one as in LBH.[34]

- The *he locale* is attached to the construct state (e.g., בֵּיתָה יוֹסֵף Gen 43:17; see also Gen 43:24; 46:1; 47:14), as found some twenty times in CBH, but never in LBH.[35]
- The infinitive construct is used without prefixed *lamed* (Gen 37:4, 8; 44:1; 48:11), as is frequent in CBH prose but uncommon in LBH prose.[36]
- The particle נָא attaches to אִם (Gen 47:29; 50:4) and אַל (Gen 47:29) in a way that is unattested in LBH.
- The imperative is continued by means of a *weqatal* form (Gen 44:4; 45:9), a type of syntax virtually unattested in LBH.[37]

The few Aramaisms signaled here must therefore be explained differently. One or another may be a foreign word used by the author of the Joseph story for literary effect. Much more likely, they are due to incidental modernization by a later scribe or reflect late glosses that crept into the text in the course of textual transmission.[38]

Linguistic Modernization

Textual alterations happen for all kinds of reasons. Many corrupt readings are generated by accident, whereas other readings may be due to unconscious adaptation of the text to the linguistic and cultural norms of the scribe. It is also possible, however, that a scribe or group of scribes sets out intentionally to modernize a text in order to render it more understandable. A well-known example of systematic modernization is the Great Isaiah Scroll from Qumran, 1QIsa[a]. As Yehezkel Kutscher showed, the scroll may be loosely characterized as a rewriting of the book in the Hebrew of the Second Temple period. The text has modernizations in the realm of orthography, morphology, vocabulary, and syntax.[39] A famous example is the substitution of דרמשק for דַּמֶּשֶׂק ("Damascus") in Isa 7:8 and elsewhere, adapting the geographical name to the form that was used in late Second Temple times. Another interesting case, involving morphology, is the replacement of the adverb דוּמָם ("silently") with the nominal form דממה in Isa 47:5. The adverbial ending *–am* fell from use in the postclassical period.[40]

Another word substitution is illustrated in the following example:

Isa 9:16
MT: עַל־כֵּן עַל־בַּחוּרָיו לֹא־יִשְׂמַח אֲדֹנָי וְאֶת־יְתֹמָיו וְאֶת־אַלְמְנֹתָיו לֹא יְרַחֵם
Therefore the Lord does not have pity on their young men, or compassion on their orphans and widows.

1QIsa[a]: על כן על בחוריו לוא יחמול אדוני ואת יתומיו ואת אלמנותיו לוא ירחם

The rare root שמח II ("to have pity") was replaced with the common Hebrew חמל with the same meaning.

An interesting instance of modernized syntax is the way infinitive constructs are systematically combined with *lamed* in the Scroll even where the MT has the older construction without the preposition: לֹא תוֹסִיפוּ הָבִיא מִנְחַת־שָׁוְא ("you shall not continue to bring vain offerings," Isa 1:13) becomes in 1QIsa[a] לוא תוסיפו להביא מנחת שוא.

Although the Great Isaiah Scroll is a thousand years older than the earliest Masoretic manuscripts, there can be no doubt that in all these examples the MT has the older reading and the Scroll the later modernization. 1QIsa[a] represents a popular version of the prophetic book, adapted to make it more easily understandable by readers of the Second Temple period.

Something similar is found in the Samaritan Pentateuch (SP). Many small changes in the consonantal Samaritan text can be explained as adaptations to the orthography, morphology, or syntax of a later type of Hebrew. Thus, in Exod 22:6, where the MT has the passive *qal* וְגֻנַּב ("and it be stolen"), the SP has the *niphal* ונגנב; in Gen 1:24, where the MT has the archaic expression וְחַיְתוֹ־אֶרֶץ ("beasts of the earth"), the SP has normalized it to וחית הארץ. A case of modernizing vocabulary is found in Gen 49:11, where the archaic סות ("robe") is replaced with the prosaic כסות ("covering"). The tendency to adapt the CBH of the Pentateuch to a later chronolect continues in the reading tradition of the Samaritans.[41]

Systematic modernization raises a theoretical problem. In the Samaritan Pentateuch and the Great Isaiah Scroll, the date of much of the language is not indicative of the date of the text. Even the criterion of accumulation fails us here: both these texts contain a plethora of linguistic features that point to the Hellenistic period, yet neither is likely to have been composed at so late a date. It is important, however, to maintain a pragmatic approach. Whether linguists would have been able to establish the relatively early date of the Pentateuch on the basis of the Samaritan Pentateuch is an interesting question, but its answer does not affect the cogency of the diachronic approach. The fact is that the MT of Isaiah and the Pentateuch does not exhibit this modernizing profile. On the whole, the MT is a rather conservative and well-preserved text. Occasional modernizations exist, but they did not affect the MT to the extent of making the diachronic approach impossible.

Textual Criticism and Redaction Criticism

An additional consideration arises in connection with textual history. In some biblical books, the comparison of textual witnesses reveals the existence of redactional (or editorial) stages. The prime exhibit is the book of Jeremiah, but scholars have shown that other books fall in the same category. The list is growing: Exodus, Joshua, 1 Kings, Ezekiel, Proverbs, Daniel, Esther, and other books are attested in differing stages of redaction.[42] This phenomenon too has relevance for the diachronic study of Biblical Hebrew.

In recent years, it has become increasingly clear that textual changes not only are caused by scribal mistakes and modernizing revisions but in some instances reflect alternative editions of the books in which they occur. Textual criticism and redaction criticism blend into one another. In the book of Jeremiah, the MT contains many elements—ranging from a single word to several verses—that are missing in the Old Greek translation.[43] The most likely explanation for this divergence between the two main witnesses is that the MT and the Septuagint reflect distinct editions of the book. Because the short edition of the Septuagint is also attested in a Hebrew manuscript from Qumran, 4QJer^{b}, it is certain that both editions existed in Hebrew. Most textual scholars hold that the shorter edition represented by the Septuagint is the older one and that the MT is the result of later expansion. The date of the expanded edition is debated, with hypotheses ranging from the sixth to the second century BCE. Nor is it certain that the expansion was made in one pass. Perhaps it reflects a longer process of incremental supplementation.

If the additional parts in the expanded edition prove to be significantly later than the shorter text, this will have repercussions for linguistic analysis. It has indeed been possible to identify a number of late elements in the Masoretic pluses. For example, the use of the adverb יוֹמָם as a noun meaning "daytime" in Jer 33:20, the use of the preposition לְ to indicate movement toward a place in Jer 3:17, and the use of an anticipatory pronoun in Jer 9:14—elements not reflected in the Septuagint version—are not typical of CBH but well attested in LBH and Qumran Hebrew.[44] These features indicate that the additional layer in the MT of Jeremiah is of a later date than most of the short text.[45] Sporadic cases of late language in Masoretic pluses have been identified in other books as well.[46]

Nevertheless, each case must be judged on its own merits. The mere absence of a passage in one textual witness does not necessarily indicate that the passage was composed in the Persian period or later. Other scenarios are possible as well.

In some cases, text may have been omitted intentionally.[47] In the book of Job, large sections of the text are missing in the Old Greek translation. This phenomenon almost certainly does not indicate textual growth. The shorter text is the creation of the Greek translator, who omitted extensive parts no doubt because he struggled to understand them or judged them to be excessively repetitive.[48]

Other omissions are due to accidents of transmission. The Great Isaiah Scroll attests several sizable minuses in comparison with the other textual witness. Ulrich has argued that these minuses reflect a relatively early stage of textual growth.[49] In his view, the corresponding pluses in the MT are secondary additions made in the Hellenistic period. However, the fact that many of the omissions occur at regular intervals in the text may suggest a different explanation.[50] It appears the exemplar from which the second part of the book was copied was defective. The missing parts were absent or illegible in the scroll from which 1QIsa[a] was copied.

Another possibility is that a textual minus indicates an insertion, but the supplementation occurred at an early date. A very interesting example in this regard is a short passage in Judges 6:

Jud 6:7–10

7 וַֽיְהִ֕י כִּֽי־זָעֲק֥וּ בְנֵֽי־יִשְׂרָאֵ֖ל אֶל־יְהוָ֑ה עַ֖ל אֹד֥וֹת מִדְיָֽן׃ 8 וַיִּשְׁלַ֧ח יְהוָ֛ה אִ֥ישׁ נָבִ֖יא אֶל־בְּנֵ֣י יִשְׂרָאֵ֑ל
וַיֹּ֨אמֶר לָהֶ֜ם כֹּה־אָמַ֣ר יְהוָ֣ה ׀ אֱלֹהֵ֣י יִשְׂרָאֵ֗ל אָנֹכִ֞י הֶעֱלֵ֤יתִי אֶתְכֶם֙ מִמִּצְרַ֔יִם וָאֹצִ֥יא אֶתְכֶ֖ם מִבֵּ֥ית
עֲבָדִֽים׃ 9 וָאַצִּ֤ל אֶתְכֶם֙ מִיַּ֣ד מִצְרַ֔יִם וּמִיַּ֖ד כָּל־לֹחֲצֵיכֶ֑ם וָאֲגָרֵ֤שׁ אוֹתָם֙ מִפְּנֵיכֶ֔ם וָאֶתְּנָ֥ה לָכֶ֖ם אֶת־
אַרְצָֽם׃ 10 וָאֹמְרָ֣ה לָכֶ֗ם אֲנִי֙ יְהוָ֣ה אֱלֹהֵיכֶ֔ם לֹ֤א תִֽירְאוּ֙ אֶת־אֱלֹהֵ֣י הָֽאֱמֹרִ֔י אֲשֶׁ֥ר אַתֶּ֖ם יוֹשְׁבִ֣ים
בְּאַרְצָ֑ם וְלֹ֥א שְׁמַעְתֶּ֖ם בְּקוֹלִֽי׃

7 When the Israelites cried out to YHWH on account of the Midianites, 8 YHWH sent a prophet to the Israelites; and he said to them, "Thus says YHWH, the God of Israel: 'I led you up from Egypt, and brought you out of the house of slavery, 9 and delivered you from the hand of the Egyptians, and from the hand of all who oppressed you, and drove them out before you, and gave you their land. 10 And I said to you, "I am YHWH your God; you shall not revere the gods of the Amorites, in whose land you live." But you did not heed my voice.'"

The passage stands out in its context and was already in the nineteenth century identified as a secondary addition.[51] The hypothesis of insertion was confirmed when a Hebrew manuscript from Qumran, 4QJudg[a], came to light in which precisely these verses are missing. The conjunction of contextual considerations and external empirical evidence has led most scholars to accept the notion that Jud 6:7–10 was secondarily added to a shorter Hebrew text of Judges. This conclusion appears to be justified. The date of the addition is a different question. Alexander Rofé, although accepting the secondary nature of the passage, has argued on the basis of its content that it is pre-Deuteronomistic.[52] The language of the passage confirms this approach: it contains no late features at all,[53] but it exhibits several usages that are uncommon in the LBH corpus:

- The first-person singular pronoun אָנֹכִי (v. 8) is typical of CBH but very poorly attested in LBH.[54]
- Temporal כִּי (v. 7) aligns with CBH against LBH.[55]
- The expression עַל אֹדוֹת ("because of," v. 7) is found nine times in the CBH corpus but never in LBH.

Thus, it appears likely that this addition was inserted during the monarchic period or soon after. There is no a priori reason textual growth could not have happened in this early period. Admittedly, it is difficult to trace the textual history of this passage in detail. Rofé argues that, after having been added secondarily, it dropped out accidentally from the textual strand represented by 4QJudg[a]. This seems unlikely. It is more likely that the shorter text illustrates the well-known fact that distinct textual stages may continue to coexist over a long period of time.

Many scholars believe the instances of textual growth confirmed by external attestation—passages missing in the Septuagint or in a Qumran fragment—are only the tip of the iceberg. Numerous other passages in the Hebrew Bible may have been added secondarily even if they are attested in all available witnesses. The extent to which this is true is open to debate, but even if it is admitted that biblical literature was created by successive supplementation, this does not make the linguistic approach infeasible. If any stratum was added in the period when the LBH corpus was composed, this should show up in its language.

Conclusions

The conclusions that we draw concerning textual variation are much the same as for the sources of variation addressed in the preceding chapter. The textual history of the Hebrew Bible creates local "noise," but it does not alter the big picture. The profiles of CBH and LBH are distinct despite textual alterations. The criterion of accumulation allows historical linguists to tell them apart.

When textual criticism is brought into the picture, it has the global effect of confirming the diachronic approach. The textual history of the Hebrew Bible provides an explanation for occasional "false positives," late features occurring in a relatively early text. In addition, such late features in the CBH corpus can often be shown to have entered the text secondarily, as scribal mistakes, as occasional modernizations, or as products of textual growth. Textual criticism and historical linguistics reinforce one another, and together contribute to a better understanding of the biblical text.

5 Inscriptions and Preexilic Hebrew Literature

Although it is relatively easy to show that the language of Ezra-Nehemiah, Chronicles, Ecclesiastes, Esther, and Daniel is later than that of the Pentateuch and Former Prophets, it is much harder to relate the two chronolects to a definite period in the history of Israel. CBH must be earlier than LBH, but setting precise limits to either of them is difficult. Nevertheless, a number of benchmarks can be established. As we will show in the present chapter, CBH must have been in use at a time overlapping that of Judean inscriptions of the monarchic era, for their language is in essential points very similar.[1]

In the early nineteenth century, when the diachronic approach to ancient Hebrew was first developed, no Hebrew inscriptions from the biblical period were known.[2] Wilhelm Gesenius related CBH to the monarchic period on the basis of the historical research of Wilhelm de Wette.[3] The first discovery of ancient Hebrew epigraphy was the Siloam inscription, which came to light in 1880.[4] Today the corpus has grown enormously, and new documents are still being discovered.[5] This makes it possible, to a certain extent, to distinguish different dialects within the epigraphic corpus. The singular feminine noun meaning "year" systematically turns up as שת in Northern Hebrew (e.g., Samaria 1.1) but as שנה in Judean Hebrew.[6] Diphthongs contract in Northern Hebrew: ין [*yēn*] "wine" (Samaria 4.3) but not in Judean Hebrew ייז [*yayin*] (Arad 1.3).[7] In these points, Biblical Hebrew goes with the Judean inscriptions.[8]

Judean inscriptions of any length and readability cluster in the period between the second half of the eighth and the beginning of the sixth century BCE.[9] Many scholars have expressed the opinion that the linguistic proximity of these inscriptions to Biblical Hebrew, and to classical prose texts in particular, is significant. George Cooke, in his textbook of Northwest Semitic inscriptions, says about the Siloam inscription: "The style is pure and idiomatic, and reads like a good prose passage out of the O.T."[10] In the recent debate, it has often been argued that such proximity indicates a date in the monarchic period for CBH.[11]

Other scholars have insisted more on the differences between the corpora.[12] Some have gone so far as to argue on this basis that Biblical Hebrew is not a genuine language contemporary with the inscriptions but an artificial idiom created later for the purpose of writing religious literature.[13]

To get a clear view of the relation between Biblical Hebrew and epigraphic Hebrew, a number of issues need to be sorted out. We attempt to do this here. We address some issues briefly, while the more important matters are discussed extensively.

Script and Orthography

An obvious difference between the inscriptions and CBH is the script. The change in script is of little importance for the analysis of the language. Nevertheless, it is interesting in its own right and deserves some remarks. The inscriptions are written in paleo-Hebrew, while most biblical manuscripts are in the later Aramaic "square" script. A number of manuscripts discovered in Qumran, limited to Pentateuchal books and Job, are written in paleo-Hebrew, and this practice continued in the Samaritan Pentateuch, whose script is a direct descendant of the old national script. Whether this indicates that some circles always copied their ancestral writings in the old script is debated.[14] It is possible that at one time all copying of biblical writings was done in the square script and that the use of paleo-Hebrew reflects a type of revival.

Even if the latter scenario should turn out to be correct, this still means that a switch occurred in scribal practice between the time the CBH writings were composed and the middle of the third century BCE, when the earliest biblical scrolls from Qumran were copied. Other evidence shows that a change from paleo-Hebrew to Aramaic script must have happened at some point. Many variant readings are difficult to explain on the basis of the square script but are immediately understandable if they were created in the old Hebrew script.[15] Note the following:

1 Kgs 3:16
MT: אָז תָּבֹאנָה שְׁתַּיִם נָשִׁים זֹנוֹת אֶל־הַמֶּלֶךְ
LXX: Τότε ὤφθησαν δύο γυναῖκες πόρναι τῷ βασιλεῖ
Then two prostitutes *came* (MT) / *appeared* (LXX) to the king.

Greek ὤφθησαν probably reflects a Hebrew reading תראנה (תראינה in the *plene* writing characteristic of the MT): third-person feminine plural of the *niphal* of ראה ("to see"). Whichever of these variants is preferable, the change of the one into the other must have happened in paleo-Hebrew script, where *beth* and *resh* (𐤁 and 𐤓) are easily confused.

What is true for the script is true for the orthography as well. The orthography of biblical manuscripts reflects the Second Temple period and differs from that of the monarchic period. One notable difference is the more developed use of vowel letters in the later period. Another is the spelling of the third-person singular suffix on singular nouns, written with *he* in the inscriptions: עבדה ("his servant," Meṣad Ḥashavyahu 1.2), but with *waw* in biblical manuscripts: עבדו (Gen 24:2). This change in orthographic practice may have been gradual, as is suggested by the remarkable spelling בו in Ketef Hinnom 1.11, considered alongside the number of cases of the *he* suffix in the biblical text.[16] Again, these differences have little implication for the date of the biblical texts. What they show is that in the transmission of the biblical text, the orthography was at some point adapted to later practice. Some of the biblical scrolls found in the Qumran caves use an even later orthography characterized by hypertrophic use of vowel letters.[17] This again shows that scribes had the latitude to modernize the orthography of older writings.[18]

Other Differences between Biblical Hebrew and the Inscriptions

Any comparison between Biblical Hebrew and the Judean Hebrew in the inscriptions has to take account of the differences between the corpora. The epigraphic corpus is much smaller than the biblical one. It also differs globally in subject matter, being primarily concerned with everyday matters, such as sending wine and ingratiating oneself with one's superiors, rather than with the famous deeds of ancestors and kings and the religious matters that loom large in the biblical corpus.

Vocabulary

Because of the quantitative and qualitative differences just described, many words of the Hebrew Bible are unattested in the inscriptions. Even some common words such as דרך ("road") or לילה ("night") are simply lacking in the inscriptions. The verb הלך ("to go"), found 1,557 times in the Bible, has a single attestation in the entire epigraphic corpus: "the water *went* (i.e., *flowed*) from the spring to the pool" (Siloam 1.4–5). This does not mean that these words were unknown to the authors of the inscriptions, let alone that they were invented later, but simply that there was no contextual need to use them in the extant texts.

The reverse is statistically more significant. Several words or usages occurring in the inscriptions are absent from the Bible. The following are characteristic examples:

- אסם (" to store"), Meṣad Ḥashavyahu 1.5,6–7; the noun is attested twice in the Bible
- בכר ("to grant"), Lachish 2.5
- זדה ("misalignment"), Siloam 1.3
- נקבה ("tunnel, tunneling"), Siloam 1.1
- תסבה in בתסבת הבקר ("at the break of dawn"), Lachish 4.9; cf. לִפְנוֹת בֹּקֶר in Biblical Hebrew[19]
- עוד ("remainder"), Arad 1:5; 5:3; elsewhere used as an adverb, as in Biblical Hebrew, e.g., Siloam 1:1, 2
- רכב ("to load"), Arad 1:6–7

Some of the formulas of politeness in the Lachish letters are also without parallel in the Bible.[20]

Although it is important to note these data, their implication is not self-evident. Some of these words may be lacking in the biblical corpus by accident. Note that the verb כול ("to measure"), which is used three times in the Meṣad Ḥashavyahu text (1.5, 6, 8), is attested just once in the Bible, in a highly poetic and theological context: "Who measured (כָּל) the dust of the earth?" (Isa 40:12). Note also that the noun מז, "extract of raisins, sweet wine" (Lachish 30.1), was unattested in the Bible until it was restored by a text-critical analysis:

> Ps 75:9
> For in the hand of YHWH there is a cup, and the wine is red and full of mixture, *and he pours out its sweet wine*, but all the wicked of the earth shall drain its dregs and drink them.
>
> MT: וַיַּגֵּר מִזֶּה ("he pours out from this")
> Conjectured original: וַיַּגֵּר מִזֵּה ("he pours out its sweet wine")[21]

Cases like this show to what degree attestation is a matter of chance.[22] The authors of the biblical text may have known the words listed above, but simply found no occasion to use them.

Even if the lack of these words indicated that they were absent from the vocabulary of the biblical authors, this would have no obvious diachronic implications. The differences between Biblical Hebrew and epigraphic Hebrew might in this case be due to regional variation or, in some cases, to the use of professional jargon.

Register

Although lapidary inscriptions such as Siloam were inscribed to last, most epigraphic texts were ephemeral. The Arad and Lachish letters deal with immediate issues that were no longer relevant shortly afterward. In a few texts one finds evidence of inattention. Thus the spellings נבשכם for נפשכם ("your lives," Arad 24.18) and, in the same document, והבקידם for והפקידם ("and he will hand them over," Arad 23.14–15) reflect the pronunciation of these words, not their etymology.[23] More generally, many inscriptions are stylistically uneven and difficult to make sense of. Some of this messiness may be due to the situated nature of the writing, in which the author and his correspondent knew what was at issue and therefore did not formulate it explicitly. But some of the disorder certainly reflects the haste with which the documents were prepared.[24]

In comparison, the biblical corpus for the most part has a literary character. The texts were written and assembled with much care, and they were meant to serve for many generations. The historical books may contain some archival material, but if so it was incorporated into a literary framework.

This difference in register explains some of the divergences between the two corpora. It has been remarked, for instance, that the Siloam inscription does not use narrative ויהי when it updates the reference time:[25]

> Siloam 1.3–4
> ובים הנקבה הכו החצבם אש לקרת רעו גרזן על [ג]רזן
> And on the day the tunneling (was completed), the masons struck toward one another, pick against pick.[26]

In CBH, such shifts in the reference time are systematically introduced by וַיְהִי:

Exod 16:22
וַיְהִי בַּיּוֹם הַשִּׁשִּׁי לָקְטוּ לֶחֶם מִשְׁנֶה שְׁנֵי הָעֹמֶר לָאֶחָד
And it came to pass on the sixth day, they gathered twice as much bread, two omers for each.

On the basis of this divergence, it has been proposed that Biblical Hebrew וַיְהִי was a literary creation of the Persian period.[27] This view is hard to accept. Not only is its evidentiary basis extremely narrow, it also does not account for the distribution of narrative וַיְהִי within the biblical corpus. As has been pointed out by several Hebraists, this stylistic device is much more frequent, and its uses far more diverse, in CBH than in LBH.[28] Some idiomatic combinations involving narrative וַיְהִי in Kings were apparently misunderstood by the Chronicler. All this makes little sense if the whole usage was created only in the Persian period. It is far more plausible to posit that narrative וַיְהִי belongs to a relatively early stratum of Biblical Hebrew. This will account for its frequency and diversity in CBH. In later Hebrew style this device was still used, under the influence of earlier textual models, but other usages competed with it. In postbiblical Hebrew, narrative וַיְהִי disappears completely. The absence of ויהי in the Siloam inscription is best attributed to a difference in stylistic register: the biblical narratives are belles lettres, the inscription a matter-of-fact account.

Stylistic differences between "high" literature that has been transmitted in a manuscript tradition and ephemeral documents uncovered by archeologists are found in other culture areas. A well-known case is that of Hellenistic Greek literature in comparison with contemporary documentary papyri.[29] It is no surprise to find similar differences between Biblical Hebrew and epigraphic Hebrew.

Systematic Similarities between Epigraphic Judean Hebrew and CBH

The differences between epigraphic Judean Hebrew and CBH that we have discussed so far are peripheral in linguistic perspective. Turning to matters that belong to the core of the Hebrew language system, we are struck instead by the far-reaching similarities between the two corpora. Phonology and, to some extent, morphology are hard to evaluate because of the nature of the writing system of the inscriptions. Medial vowels are rarely indicated with a vowel letter, and final long vowels are not necessarily marked. While some of the morphology of the inscriptions may have diverged from Biblical Hebrew,[30] there are hardly any cases in which such divergences can be demonstrated.[31] However, the bulk of the vocabulary of the inscriptions and all the syntax can be paralleled from passages in the Hebrew Bible.[32]

Particularly relevant in the present context is the fact that epigraphic Hebrew exhibits several features, both lexical and grammatical, that are characteristic of CBH but rare or unattested in LBH.[33] Some of these may be due to accident, similar to the situation for epigraphic vocabulary not attested in Biblical Hebrew. Thus, the noun צמד ("pair [of animals]") is attested once in Arad 3.4–5, five times in CBH, twice in First Isaiah, and once in Job,[34] but never in LBH.[35] The absence of the word from LBH is not necessarily significant, however, because the corpus contains no passages that mention pairs of animals. Similarly, the verb ענה ("to answer") is used twice in the Meṣad Ḥashavyahu text (1.10, 11) in the sense "to testify." This meaning is attested in CBH and elsewhere,[36] but not in LBH. But again, there may be no passages in the LBH corpus where this meaning was needed.

The situation is different when LBH uses an equivalent expression. The Arad and Lachish letters systematically refer to themselves and other written missives with the Hebrew noun ספר ("letter"). The same word is used in Kings wherever letters are mentioned. In LBH, the noun סֵפֶר tends to express different meanings, primarily the meaning "book." Letters are referred to with the Aramaic loanword אִגֶּרֶת.[37] This constellation suggests that the book of Kings is from the same general period as the Arad and Lachish letters. Admittedly, the demonstration is not watertight, because some LBH passages still use the older word סֵפֶר ("letter").[38] One could argue that the passages in Kings were written in the Persian period and that the author intentionally used a native Hebrew word for "letter" when writing about the distant past.

The official title אשר על הבית ("royal steward," lit. "which is over the house") is attested in the Silwan tomb inscription, in at least three seal impressions from the late monarchic period, as well as six times in Kings and four times in First Isaiah.[39] It is not found elsewhere. The royal steward is not as important a figure in Chronicles as in Kings, but he does seem to be mentioned at least once in 2 Chr 28:7, and his title there is נְגִיד הַבָּיִת (lit. "prince of the house").[40] These data may indicate that the CBH title had fallen into disuse by the time of the Chronicler.

The idiom חי יהוה ("by the life of Yahweh") is found four times in Judean inscriptions, and thirty-one times in the Bible.[41] It is attested only once in LBH, in 2 Chr 18:13, where the phrase was taken over from the parallel in 1 Kgs 22:14. The formula is not found in Ben Sira, the Qumran documents, and Rabbinic Hebrew. The diminished use of this formula in the LBH corpus may be due to theological scruples, as suggested by the more cautious Dan 12:7, חֵי הָעוֹלָם ("[an oath by] the one who lives forever").

The scarcity of lexical and phraseological data should be evaluated in relation to the size of the epigraphic corpus. Each newly discovered Judean inscription of any size adds new words to the lexicon of words in epigraphic Hebrew.[42] Moreover, the limited scope of the inscriptions privileges the use of words from daily life that were the least susceptible to diachronic change.

More systematic evidence of the linguistic proximity between epigraphic Hebrew and CBH comes from the area of grammar. Morphosyntax, the use of particles, and verbal syntax all provide features common to those two corpora but absent, or nearly so, from LBH. In most cases LBH uses a different set of features than CBH and inscriptional Hebrew, thus conforming to Hurvitz's contrastive principle.

He Locale

The directional suffix *–ah* is attested six times in the inscriptional corpus, more than seven hundred times in CBH, and a little less than one hundred times in LBH.[43] In spite of the limited number in the inscriptions, the use of this feature clearly aligns with CBH as distinct from LBH. This can be seen in the functional force of the *he locale* in the inscriptions. Adverbial שמה is used twice implying motion to a place. This is the normal function in CBH, but in LBH שָׁמָּה designates simple location, not motion in space, three times out of five.

More impressively, Arad 17.2 uses the feature in a construct chain: ביתה אלישב ("to the house of Elyashib"). This type of syntax is found more than twenty times in CBH (e.g., בֵּיתָה בְתוּאֵל, Gen 28:2) but not even once in LBH. LBH invariably instead uses the construction: preposition + *status constructus* + nominal phrase (e.g., Esth 2:8, אֶל־בֵּית הַמֶּלֶךְ, "to the house of the king").[44]

The directional suffix becomes obsolete after the biblical period. In Qumran Hebrew it is relatively rare and does not always express direction.[45]

In Mishnaic Hebrew it is found only in petrified expressions like חוצה ("outside"), מטה ("downward"), and מעלה ("upward"). Judean epigraphic Hebrew and CBH reflect the same stage in its development. LBH reflects a later stage.

Infinitive Construct without *lamed*

One of the main functions of the infinitive construct is in complement clauses depending on verbs such as אבה ("to want"), ידע ("to know"), יכל ("to be able"), or יסף ("to continue"). A clear development can be traced from a situation in which the infinitive can stand on its own or be introduced by the preposition לְ ("to") to a situation in which the preposition and the infinitive practically coalesce into one single form.[46] In the inscriptions, most instances of the infinitive construct in complement clauses have the preposition, but in one example the preposition is missing: לא ידעתה קרא ("you cannot read," Lachish 3.8–9).[47] This construction finds parallels in CBH (e.g., לֹא אֵדַע צֵאת וָבֹא, "I do not know how to go out and come in," 1 Kgs 3:7),[48] but not in LBH, where infinitive constructs in complement clauses are always introduced by the preposition לְ.[49]

טרם ("before")

The temporal particle טרם ("before") is found in Arad 5.12. It occurs twenty-seven times in CBH and twenty-nine times in other writings, but never in LBH. Temporal "before" clauses are rare in LBH, but where they do occur they are constructed differently (לִפְנֵי + infinitive in 2 Chr 33:19; עַד אֲשֶׁר לֹא in Eccl 12:1, 2, 6). The particle reemerges in Ben Sira and Qumran Hebrew as an archaism.

כים ("first")

The expression כים, literally "as today," is used in Lachish 2.3 and 4.1 with the idiomatic meaning "first of all." The same meaning is found six times in CBH.[50] This feature occurs in 2 Chr 18:4, where it was copied from the source text (see 1 Kgs 22:5), but nowhere else in LBH.

בעוד ("while . . . still")

The composite particle בעוד occurs in Siloam 1:2: "*while there were still* three cubits to be tunneled through." It is found eight times in CBH (e.g.,

Gen 48:7, "*while there was still* a certain distance to come to Ephrath"), twelve times in other writings, but never in LBH.[51] In 1 Chr 12:1, simple עוֹד is used instead: "These are those who came to David at Ziklag, *while* he *still* (עוֹד) was in hiding from Saul the son of Kish."

פן ("lest")

The telic particle פן occurs in Arad 24.16, 20. It is used over 80 times in CBH, 133 times in Biblical Hebrew in all, but only once in LBH, in a passage the Chronicler copied from his sources (1 Chr 10:4, parallel 1 Sam 31:4). LBH uses other means to express negative purpose (e.g., אֲשֶׁר לֹא in Eccl 7:21; אֲשֶׁר לָמָּה, Dan 1:10). Like טֶרֶם, פֶּן was revived in early postbiblical Hebrew. The particle is used frequently in Ben Sira and in Qumran Hebrew.

לקראת/לקרת ("toward")

The compound particle לקרת ("toward") occurs in Siloam 1.4: "The masons struck toward one another." Although there is an interesting difference in orthography, the feature is functionally identical with Biblical Hebrew לִקְרַאת (1 Sam 17:21, "Israel and the Philistines drew up their battle lines facing toward one another"). This feature occurs well over one hundred times in CBH and a dozen times in other writings. In LBH, it is found only in passages where the Chronicler copied the feature from his sources: 1 Chr 19:5, 11, 17 (parallel 2 Sam 10:5, 10, 17); 2 Chr 35:20 (parallel 2 Kgs 23:29). The idiomatic equivalent in LBH, curiously, is לִפְנֵי.[52] Like טֶרֶם and פֶּן, לִקְרַאת resurfaces in Qumran Hebrew.

Performative Use of *qatal*

Performative *qatal* occurs in Arad 16.2–3; 21.2, ברכתך ("I bless you").[53] Performative *qatal* is frequent in CBH,[54] where it is used with a wide variety of verbs of speech.[55] LBH has a few cases of נָתַתִּי ("I give," 1 Chr 21:23; 29:3; 2 Chr 2:9), but they seem to be the last formulaic attestations of a dying usage.[56]

Infinitive Absolute in Commands

In the Arad letters, the infinitive absolute נתן ("to give") is used five times with an imperative function (Arad 1.2; 2.1; 7.2; 8.1; 11.2). The use of the infinitive absolute in commands, always uttered by a superior as in the Arad letters, is frequent in CBH.[57] The usage is found in Jer 32:14 and 35:2, and Zech 6:10, but there are no certain examples of it in the LBH corpus or in postbiblical Hebrew.[58]

Paronomastic Use of the Infinitive Absolute

The paronomastic (or tautological) infinitive occurs in Murabba at 1.1, [ש]לח שלחת ("sending I have sent").[59] The usage is attested over three hundred times in CBH and is frequent in other books, too. In LBH it becomes rare: 1 Chr 4:10; 21:17, 24; 2 Chr 18:27; 32:13; Esth 4:14; 6:13 (a total of seven occurrences).

Continuing Imperatives with *weqatal*

The *weqatal* form continues an imperative in Arad 17.1–4: בא . . . ולקחת ("go in . . . and take"; see also Arad 2.1–5).[60] There are around two hundred instances of this syntax in CBH, and it is also common in the Latter Prophets. In the LBH corpus it is found only five times: 1 Chr 14:14; 15:12; 17:4; 21:10; 2 Chr 18:33.

Many of these features occur only once or twice in the epigraphic corpus. Nevertheless, the fact that there are so many features in the inscriptions that in the Bible are almost entirely limited to CBH is significant. It shows that the writers of the inscriptions draw upon the same language system as the authors of the CBH corpus.

LBH in the Inscriptions?

The epigraphic corpus exhibits a few features adumbrating LBH and even postbiblical Hebrew.[61] An interesting feature in this regard is the construction [אי]ננו יכלם ("we cannot") in Arad 40.13–14. In Biblical Hebrew the negated form of this verb in reference to the present is systematically expressed with לֹא + *yiqtol* (e.g., Gen 29:8, לֹא נוּכַל, "we cannot"). The participial construction is typologically later. After Arad 40, its next attestation is in Mishnaic Hebrew (e.g., m. Kelim 17:4, אינן יכולים, "they cannot").

The presence of such a typologically late feature in the inscriptions is not wholly unexpected. First, it may be connected to the relatively low stylistic register of many inscriptions. It has been established in general linguistic literature that many innovations appear first in speech and only much later in written literature.[62] The literary style of the Hebrew Bible may have held on to certain types of expression long after the spoken language abandoned them. Occasional modernisms, in Biblical Hebrew as in epigraphic Hebrew, may indicate the more or less inadvertent intrusion of spoken forms into the written language. Second, we should take into account that most of the Judean inscriptions are relatively late. The date of Arad 40 is a famous conundrum. Aharoni dated the letter to the latter half of the eighth century, and several other epigraphers followed him.[63] But Pardee and Aḥituv independently have proposed a later date, at the end of the seventh or the beginning of the sixth century.[64] The question cannot be decided here. But it is clear that the other Arad letters and all the Lachish letters come from the very latest period of the monarchy. In light of this time frame, it is no great surprise to find that epigraphic Hebrew should exhibit a profile that is closer to Jeremiah and Ezekiel than to pure CBH.

Conclusions

The language of Judean inscriptions from the eighth to sixth centuries BCE stands close to CBH. Admittedly, some of the specialized vocabulary of the inscriptions, closely related to their subject matter, is not found in the biblical corpus. In regard to style, too, the two corpora are rather distinct, with the inscriptions reflecting a lower, less literary register than the biblical texts. However, in regard to the essential linguistic system—basic vocabulary, morphosyntax, use of particles, function of verbal forms—epigraphic Hebrew and CBH are essentially identical. This observation has historical implications. It indicates that the CBH corpus and the inscriptions are coeval. The two corpora tap into the same reservoir of linguistic forms.

The proximity of the two corpora cannot reveal when CBH began. The type of language to which they jointly testify came into being before the earliest inscriptions attesting it, that is, before the second half of the eighth century. But it is impossible to say how long before. Similarly, inscriptional Hebrew cannot tell when this type of language fell out of use. In spite of occasional modernisms, the latest Arad and Lachish letters still basically reflect the same forms of expression. It is implausible that this type of language would suddenly disappear immediately afterward.

Between the beginning of the sixth and the middle of the third century, there is a large gap in our documentation. Practically no epigraphic texts in Hebrew have been found from this period.[65] This gap makes it impossible to map the evolution of Hebrew against the language of dated inscriptions. What we see is that CBH is close to epigraphic Hebrew of the monarchic period, whereas LBH shows much greater proximity to the corpus of epigraphic Hebrew after the large gap, Qumran Hebrew. The essential transformation happened in the "dark ages" (speaking from the point of view of the Hebrew epigrapher): somewhere between 600 and 250 BCE.

6 Transitional Biblical Hebrew

As we showed in chapter 3, language evolution in the Hebrew Bible manifests itself mainly in the massive and systematic differences between two subcorpora: Genesis to 2 Kings versus Esther, Ezra-Nehemiah, Chronicles, Daniel, and Ecclesiastes. The clear demarcation of a relatively early group of writings and a relatively late one provides firm ground for the diachronic approach. At the same time, this state of affairs is somewhat surprising from a general linguistic point of view. As linguists have been able to observe empirically, languages evolve gradually. Each state of language contains early modes of expression, some of which are on their way out, alongside recent innovations, some of which will become generally adopted. Archaisms and new coinages coexist in a dynamic equilibrium, without which the speakers of any language could not communicate. Change is, for the most part, incremental and imperceptible. Successive chronolects emerge slowly; they do not spring up full blown.

In light of these considerations, the CBH and LBH corpora should be regarded as snapshots of distinct periods in the history of the language, separated by a significant lapse of time. Although ancient Hebrew evolved continuously, our documentation allows us to see only segments of that evolution. Partly this situation is due to the limitations of our knowledge: if it were possible to chart developments within CBH and within LBH, it might be possible to trace the gradual development of Hebrew more closely.[1] "Early CBH," "late CBH," "early LBH," and "late LBH" could be situated along a time line. Even in this case, however, an important gap would remain between the latest phase of CBH and the earliest phase of LBH.

The gap is not completely empty, however. A set of writings stands between CBH and LBH. In recent years, we have seen the publication of thorough studies on a number of books that may be regarded as belonging to Transitional Biblical Hebrew (TBH): Ezekiel, Lamentations, Jeremiah, Second Isaiah, Job, Jonah, Haggai, and Zech 1–8.[2] The linguistic profile of these books is characterized by a combination of CBH and LBH features. Some of these texts are explicitly situated in the sixth century, and all except the books of Job and Jonah contain subject matter that interacts with the exilic or early postexilic period. On the face of it, they confirm not only the relative but also the absolute dating of the CBH and LBH books: preexilic CBH precedes TBH, which is followed by postexilic LBH.

The apparent neatness of this scheme should not obscure a number of problems: the books at issue are largely written in poetry, thus impeding the diachronic approach; their redaction history is uncertain, and one cannot date them in their entirety to the sixth century without further qualifications. In the present chapter we take a look at some of the writings involved and discuss the issues they raise.

Prose and Poetry

TBH stands between CBH and LBH. A typical TBH text contains LBH elements, but not as many as one expects in core LBH texts. It will also contain CBH features that are not normally found in LBH. The physiognomy of TBH differs from that of both classical and late Biblical Hebrew. Because the differences are less marked than between CBH and LBH, the definition of TBH as a distinct phase of the language is less well established than the other two. If the canon for some reason had not included the *Ketuvim* (which has all the LBH books), a historical approach to Biblical Hebrew would still be possible. Presumably Hebraists would be able to determine that the bulk of the Pentateuch and Former Prophets reflects an earlier chronolect than Jeremiah, Ezekiel, Second Isaiah, and Haggai-Zechariah. However, the whole approach would be much weaker than it is at present, based on the contrast between two corpora that differ as a whole and in many details (see chapter 3).

Adding to this difficulty is the fact that much of the TBH corpus is written in poetry. Poetry is intrinsically more difficult to analyze in diachronic terms than prose. Poetry typically makes use of a much wider range of forms, including archaisms and modernisms. An additional hurdle is that the diachronic approach to ancient Hebrew was largely developed on the basis of prose texts, because the CBH and LBH corpora consist largely of narrative. Extending the approach to poetic texts violates the requirement to compare like to like. A small portion of the TBH corpus is written in prose, however: most of Jonah, parts of Jeremiah, the narrative framework of Job, and shorter sections in other books.[3] These prose sections belong roughly to the same literary genre as most of CBH and LBH. They can therefore more easily be compared.

The story in Job 1–2 and 42 can serve as an illustration. A short stretch of text, it reads as a smooth narration not unlike the patriarchal stories in Genesis. On close inspection, however, it turns out to exhibit several features otherwise found exclusively, or nearly so, in LBH. For instance, Job 42:8 uses the expression הִתְפַּלֵּל עַל ("to intercede for"). In classical Hebrew the notion of intercession is expressed instead by the set phrase הִתְפַּלֵּל בְּעַד (Gen 20:7; Num 21:7; Deut 9:20; 1 Sam 7:5; 12:19, 23; 1 Kgs 13:6), and this idiom is found also in Ps 72:15, Job 42:10, and seven times in Jeremiah (Jer 7:16; 11:14; 14:11; 29:7; 37:3; 42:2, 20). In contrast, הִתְפַּלֵּל עַל is otherwise found only in LBH: Neh 1:6; 2 Chr 30:18. In the use of הִתְפַּלֵּל עַל, the prose tale of Job aligns with LBH and contrasts with CBH, thus suggesting that it is a relatively late composition. One feature alone would not establish this, but other features corroborate the analysis. In a very precise investigation, Avi Hurvitz found seven late features in Job 1–2, 42.[4]

The conclusion that the Job story is later than the CBH corpus is warranted, but the question remains: how much later? Seven features are not much in nearly three chapters. Moreover, alongside the LBH features, the prose tale also contains some distinctive CBH features. As we pointed out earlier, the classical expression הִתְפַּלֵּל בְּעַד is also found in Job, two verses later in Job 42:10. The prose tale contains several features typical of CBH that are unattested in LBH. Some of these may be due to conscious archaizing. For instance, in Job 42:11 the word קְשִׂיטָה (a unit of money), known otherwise only from Gen 33:19 and Jos 24:32, may well have been borrowed from the patriarchal narratives. But the author of the prose tale also uses iterative *weqatal* (Job 1:4–5), temporal כִּי (Job 1:5), the conjunction לָכֵן ("therefore," Job 42:3), and adversative אוּלָם (Job 1:11; 2:5) in ways that are normal in CBH but unparalleled in LBH. Such syntactic and morphosyntactic features would have been difficult to imitate if they had disappeared from active use.[5] Their presence in the prose tale indicates that the text was composed before these features became obsolete, that is, before the period when the LBH books were written. The upshot is that Job 1–2 and 42 reflect a state of language later than CBH and earlier than LBH: the chapters are transitional. Similar demonstrations have been advanced for the prose portions of Jonah and Jeremiah.[6]

What about TBH poetry? The literary relation between the different parts of the book of Job is hotly debated.[7] Some scholars think that the narrative framework is older and the poetic dialogues were introduced later. Others contend that the poetic dialogues preceded the prose tale. The poetic chapters have not been subjected to a systematic language-historical investigation in the way the prose tale has. Preliminary soundings suggest that, when stylistic considerations are bracketed, the basic grammatical profile of the poetry is similar to that of the prose.[8] On the one hand, the dialogues contain many late features, including אמר as "to command" (9:7), גזר ("to decree," 22:28), מִלָּה, plural מִלִּין and מִלִּים ("word, words," thirty-four times), מנה ("to appoint," 7:3), תקף ("to prevail," 14:20; 15:24). On the other hand, the poetry of Job exhibits several features typical of CBH and virtually absent from LBH: adversative אוּלָם (eight times), הִנֵּה־נָא (13:18; 33:2; 40:15, 16) and אַל־נָא (32:21), the passive *qal* (3:3; 28:2, 15), temporal-conditional כִּי (7:13; 27:9; 31:14, 21, 29; 36:13; 37:4; 38:40), the compound preposition לִקְרַאת ("toward," 39:21), and the conjunction לָכֵן (20:2; 32:10; 34:10, 25; 37:24). Note that several of these features are common to the prose and poetry of Job (אוּלָם, temporal כִּי, לָכֵן). These data suggest that the time frames during which the prose and poetry of Job were composed overlap.

For other poetic corpora, thorough diachronic analysis is already available. Although poetry is more difficult to analyze than prose, there is no principled reason to exclude it from diachronic research altogether. Poetry and prose are different, but not incommensurable. In a fine study of the language of Lamentations, Chip Dobbs-Allsopp has stated this principle clearly: "The belief that somehow poetry is not amenable to typological study and analysis in the same way that prose is . . . is patently false. It is true that our poetic remains in Hebrew are not as strategically distributed as one might ideally like and that one must allow for certain peculiarities which are especially characteristic of poetry (e.g., dearth of the so-called prose particles, higher incidence of archaisms), but otherwise there is no sound basis for believing that at the linguistic level poetry differs substantively from prose."[9] He goes on to show that Lamentations has a number of late features, both lexical and grammatical, but not as many as one would expect in a LBH text. This corpus also has a significant number of CBH features. The conclusion, as in the case of the prose tale of Job, is that the language of Lamentations is transitional, a phase Dobbs-Allsopp situates in the sixth century. Similar results have been reached in studies of Ezekiel and Second Isaiah.[10]

Historical Linguistics and Redaction History

When one starts out from the CBH-LBH divide, transitional Hebrew may appear Janus faced, a mixture of early and late features. This view, and the term "transitional" itself, are misleading inasmuch as they suggest that such a mixture is exceptional. It is not: all languages are transitional in that they continue earlier modes of expression while also containing the seeds of later developments. If TBH comes between CBH and LBH, it only stands to reason that the intermediate phase should exhibit elements typical of the other two. Nevertheless, as a practical designation of the linguistic phase found in the books enumerated here, Transitional Biblical Hebrew is a useful term.

Before continuing along these lines, however, we need to take a step back and ask whether the approach in this chapter is really the correct one. A different scenario is imaginable: perhaps the mixture of early and late features reflects not the transitional character of the language but the stratified nature of the writings. Perhaps the earliest form of a given book was written in pure CBH, to which a later redactor made a number of additions written in LBH. This would account for the linguistic mixture that we have observed. Or perhaps the book was a "rolling corpus" to which successive generations of scribes added as they saw fit, each in their own type of Hebrew.

As we showed previously (chapter 4), the linguistic profile of some TBH books is indeed complex. Notably, the book of Jeremiah is composed of at least two strata: the short text reflected in the Old Greek and the Masoretic additions. Many Hebrew words, expressions, and constructions found in the Masoretic additions are late.[11] Note the following three instances:

Jer 3:17
MT: וְנִקְווּ אֵלֶיהָ כָל־הַגּוֹיִם לְשֵׁם יְהוָה לִירוּשָׁלִָם
And all the nations shall be gathered to it, *to the name of YHWH, to Jerusalem.*

LXX: καὶ συναχθήσονται εἰς αὐτὴν πάντα τὰ ἔθνη
And all the nations shall be gathered to it.

The Masoretic plus uses the preposition לְ ("to") to express movement toward a definite location. This syntax is unattested in CBH and typical of LBH.[12] In Jer 31:17, the MT again uses לְ in this way in a phrase not attested in the Old Greek.

Jer 9:14
MT: הִנְנִי מַאֲכִילָם אֶת־הָעָם הַזֶּה לַעֲנָה
I am feeding *this people* with wormwood.

LXX: Ἰδοὺ ἐγὼ ψωμιῶ αὐτοὺς ἀνάγκας
Behold, I will feed *them* anguish.

Literally, the MT means "I am feeding them, this people." The use of an anticipatory pronoun is found once or twice in CBH texts, but it is far more typical of LBH and Aramaic.[13] The shorter Greek text does not reflect this syntax:

Jer 20:5
MT: וְנָתַתִּי אֶת־כָּל־חֹסֶן הָעִיר הַזֹּאת וְאֶת־כָּל־יְגִיעָהּ וְאֶת־כָּל־יְקָרָהּ
וְאֵת כָּל־אוֹצְרוֹת מַלְכֵי יְהוּדָה אֶתֵּן בְּיַד אֹיְבֵיהֶם
I will deliver all the strength of this city, and all its labors, *and all its precious things*; and all the treasures of the kings of Judah I will give into the hand of their enemies.

LXX: καὶ δώσω τὴν πᾶσαν ἰσχὺν τῆς πόλεως ταύτης καὶ πάντας τοὺς πόνους αὐτῆς καὶ πάντας τοὺς θησαυροὺς τοῦ βασιλέως Ιουδα εἰς χεῖρας ἐχθρῶν αὐτοῦ
And I will give all the strength of this city, and all its labors, and all the treasures of the king of Judah into the hands of his enemies.

Along with some other elements, the phrase אֶת־כָּל־יְקָרָהּ ("all its precious things") is missing in the Greek translation. The noun יְקָר ("glory, wealth") is a late Aramaism.[14]

Such examples, which could be multiplied,[15] indicate that additions to the MT were made by scribes whose language was more evolved than that of the text to which they were adding. The earlier text was not, however, written in pure CBH. In a recent investigation, Aaron Hornkohl has shown that the short text of Jeremiah (i.e., the text reflected in the Old Greek) also contains late forms and expressions.[16] For instance, the word אֲרֻכָה ("healing") is found in Jer 8:22, 30:17, and 33:6, all three times in passages attested in Greek. The word otherwise occurs in Isa 58:8, Neh 4:1, and 2 Chr 24:13, and several times in Mishnaic Hebrew.[17] CBH uses other words for "healing." Again, the use of the preposition לְ ("to") to express movement toward a definite location is found in Jer 51:2 in a passage attested in the Old Greek.[18] This analysis shows that although the language of Masoretic pluses is later than that of the short text, it is perhaps not much later. Some of the pluses are extensive, yet they do not read like LBH. They exhibit late features but not as many as core LBH texts, such as Chronicles or Esther. In a global view, the language of the book suggests that few, if any, of the longer sections were added later than the end of the sixth century.

The book of Isaiah presents a different profile. After First Isaiah, brought to closure with the historical chapters paralleling Kings (Isa 36–39 parallel to 2 Kgs 18–20), comes a collection of prophetic texts reflecting a much later age. The linguistic differences between the two parts of the book leap to the eye. A famous example occurs in the two passages announcing how in the idyllic future peace will reign among the animals: Isa 11:6 uses the adverb יַחְדָּו ("together"), but Isa 65:25 substitutes the adverbial phrase כְּאֶחָד ("together"). The former is typical of CBH (although it occurs three times in Nehemiah), and the latter is a calque from Aramaic never found in CBH but well attested in LBH (Eccl 11:6; Ezra 2:64; 3:9; 6:20; Neh 7:66). There are many more instances: Isa 40–66 has around thirty elements characteristic of LBH.[19] As against this, even Isa 24–27, probably the latest section among the prophecies of Isa 1–35, hews closely to CBH and uses only a few late forms.[20]

Isa 40–66 is not representative of LBH, however, but rather of TBH. One finds several elements characteristic of CBH: אָנֹכִי (about twenty times including 66:13, 18), temporal-conditional כִּי (e.g., 43:2), passive *qal* (e.g., 49:24, 25; 52:5; 53:8), טֶרֶם (42:9; 48:5; 65:24; 66:7), פֶּן (48:5, 7), אֵי־זֶה ("where?" 50:1; 66:1),[21] and others. Some of these features may be due to the poetic genre, which is more prone to use archaic language than prose. But in aggregate, the features show that the language of Isa 40–66 is not yet that of the LBH corpus.

Transitional Hebrew and the Sixth Century

Jeremiah, Ezekiel, Haggai, and Zech 1–8 are set partly or wholly in the sixth century. Lamentations was likely written in reaction to the destruction of Jerusalem in 587/586 BCE. Second Isaiah mentions Cyrus and looks forward to an imminent return from the Babylonian Exile. The majority of the books that have been qualified as TBH—the exceptions are Job and Jonah—are linked to the century that stretches from the death throes of the state of Judah to the beginning of the Second Temple period. In historical-critical scholarship, this link has admittedly been loosened: sections and strata, sometimes even books in their entirety, have been dated to later

Persian or even Hellenistic times. In principle, it is entirely possible that a prophetic book from the sixth century was supplemented or rewritten during the later postexilic period. It is also possible that an account of a prophetic figure from the Babylonian period could be created more or less from whole cloth a long time after the return—a scenario illustrated by the book of Daniel.[22] The prima facie likelihood that the TBH books are mainly products of the sixth century does not by itself suffice to demonstrate absolute dates of CBH, TBH, and LBH as before, during, and after the exile respectively.[23]

However, with regard to at least one TBH book there is strong linguistic evidence tying it directly to the Neo-Babylonian period. Hebraists have consistently regarded the book of Ezekiel as representative of transitional Hebrew. Gesenius already named Ezekiel, along with Job, as standing "auf der Gränze beyder Zeitalter" ("on the borderline between the two ages") of Hebrew literature.[24] Monographs by Avi Hurvitz and Mark Rooker buttressed this judgment with extensive linguistic analysis.[25] Ezekiel contains many late linguistic features, but it also continues CBH usages that became obsolete in LBH. Late features include the lexemes מִקְטֶרֶת ("censer," 8:11) and הדיח ("to wash [a sacrifice]," 40:38),[26] and the frequent use of nonvolitive *we-yiqtol*,[27] as well as of the bare participle as a verbal form.[28] The use of CBH vocabulary can be discounted as archaizing, but grammar characteristic of CBH and rare or absent in LBH shows that Ezekiel reflects an earlier stage of the language: passive *qal* (15:3; 16:4), *weqatal* continuing the imperative (twenty-one times), paronomastic infinitive (more than twenty times), infinitive absolute used imperatively (24:5), and the particles טֶרֶם 16:57)) and לָכֵן (sixty-three times).

Ezekiel, then, reflects TBH. At the same time, the book of Ezekiel contains many linguistic features reflecting Babylonian influence.[29] Some of these are loanwords, such as נְחֻשֶׁת ("abundance [of vaginal outflow]," 16:36)[30] and קְבָל ("battle," 26:9);[31] others are loaned expressions, such as אֲמֻלָה לִבָּתֵךְ ("I am filled with anger against you," 16:30).[32] The Babylonian element is pervasive, extending through the entire book.[33] It is also distinctive: many of these words and expressions are found only in Ezekiel. The phenomenon almost certainly indicates that the book originated in Babylonia, as indeed it claims. The loans are tokens of acculturation to the environment in Tel Aviv on the river (or canal) Chebar.[34] The implication is not that the entire book was written in Babylonia by a single author. There may well be segments of text that were added later in different cultural milieus. But the core of the book and its distinctive linguistic cast must go back to the Babylonian period—in other words, the sixth century.

Babylonianisms can be found also in Jeremiah and Second Isaiah. The loanword שָׁשַׁר ("red clay or paste") is found in Jer 22:14 and Ezek 23:14 but nowhere else. In Isa 40:20 the *hapax legomenon* מְסֻכָּן, designating a kind of tree or wood, is almost certainly an Akkadian loanword as well.[35] But we need not elaborate on this issue. The case of Ezekiel suffices to show that the link between TBH and the sixth century is not merely suggested in a naïve reading of the texts but can be supported with solid evidence.

TBH in the Pentateuch and Former Prophets?

The definition of TBH differentiates it from CBH and LBH. Consequently, the notion of transitional Hebrew has been applied almost exclusively to books that figure in neither corpus. However, it could prove fruitful also to discuss some allegedly late passages in the CBH corpus. A good example is Gen 24. Alexander Rofé has developed several lines of argument contending that this chapter in its present form was added to the Pentateuch during the Persian period.[36] The linguistic evidence he brings to bear includes the expression "God of Heaven" (vv. 3, 7),[37] the noun מִגְדָּנֹת ("gifts," 24:53),[38] the rare verbs גמא ("to swallow," v. 17), ערה ("to pour," v. 20), and שאה ("to gaze," v. 21), and a few items of syntax. Only the first two items are well attested in LBH, but the overall demonstration remains impressive.

As we have noted previously, Gary Rendsburg has reconsidered the linguistic evidence and reached different conclusions.[39] In his view, most of the features adduced by Rofé can be explained as instances of style switching: the author of Gen 24 used Aramaic-like turns of phrase in respect of the Aramaic milieu in which most of the story happens. The story otherwise reflects good CBH grammar and style. The explanation from style switching works in one or two instances,[40] but it cannot account for all the evidence gathered by Rofé.[41] However, the observation that Gen 24 overall reflects good CBH is correct. The chapter uses the following features that are typical of CBH but rare or unattested in LBH:

- אוּלַי ("perhaps," vv. 5, 39)[42]
- טֶרֶם ("before," vv. 15, 45)
- temporal-conditional כִּי (v. 41)

- פֶּן ("lest," v. 6)
- לִקְרָאת ("toward," vv. 17, 65)
- אָנֹכִי (vv. 13, 24, 27, 31, 34, 37; אֲנִי occurs in v. 45)[43]
- passive *qal* (v. 15)
- infinitive construct used as complement without לְ (v. 50)
- the modal particle נָא following a pronominal element (v. 42)

The absence of these features from the LBH corpus suggests that they had fallen into disuse when the late books were composed. If Gen 24 had been created from whole cloth in the Persian period it would amount to a tour de force. While one can see later authors using expressions such as לָקַח אִשָּׁה ("to take a wife," Gen 24:4, 7, 37, 38, 40; contrast נָשָׂא אִשָּׁה in LBH) or רְבָבָה ("myriad," Gen 24:60; רִבּוֹ or רִבּוֹא in LBH), which they had found in earlier texts, it is much more difficult to imagine them recreating a whole network of grammatical features that had long been obsolete.

The linguistic evidence seems to lead to an impasse. Rofé's observations indicate a late date of composition for Gen 24; the CBH features indicate, on the contrary, that it is early. The best solution may be to attribute Gen 24 to the transitional period and to define its language as TBH. Many of the early grammatical features we have listed have parallels in the transitional corpus. The telltale indications of lateness are of the same kind as what we find there. For instance, the expression "God of heaven" is found in Jon 1:9, and the root גמא ("to swallow") occurs in Job 39:24 (although in a different verbal stem).

As we pointed out in chapter 4, there is no reason to situate scribal expansions of the CBH corpus exclusively in the Persian period or later. If most of the book of Genesis was written in the monarchical period, as its language suggests, supplements may have been added during the long sixth century.

Conclusions

Transitional Biblical Hebrew is a useful label to apply to such books as Jeremiah, Ezekiel, Lamentations, Second Isaiah, Job, Jonah, Haggai, and Zechariah 1–8.[44] Of course, these books all present their own special problems. Linguistically the books are extremely diverse, and it is difficult to find features characterizing all of them. Nevertheless, there is an unmistakable family relationship. They all present a linguistic profile combining elements from CBH with elements that will become characteristic of LBH. Regarding the CBH features, what is particularly relevant is the way grammatical features that become extinct in LBH are still used freely in the TBH corpus: passive *qal*, *weqatal* continuing the imperative, the particles אוּלָם, טֶרֶם, and פֶּן, and several others.[45] Other CBH features, such as the expression בִּי אֲדֹנִי ("excuse me, sir") or the use of directional *he* in a construct chain (בֵּיתָה יוֹסֵף, "to the house of Joseph"), disappear earlier and are not found in TBH. Regarding the LBH features, many occur sporadically in TBH: for example, the noun יְקָר ("glory"), or the preposition לְ ("to") expressing movement toward a definite location. Other typical LBH features are missing from TBH. Particularly striking is that in the sizable TBH corpus one does not find a single Persian word.[46] Also, several Aramaic loanwords that are well established in LBH are lacking in TBH: זְמָן ("time"),[47] צָפִיר ("he goat"),[48] שלט ("to rule").[49] Similarly, several distinctive LBH grammatical elements are lacking, such as אִלּוּ ("if"), בְּכֵן ("then"), and iterative *we-yiqtol*.[50]

In sum, as a transitional phase, TBH is less distinct from CBH and LBH than the latter two are from each other. Nevertheless, the evidence suffices to recognize TBH as a distinctive chronolect. The intermediate phase differs from the other two in systematic and typologically expected ways. The influence of Aramaic on Hebrew was exerted over a very long period, and its impact grew stronger with time. One would expect to find an increase of Aramaic loanwords in LBH if it is later than TBH. Similarly, the absence of Persian words in TBH is natural only if it precedes LBH: it would have taken time for Persian loanwords to penetrate into Hebrew. The development of Hebrew syntax too was slow. Some late features show up already in TBH, while others first emerge in LBH. Because language development is gradual, the evolution from CBH to LBH will have gone through many intermediary steps, only some of which have left a trace in our documents.

The identification of TBH as an intermediary phase lends strong support to the diachronic approach to Biblical Hebrew. Although we are still far from being able to trace the continuous evolution of Biblical Hebrew, the TBH corpus provides material to fill the gap between CBH and LBH. In this way TBH confirms the relative dating of the two main phases and demonstrates at the same time that they are not contiguous or overlapping, but more likely separated by a considerable time span. TBH also crucially contributes to the question of the absolute chronology of Biblical Hebrew.

The bulk of the TBH corpus—Jeremiah, Ezekiel, Second Isaiah, Haggai, and Zechariah, as well as Lamentations—has strong links to the sixth century. Some of it, notably the core parts of these prophetic books, can hardly be situated elsewhere. By implication, CBH, which precedes TBH, must be preexilic, and LBH, which follows it, postexilic. It is worth emphasizing that this result, while based on different evidence and arguments, tallies with the conclusions of the preceding chapter on CBH and preexilic Judean inscriptions.

7 Pseudoclassicism: Late Biblical Hebrew and Qumran Hebrew

As we have argued in the preceding chapters, Hebrew went through major changes during the exilic and postexilic periods. The principal factor was foreign influence, notably Aramaic, although internal developments also played a part. An additional factor of change forms the subject matter of this chapter: some innovations in LBH, perhaps paradoxically, arose out of the desire of later authors to continue in the footsteps of earlier writers. Imitation of literary models led to linguistic usages that superficially resemble classical features but on closer inspection reveal real differences. These "pseudoclassicisms" are important evidence of changing attitudes toward older Israelite literature. To the historical linguist, they also demonstrate that archaizing composition was never perfect. Although postclassical authors tried to imitate the language they knew from old texts, they never fully succeeded.

Books written in LBH testify in a variety of ways to the influence and growing authority of earlier writings. Chronicles widely draws on a source that must have been nearly identical to the book of Kings.[1] Parts of Ezra-Nehemiah describe the application of religious laws that are in the Pentateuch.[2] Much of Dan 8–12 reflects exegesis of prophetic texts.[3] And Esther freely draws motifs from the Joseph story and other earlier narratives.[4] Only Ecclesiastes and Song of Songs, on the face of it, do not depend on classical models.[5]

In their language, too, the LBH books often draw on CBH models. They use phrases and expressions drawn from (or alluding to) classical passages, and they maintain traditional stylistic features. The effect is not always a seamless linguistic continuity. CBH expressions at times turn up in

LBH with a different meaning or a different form. Although some of the differences may be due to natural development or Aramaic influence, others reflect the fact that later writers did not perfectly master the language in which they tried to express themselves. Words and phrases that were no longer current were taken from old texts only partly understood and were used with new meanings disconnected from the old ones.

The Reuse of Classical Expressions in LBH

Many expressions in the LBH books closely resemble classical Hebrew expressions. Of course, some Hebrew vocabulary remained relatively stable throughout the history of the language. A clause like וַיֵּלֶךְ אַחֲרֵיהֶם הוֹשַׁעְיָה ("Hoshaiah went after them," Neh 12:32) is as much at home in LBH as it is in CBH (cf. Num 16:25). But LBH also has some distinctively CBH expressions. For instance, in Neh 4:1 the phrase וַיִּחַר לָהֶם מְאֹד ("they were very angry," lit. "it burned for them strongly") reproduces an idiomatic expression well known from earlier texts (see, e.g., Gen 34:7) but otherwise rare in LBH.[6] Moreover, this expression is unattested in later phases of the language—Ben Sira, Qumran, Rabbinic Hebrew. Nevertheless, as long as such expressions agree in form and meaning with the CBH usage, we cannot be sure about the process by which they were produced. The author of Neh 4:1 may have known the expression חָרָה לְ ("to be angry") from his study of earlier texts and may have used it because he wanted to give his story a "scriptural" ring. In this case, the usage would be due to conscious archaizing on the part of the later author. But the author may equally well have known the expression from the living Hebrew of his time and used it spontaneously. There is simply no way to know when it disappeared from use. Many other expressions in the LBH corpus recall phrases from the Pentateuch or the Former Prophets, but for the most part we cannot tell whether they were consciously borrowed.[7]

The case is different when the late usage resembles the early one in some regards yet differs from it in others. Where the LBH expression recalls the CBH one but diverges from it formally or semantically, the case for conscious archaizing becomes much stronger. Examples illustrating this situation are sufficiently numerous to stand out as a group. An interesting case is the use of לְבוֹא followed by a geographical name apparently meaning "to the entrance (or border) of GN":

2 Chr 26:8
וַיִּתְּנוּ הָעַמּוֹנִים מִנְחָה לְעֻזִּיָּהוּ וַיֵּלֶךְ שְׁמוֹ עַד־לְבוֹא מִצְרַיִם
The Ammonites paid tribute to Uzziah, and his fame spread up to the border of Egypt.

Although the phrase is unique in combination with מִצְרַיִם ("Egypt"), it recalls a CBH usage with a different geographical name:

Josh 13:5
וְכָל־הַלְּבָנוֹן מִזְרַח הַשֶּׁמֶשׁ מִבַּעַל גָּד תַּחַת הַר־חֶרְמוֹן עַד לְבוֹא חֲמָת
And all Lebanon, toward the sunrising, from Baal-gad under Mount Hermon unto the entering into Hamath (KJV)
And all Lebanon, toward the east, from Baal-gad below Mount Hermon to Lebo-hamath (NRSV)

However, in CBH the original meaning of לְבוֹא is not "to the entrance (or border) of," as is presupposed in the KJV. As the NRSV indicates, לבוא is part of the geographical name. At the time the texts were written, it designated a place named Lebo situated in the land of Hamath.[8] Only in later times, when this location was no longer known, was the first part of the name reinterpreted as the preposition לְ followed by the infinitive of בוא ("to come"). This reanalysis shows up in the versions: עַד לְבוֹא חֲמָת in Josh 13:5 is rendered ἕως τῆς εἰσόδου Εμαθ ("up to the entrance of Emath") in the Septuagint, and similar renderings are found elsewhere in the Septuagint as well as in the other ancient (and less ancient) versions.[9] The true meaning of the name was rediscovered in the twentieth century thanks to close study of cuneiform and hieroglyphic texts mentioning the city of Lab'u in the land of Hamath.[10]

Because nothing is known of a city called Lebo in Egypt, the expression לְבוֹא מִצְרַיִם needs a different explanation. It appears that it owes its origin to the same interpretation of לְבוֹא חֲמָת as is found in the versions.[11] The author of Chronicles analyzed the geographical name לבוא as an idiomatic expression meaning "to come up to (the border of)."[12] He then used this phrase in a completely different context, thus revealing his misunderstanding of the expression. LBH לְבוֹא מִצְרַיִם looks like CBH לְבוֹא חֲמָת, but the meaning of לבוא is not the same. The usage is pseudoclassical. Examples of this type provide strong evidence for deliberate archaizing. The usage found in 2 Chr 26:8 came to the author not from the living Hebrew of his day but from his study of passages like Josh 13:5.

Pseudoclassicisms come in various guises.[13] The divergence between the late and earlier usages may be situated in their meaning or in their form. In the case of לָבוֹא in 2 Chr 26:8, the divergence is seen on two levels at once, the proper noun being analyzed as an infinitive and a different meaning being attributed to it. But in other cases, only one of the two is affected.

An example of a semantic pseudoclassicism is the way Chronicles uses the idiomatic expression מִלֵּא יָד, "to fill someone's hand," in the meaning "to bring an offering":

> 1 Chr 29:5
> וּמִי מִתְנַדֵּב לְמַלֹּאות יָדוֹ הַיּוֹם לַיהוָה
> Who will willingly bring an offering (lit. *fill their hands*) today to YHWH?[14]

The usage recalls the expression, "to fill someone's hand" in the Pentateuch and Former Prophets:

> Jud 17:5
> (Micah) had a shrine, and he made an *ephod* and *teraphim*, and installed (וַיְמַלֵּא אֶת־יַד, lit. "filled the hand of") one of his sons, who became his priest.

In CBH the expression "to fill someone's hand" means "to ordain to a sacred office."[15] This idiom became rare during the Persian period.[16] Consequently, its meaning became uncertain, and new interpretations were made on the basis of the literal meaning of its components. One meaning that emerged in the exegetical tradition was "to give offerings." This interpretation is attested in the Targums. The end of the verse from Jud 17:5 quoted above is translated in Targum Jonathan: "He brought the offering of one of his sons (וקריב ית קרבן חד מבנוהי), who became his priest"; this is the standard translation of the expression in all the Jewish Targums. This corresponds to the meaning with which the word was used anew in Chronicles.

In other cases of pseudoclassicism, the meaning remains roughly the same and the divergence concerns the formal analysis of the CBH expression:

> Neh 10:32
> וְנִטֹּשׁ אֶת־הַשָּׁנָה הַשְּׁבִיעִית וּמַשָּׁא כָל־יָד
> And we will forgo (the crops of) the seventh year and the exaction of every debt.

As scholars have recognized, the expression מַשָּׂא כָל־יָד is to be understood in light of a passage in the Pentateuch:

> Deut 15:2
> וְזֶה דְּבַר הַשְּׁמִטָּה שָׁמוֹט כָּל־בַּעַל מַשֵּׁה יָדוֹ אֲשֶׁר יַשֶּׁה בְּרֵעֵהוּ
> And this is the manner of the remission: every creditor (lit. "master of the loan") shall remit his claim (lit. "his hand") to what he has lent to a neighbor.

In both passages, the implication is that of debt relief. Syntactically, however, the expressions differ. In Nehemiahמַשָּׂא כָל־יָד is a genitive construction, literally "a loan of any hand." But this analysis is not satisfactory for the Deuteronomy verse. Here מַשֵּׁה qualifies בַּעַל: the "master of the loan" is the creditor. The fact that the verb שמט is elsewhere constructed with יָד shows that we should take "his hand" as the direct object of the verb.[17] If this analysis is correct, then the text of Neh 10:32 represents a misunderstanding of the construction, showing that the author was not expressing himself in the living Hebrew of his day but imitating a biblical phrase.[18]

As in the examples of לָבוֹא and מִלֵּא יָד, so here the misunderstanding is not unique to the LBH author but is attested in other sources as well. The Masoretic vocalization of Deut 15:2 indicates a genitive construction, "the loan of his hand," against the plain meaning of the verse. The same interpretation is found in Targum Onkelos, Targum Pseudo-Jonathan, and the Peshitta.[19]

Grammatical Pseudoclassicisms

Pseudoclassical usages are not limited to the domain of words and idioms. In their grammar, too, the LBH books show signs of pseudoclassicism. Grammatical features characteristic of CBH turn up in LBH with diverging form or meaning due to reanalysis.

An illustrative example is the "long" imperative: the 2ms imperative followed by paragogic *he* (קוּמָה, "stand up," instead of קוּם). Long imperatives are found across the biblical corpus. In the CBH corpus the form expresses a distinct nuance compared to the normal, "short" imperative. As was discovered more or less simultaneously by Ahouva Shulman and Steven Fassberg, the lengthened form adds a notion of movement toward the speaker (or sometimes more generally, interest of the speaker): לֵךְ means "go away" (Gen 12:19) or "go from A to B" (Gen 12:2), but לְכָה means "come"

(Num 10:29).[20] The paragogic ending is in all likelihood related to the Akkadian ventive, which has a similar function (although it is not limited to the imperative).[21]

In later stages of ancient Hebrew, this form became defunct. Long imperatives are about six times more frequent in CBH than in LBH.[22] The form still occurs a number of times in Qumran Hebrew and once in Ben Sira, but in Mishnaic Hebrew it is not attested.[23] More significant than the statistics is the change in the function of the form from LBH onward. In some passages, we still find the notion of movement toward the speaker, but in other passages it is absent, showing that this is no longer the meaning of the form. Instead the form functions as a free variant for the normal imperative, selected occasionally to give the text an aura of antiquity:

> 2 Chr 25:19
> עַתָּה שְׁבָה בְּבֵיתֶךָ
> Now stay at home.

Here, the lengthened form is used in a way that does not agree with the CBH rule. Significantly, the parallel text in 2 Kgs 14:10 has the normal imperative, שֵׁב בְּבֵיתֶךָ, as expected in CBH, because the clause does not express movement toward or interest of the speaker. In other LBH passages as well, the long imperative is used in a way that deviates from the CBH rule,[24] and this tendency continues in Qumran Hebrew.[25]

Another example of grammatical pseudoclassicism is the use the jussive in nonvolitive contexts. As is well known, in CBH a short imperfect, attested only for certain forms of second and third weak roots and certain forms of the *hiphil*, expresses volition: יְהִי אוֹר means "*let there be* light" (Gen 1:3). Because of the CBH rules of word order, the short form occurs almost invariably at the head of the clause and is therefore often preceded by *waw*. In some contexts, *waw* followed by the jussive has a special subordinating function:

> Exod 8:4
> הַעְתִּירוּ אֶל־יְהוָה וְיָסֵר הַצְפַרְדְּעִים מִמֶּנִּי וּמֵעַמִּי
>
> Pray to YHWH *to take away* [lit. "and let him take away"] the frogs from me and my people.

Even in this case, however, the form preserves its basic volitive function.

In LBH, the jussive form still occurs many times, but its function is not the same as in CBH. In some contexts the volitive or subordinative functions are discernible, but in many others they are not. Nonvolitive jussives stand out particularly when they are preceded by *waw*:

Dan 11:4
וּכְעָמְדוֹ תִּשָּׁבֵר מַלְכוּתוֹ וְתֵחָץ לְאַרְבַּע רוּחוֹת הַשָּׁמָיִם
And while still rising (in power), his kingdom shall be broken *and divided* to the four winds of heaven.[26]

The use of the imperfect is due to natural development of the language: CBH would have used *weqatal* (וְנֶחֶצְתָה) here in predictive discourse. The use of the short form, however, almost certainly reflects a desire to follow the classical syntax. The authors of postclassical texts noted that scriptural texts tend to use the jussive following *waw*, but failed to pay attention to the distinct function expressed by the form. They imitated the morphology and syntax of the classical texts, even where the meaning is unsuitable.

These two grammatical pseudoclassicisms occur in more than one LBH book, the lengthened imperative occurring in Nehemiah and Chronicles, and the jussive form in Daniel and Ecclesiastes. Both continue in Qumran Hebrew. This distribution shows, once again, that pseudoclassicisms are not necessarily innovations of individual late authors but reflect more general interpretive knowledge disseminated in Jewish circles during the postexilic period.

The Significance of Pseudoclassicisms

Although scholars have long recognized internal developments and Aramaic influence as factors of change in the history of ancient Hebrew, pseudoclassicism has only been diagnosed more recently. Only in the light of the Hebrew of the Dead Sea Scrolls, where pseudoclassical features are more prominent, have scholars realized that similar processes also affected LBH. Identifying pseudoclassicisms involves drawing subtle distinctions in meaning or form, and there often remains a degree of uncertainty. Some cases, including some of those described already, are contestable. At times, it is possible to argue that the usage in the late books is the same as in the CBH corpus, or that the difference between them is due to the development of the language or to nonlinguistic factors such as textual corruption. Taken together, however, the examples demonstrate that the process of pseudoclassicism certainly exists.

Where later interpretation succeeds in regaining the original meaning of a word, the interpretation is indistinguishable from linguistic continuity.

Only where the interpretation is "off" in one way or another can it be recognized for what it is. The pseudoclassicisms that we can detect are the proverbial tip of the iceberg, revealing the essentially archaizing nature of most of the LBH books.

This phenomenon ties in with several other features of the use of authoritative texts in Second Temple Judaism. Pseudoclassicisms indicate that CBH texts were studied intensively in scribal circles, perhaps in a school setting. As we have observed, the divergent interpretation underlying them often turns up independently in the ancient versions or in other sources. The interpretation of לבוא + GN as "to come to (i.e., up to the border of) GN" underlying 2 Chr 26:8 is found in all the ancient versions of this verse, and also in most occurrences of the expression לְבוֹא חֲמָת. Similarly, the meaning attributed to the expression מִלֵּא יָד ("fill the hand of") in Chronicles was clearly known by the later Targumists. Yet we should not conclude that the later usages were created by the Chronicler and adopted from Chronicles in the other sources. A more likely explanation is that the pseudoclassical interpretation was taught as an oral tradition in various Jewish circles. Classical texts were considered authoritative, but some of the rarer words and expressions they contained had been forgotten and needed interpretation. By the time the Pentateuch was translated into Greek, early in the third century BCE, many interpretations had become more or less traditional. Pseudoclassicisms in LBH show that traditional exegesis of classical texts had begun much earlier than the Hellenistic era, and that some interpretations were widespread already by the end of the Persian period.

The phenomenon of pseudoclassicism reveals a striking attitude to language, one might even say a language ideology. It is one thing to interpret old texts and to search for the meaning of rare words and expressions occurring in them; it is quite another to use those old words, in the meaning arrived at by antiquarian interpretation, in one's own writing. Hebrew did not die out in the sixth century BCE: it continued as a living language through the exilic and postexilic periods up to the time of the Jewish wars in 70 and 135 CE. Many vernacular developments show up in LBH. But the authors of the LBH corpus did not simply write in the Hebrew of their own period. At times they used features of classical Hebrew that had long fallen from use in the living language. Their literary practice reflects the increasing authority of religious texts that would come to constitute the Bible. Jewish authors of the Persian period and later defined their cultural identity in terms of those texts. Judaism gradually turns into a book-based religion. To belong to the community was to accept the authority of the ancient writings it recognized. Pseudoclassicism testifies to this attitude. Reuse of expressions occurring in ancient religious writings was one way to recognize and reappropriate their authority.

From a historical linguistic perspective, pseudoclassicisms also highlight the temporal distance between CBH and LBH. Pseudoclassical usage is the end result of a lengthy process comprising at least the following stages:

1. A linguistic feature occurring in the transmitted text falls from active use.
2. Consequently, its meaning or grammatical structure is forgotten.
3. The passage becomes hard to understand and gives rise to commentary.
4. One particular interpretation of the feature comes to be accepted as correct.
5. On the basis of this new understanding, the feature is revived in LBH.

For this complex process to take place, we must allow for at least two or three generations, and possibly many more.[27] Such a time frame is compatible with the argument we have developed in the previous chapters: if CBH is preexilic and LBH postexilic, this leaves a long period between the two.

Perhaps it is possible to go further. The occurrence of pseudoclassicisms in LBH may be indicative not only of a long lapse of time but also of some type of cultural disruption. After all, even when words drop from active use, this does not necessarily lead to their being forgotten. Literary texts in any language use words and forms that are rarely if ever used in speech. To cast such words into oblivion requires a shift, a cultural change of major proportions. Just such a shift happened in the history of the Hebrew language, if one accepts that CBH goes back to the monarchical period. The destruction of the city of Jerusalem and its temple, the end of the monarchy and other institutions, and the exile of a large part of Judah's cultured classes, all of which happened in 586 BCE, are just the type of cataclysm that could create a break in the transmission of traditional knowledge. If these reflections are accurate, the phenomenon of pseudoclassicism not only confirms the time span separating LBH from CBH but also gives an indication of their absolute dates.

Pseudoclassicism in Qumran Hebrew

While pseudoclassical features are sporadic in LBH, they become frequent in Qumran Hebrew. As we have noted, the phenomenon of pseudoclassicism was first observed in Qumran Hebrew.[28] The sectarian Dead Sea Scrolls are written in a biblicizing jargon that draws heavily on the language of the Torah and the Prophets. When medieval manuscripts of the Damascus Document—a work that later turned up among the Dead Sea Scrolls—were discovered in the Cairo Geniza at the end of the nineteenth century, Solomon Schechter, their discoverer and editor, described the language as follows: "The language of the MS. is for the most part pure Biblical Hebrew. The first three pages rise even to the dignity of Scriptural poetry, though a good deal of it is obscured by the unfortunate condition in which the text is at present. But there are in it terms and expressions which occur only in the Mishna or even only in the Rabbinic literature dating from the first centuries of the Middle Ages."[29] Schechter's judgment remains cogent today. In a more recent study, Ian Young has shown that Pesher Habakkuk contains very few LBH features and is written almost entirely in Classical Hebrew.[30]

This is not to say that the Hebrew of the sectarian scrolls equals CBH in all details. Some of the vocabulary, such as the word פֶּשֶׁר ("interpretation") itself, is late, as is some of the phraseology and the syntax. In addition, several classical expressions in the scrolls do not match their CBH counterpart:[31]

אות — The verb means "to consent" in CBH. It is used in the Damascus Document with a different meaning: "to share (in an economic venture)." The new meaning reflects an interpretation based on the context in Gen 34 (the rape of Dinah), where the verb is used three times. The interpretation "to share" is found also in Targum Neofiti.[32]

אֶפְעֶה — Designating a type of snake in the Hebrew Bible, the noun אפעה is used three times in the Hodayot with the meaning "nothingness."[33] The secondary interpretation may have been influenced by the *hapax legomenon* אֶפַע ("nothingness") in Isa 41:24.[34]

אִישׁ־בֵּנַיִם — In 1 Sam 17: 4, 23, אִישׁ־הַבֵּנַיִם means "man of the middle, champion representing an army in single combat." In the War Scroll, the plural אנשי בנים occurs several times with a rather different meaning, probably "foot soldier."[35] The new meaning was probably arrived at on the basis of the context in 1 Sam 17, where it refers to Goliath. The ancient versions reflect widespread ignorance of the meaning of the expression.

בַּד בְּבַד In Exod 30:34, where it is a *hapax legomenon*, the expression means "in equal measure." In 1QS IV, 16, 25, it expresses a different meaning: "separately."[36] The interpretation probably reflects influence from the phrase לְבַד ("separately").

הוֹן In the Bible הוֹן means "riches, wealth." In Qumran Hebrew the word is used interchangeably with ממון ("money"). In the Targums הון is occasionally rendered as ממון.

מגן In Biblical Hebrew, this verb in the *piel* means "to give" (Gen 14:20; Hos 11:8; Prov 4:9). In 1QM XVIII, 13, the verb has a different meaning, probably "to break," "to shatter (the heart)."[37] The reinterpretation was based on Lam 3:65, taking מְגִנַּת as derived from the same root. The meaning "to break" is attributed to מגן in Targum Neofiti at Gen 14:20.

מַדְהֵבָה The *hapax legomenon* in Isa 14:4 probably came into being by a scribal mistake. In Qumran Hebrew it was given a specific meaning, perhaps "thirst," and adopted into active use.[38]

מָעוֹז In Biblical Hebrew, this noun means "refuge," "stronghold" and derives from the root עוז ("to take refuge"). In Qumran Hebrew the word is often used in the meaning "strength," from עזז ("to be strong"). The versions also interpret Biblical Hebrew מָעוֹז as "strength" in many passages.[39]

שַׁחַת In Biblical Hebrew, this noun, derived from the root שחה ("to be deep"), means "pit." In Qumran it is used most often with the meaning "perdition," "utter destruction," probably reflecting reanalysis on the basis of the root שחת ("to destroy").[40]

תְּשׁוּקָה In the Bible this noun means something like "desire" (Gen 3:16; 4:7; Song 7:11). In Qumran, it is a synonym of תשובה ("return").[41] The meaning "return" is reflected also in the ancient versions.

This list is offered without any claim of exhaustiveness.[42] Even so, it amply illustrates how the phenomenon of pseudoclassicism is anchored in the language of the sectarian scrolls. These data demonstrate that Qumran Hebrew differs essentially from CBH. Their superficial resemblance does not support the argument that CBH could have been readily written in the Hellenistic period, if the author desired to do so. On the contrary, pseudoclassicisms demonstrate that later authors, however much they desired to adopt the language of scripture, were incapable of writing classical Hebrew. The cases where they get it wrong show that even where Qumran authors correctly reproduce CBH phraseology and syntax, they were imitating literary models. If a CBH feature unattested in LBH resurfaces in Qumran Hebrew, we should always consider the possibility that it is an archaizing revival rather than an indication of linguistic continuity.[43]

The Dead Sea Scrolls are later than the biblical books and have probative value only for the Hebrew of their time. Nevertheless, the study of their language can contribute much to the historical approach to Biblical Hebrew. Qumran Hebrew is an important heuristic for identifying pseudoclassicisms in LBH. LBH and Qumran Hebrew share many features and are generally close to one another. After several instances of reanalyzed biblical expressions were observed in Qumran Hebrew, it made sense to consider whether similar phenomena occurred in LBH. This turned out indeed to be the case. In addition, Qumran Hebrew allows one to have a more global view of pseudoclassicisms as an historical phenomenon: what started out as a sporadic array of features has since become a pervasive characteristic. As in the case of LBH, pseudoclassicisms in Qumran Hebrew have striking implications for their underlying view of language. Among the sectarians, classical Hebrew was defined expressly as God's own language.[44] Their ideology of Hebrew explains their active effort to produce new texts in the language of scripture.

Conclusions

Pseudoclassicisms first emerge as a feature of style and register. The postclassical authors spoke their own variety of postclassical Hebrew, but in their written texts they at times preferred to clothe their thoughts in language borrowed from classical texts. This practice seems to have been a conscious one, involving the writer's decision to imitate CBH. Texts from the same period and milieu show different degrees of this tendency: while Chronicles has several pseudoclassicisms and the Hodayot have many, Ecclesiastes has very few and the Copper Scroll none at all. Although the phenomenon seems to affect the entire corpus of literary Hebrew of the late Persian and Hellenistic periods, it is more characteristic of individual texts and their genres than of the language itself. Of course, over time a usage that starts out as a stylistic feature can become entrenched in the language system. Some pseudoclassicisms eventually become part of the dictionary.

Pseudoclassicisms are not very numerous in LBH, and they are hard to demonstrate beyond a reasonable doubt. They are nevertheless important in a diachronic approach to Biblical Hebrew. They undermine the idea of "perfect archaizing": however proficient later authors may have been in classical Hebrew, they inevitably tripped up in one way or another. What may look like identical languages can in reality be shown to be only superficially similar but divergent in meaning or form. Pseudoclassicisms also attest the temporal distance between CBH and LBH: it took time for CBH expressions to be forgotten, revived in interpretation, and exploited anew in original writing. Finally, pseudoclassicisms give unique insight into the way Hebrew evolved after the monarchic period. From a national language, Hebrew turned, slowly and gradually, into the property of a community, an "ecclesiolect."

8 Consilience and Cultural History: The Ages of Biblical Literature

To sum up our book so far, we have shown that Biblical Hebrew—like all languages, literary and spoken—has a history that we can trace, even among the welter of other variations due to textual transmission, dialects, and literary style. We are able to specify three main phases or "chronolects" of Biblical Hebrew: classical (CBH), transitional (TBH), and late (LBH). The similarities between CBH and preexilic Hebrew inscriptions allow us to locate the historical context of CBH in the preexilic period. The characteristics of TBH and the books written in it indicate that its historical context is the "long" sixth century BCE. The phenomenon of pseudoclassicisms and the other features of LBH illuminate its context in the postexilic period. We have established a relative and absolute dating for these chronolects and have described their distinctive features, focusing on changes in morphosyntax and semantics. As our many examples illustrate, this model of the history of Biblical Hebrew has obvious implications for the dating of biblical texts.

In this chapter we broaden the scope of our inquiry to include other historiographical concerns. As Alexander Rofé aptly observes, to determine confidently the date of the biblical books and sources, we must supplement linguistic inquiry with other kinds of historical scholarship. We can accomplish our task "not by language alone," but by using all the tools of historical-critical research.[1] Recently Erhard Blum has advanced similar cautions. He urges that "linguistic arguments should be part of a much more comprehensive historical-philological endeavor."[2] We concur. Historical linguistics and other modes of historical scholarship must be integrated if we wish to achieve results that are cogent and convincing. In this chapter, we situate the results of the previous chapters within the larger horizons of historical research. We aim to show how Hebrew linguistics and other types of historical inquiry work together to provide a "thick description" of the ages of biblical literature.[3]

The evidence that we consider alongside the linguistic data consist primarily of casual or inadvertent details in the texts about political institutions, cultural realia, and foreign affairs, which can be checked against extrabiblical sources. These peripheral details are key evidence for historical context. As we will see, these traces of the past are better clues for literary history than is the currently dominant approach, which, as Blum remarks, relies on "dating based on specific traditions in terms of conceptions, ideas, or *theologumena*."[4] We criticize this approach as overly impressionistic and wedded to a "pigeon-holing" model of history. Moreover, it tends to dismiss the evidence of linguistic history.

We use as our guiding threads two methodological principles: consilience and cultural history. The principle of consilience states that different types of evidence converge in a true (or well-warranted) theory. Cultural history is a mode of historical inquiry that takes its cues from incidental features of texts—rather than their explicit discursive claims—to elucidate the milieus and mentalities of the past. The method of cultural history includes in its focus literary fictions and the social *imaginaire* as well as actual events. It attends to the interweaving tracks of real and invented history. Let us unpack these two guiding ideas.

William Whewell, who coined the term *consilience*, describes the principle as follows: "The Consilience of Inductions takes place when an Induction, obtained from one class of facts, coincides with an Induction, obtained from another different class .... Consilience is a test of the truth of the Theory in which it occurs."[5] Individual inferences based on different classes of evidence can be weak or strong; it is their convergence that establishes the relative strength of a theory. To put it differently, in the words of biologist Stephen Jay Gould, consilience denotes "the confidence gained when many independent sources 'conspire' to indicate a particular historical pattern."[6]

The principle of consilience is important in historical inquiry because our knowledge of the past is necessarily partial and incomplete. We are limited to what Marc Bloch calls the "tracks" of the past, that is, "the mark[s], perceptible to the senses, which some phenomenon, in itself inaccessible, has left behind."[7] To assess the historical implications of these tracks, we are required to use all the modes of inquiry at our disposal. If the linguistic tracks seem to tell a certain story, then we must test—and revise—this story in the light of other relevant inferences. To reach warranted historical knowledge, we must seek consilience.

To seek consilience between inferences from language and other historical tracks, we turn to cultural history, which is the approach best suited to our texts, which are an amalgamation of folklore, history, politics, and cultural memory.[8] The materials of cultural history—as we will see—include peripheral details like coins, musical instruments, place names, curses, titles, loanwords, artistic motifs, and literary traits like style switching. These are the kinds of involuntary tracks that, in Bloch's formulation, permit us to "know . . . far more of the past than the past itself had thought good to tell us."[9]

The historian Jacob Burckhardt pioneered this kind of inquiry in his cultural histories of ancient Greece and Renaissance Europe. He describes the orientation of cultural history as follows: "Cultural history . . . possesses a primary degree of certainty, as it consists for the most part of material conveyed in an unintentional, disinterested or even involuntary way by sources and monuments; they betray their secrets unconsciously and even, paradoxically, through fictitious elaborations, quite apart from the material details they may set out to record and glorify, and are thus doubly instructive for the cultural historian."[10] The "doubly instructive" quality of the evidence refers to its explicit and implicit meanings. The explicit meanings of the sources are of course important for the historian, whether they are historically reliable or not. But even more significant are the implicit concepts and beliefs, which are often more reliable than the explicit meanings, because they are not distorted by an ideological *Tendenz*. These casually revealed "secrets," often embedded in small details, shed considerable light on the cultural history of biblical literature.

In our search for consilience and cultural history we disregard the type of arguments commonly made by biblical scholars that try to locate ideas—often theologumena, as Blum observes—in a particular period of Israelite history, when they were most salient. R. G. Collingwood criticizes this approach as "pigeon-holing." It construes history "not [as] a chronological scheme merely, but a qualitative scheme, in which 'periods' each with its own pervasive character follow one another in time."[11] This approach was regarded as genuinely scientific in the nineteenth century. Although its value is, in Collingwood's estimation, "exactly nil" in the absence of corroborating evidence,[12] it endures in biblical scholarship, perhaps because the ancient historical evidence is so sparse.

Benjamin Sommer has recently subjected this method of dating texts in biblical scholarship to detailed criticism.[13] He describes the usual procedure as follows: "A scholar ascertains the themes of a passage, then thinks about when that theme would be relevant, crucial, or meaningful to ancient Israelites, then dates the text to that time-period. It should be immediately clear that this method of dating holds no validity whatsoever."[14] The reasons for its lack of validity are straightforward. As Sommer observes, "It is always possible that an author at one period came up with ideas that turned out to be peculiarly relevant at another period." It is incorrect to assume, as do "so many biblicists . . . [that] certain ideas can only have been thought at a particular moment." Sommer concludes, with some dismay, "Unfortunately, these sorts of reasoning compose . . . a great part of the argumentation of most biblical critics who attempt to date biblical texts."[15] This procedure fails to account for the unpredictability of literary creation and the complexity of religious thought. Nor does it take into account the ebb and flow of cultural ideas. It is a "simplistic reductionism."[16] At best it yields weak inferences, which are viable only when combined with other linguistic and historical evidence and inferences.

Our samples of consilience and cultural history are arrayed chronologically from the early Iron Age to the Hellenistic era, including the Iron II, Neo-Assyrian, Neo-Babylonian, and Persian periods. The evidence becomes more abundant beginning in the Neo-Assyrian period, but in each era there is a striking degree of consilience in the inferences drawn from different classes of linguistic and historical data. Our examples are only a selection out of a much greater pool, but they suffice to indicate that the picture we have drawn from the linguistic evidence is well grounded. A comprehensive presentation of the evidence would take many volumes and lifetimes; consequently, this sample is provisional. But it shows the cogency of our model.

Canaanite Duals and the Community of Early Israel

The dual forms in the last stanza of the Song of Deborah (Judges 5) have literary and historical implications that have yet to be explored.[17]

Judg 5:30
Are they not finding and dividing the spoil?
  A young woman (רַחַם), two young women (רַחֲמָתַיִם) for every man,
Spoil of colored cloth for Sisera,
  Spoil of colored embroidery (רִקְמָה),
  Two colored embroideries (רִקְמָתַיִם) for the necks of the despoilers.[18]

The two dual forms, רַחֲמָתַיִם ("two young women") and רִקְמָתַיִם ("two embroidered cloths"), are wordplays in sound and meaning: they are onomatopoetic kinds of war booty, valuable goods that warriors bring home to signify victory. Both kinds of spoil are gendered as feminine, one physically—note the sexual and reproductive resonance of the noun רַחַם ("young woman," lit. "womb")[19]—and the other as a product of women's labor.[20] The conquering heroes take home wives, concubines, and luxury goods made by women. With these spoils, victory implies reproductive success and wealth.

These dual forms, and the ideology of war that they express, are in a speech by a Canaanite woman. She is a courtier to Sisera's mother and is attempting to allay her mistress's anxiety about her son's delay in returning from battle. In the scene painted by her speech, Sisera's delay is due to the distribution of spoil among his men. What she does not know is that Sisera lies dead at the feet of his killer, a woman named Jael, as related in the previous stanza (Judg 5:24–27). There are many ironies in this sequence of scenes, as Jael's heroic victory is juxtaposed to Sisera's defeat and the impending sorrow of Sisera's mother.[21]

Linguistically and stylistically, the use of these duals is striking. As far as we know, in Hebrew and other Iron Age Northwest Semitic languages the dual was not a productive form. It is mostly limited to natural or temporal pairs, plus a few other fixed expressions. This contrasts with earlier Northwest Semitic (i.e., Ugaritic), where the dual is a productive form for any noun.[22] Because the Canaanite woman uses the dual as a productive form for רַחַם ("young woman") and רִקְמָה ("embroidery"), this scene represents a Canaanite dialect in which the dual was productive. This points to a very early period. The text either knows or remembers a period when Canaanite languages had a productive dual. This is a small, casual detail that reveals a glimpse of the linguistic culture at the time of the text's composition.

The use of these duals in the speech of a Canaanite woman is intelligible in Hebrew, as the dual form was well known. Here both duals are parallel (either within the line or in successive lines) to the corresponding singular noun. A comparable instance is in a brief poetic speech by Samson in which he says, חֲמוֹר חֲמֹרָתָיִם ("a heap, two heaps," Judg 15:16). Samson's juxtaposition of singular and dual is a wordplay on חֲמוֹר ("he-ass"), whose jawbone he is using to kill heaps of Philistines.[23]

The effect of these duals in represented speech is to mark the speech as archaic. In Judg 5:30 it marks the speech as archaic and foreign. This is the literary technique of style switching, in which the use of unusual or foreign elements adds a particular color to a text, often in direct discourse.[24] The technique of style switching presumes that the linguistic feature corresponds to an actual or remembered feature, in this case the productive use of the dual in proto-Hebrew or proto-Canaanite.

This is not an isolated old feature in Judg 5. The text swarms with them. To limit ourselves to the passage quoted above, the present progressive in the first line is expressed by two *yiqtol* forms, יְמַצְאוּ יְחַלְּקוּ ("finding and dividing"). As Tania Notarius observes, this is an archaic feature, as this function of *yiqtol* was replaced in CBH by the predicate participle.[25] The only exception is in direct questions, where the older usage is preserved. She concludes, "The present progressive use of imperfective יקטל in Judg 5:30 is a rare and typologically archaic phenomenon."[26] There are other archaic features throughout the poem, in morphology, lexicon, and syntax.[27]

The old linguistic details in the Song of Deborah are consilient with the poem's cultural content. As scholars have long noted, there are many antique traces in the text's picture of Israelite society. Only ten Israelite tribes are listed, and the names of two of them, Machir and Gilead, occur only here. In later texts, they are tribal clans within Manasseh and are replaced in tribal lists by Manasseh and Gad.[28] The tribes of Judah, Simeon, and Levi are not mentioned at all. There is no king and no standing army. Israel is a tribal society in which the internal segments and allied polities (including the unknown Meroz) must be shamed or cajoled into action, with curses as the only recourse if they refuse. The poem describes its own context as rural and oral: "There, by the watering places, they recount the righteous deeds of Yahweh, the righteous deeds of his villagers in Israel" (Judg 5:11). This is a self-reference to the oral setting of the poem and the genre to which it belongs. Both the overt content and the social and linguistic details of the song are consonant with a premonarchical social setting.

The Song of Deborah evokes a clear picture of early Israelite society. But there are also more subtle sociopolitical meanings. As Mark Smith has recently commented, "The poem may in fact both express and repress the problem of social-political identity in early Israel."[29] On the one hand, the tribes are in disarray, only loosely allied and dependent on exhortations and curses for joint action against the Canaanite troops. Only six tribes respond to the call to battle, and four stay home. On the other hand, the tribes are, in theory, a unified community. The assembled troops are called the עַם יְהוָה ("people of Yahweh," Judg 5:13), and their charismatic leader, Deborah, is אֵם בְּיִשְׂרָאֵל ("mother of/in Israel," Judg 5:7). These terms describe a single people unified under a single God. These two portraits—of unity and disarray—are in tension.

The song in praise of the victory of Yahweh and his heroic villagers exposes the internal complications of the political idea of Israel in this early period. The six tribes that participate in the battle—Ephraim, Benjamin, Machir, Zebulon, Issachar, and Naphtali—are geographically contiguous. They are directly affected by the disruption of travel (חָדְלוּ אֳרָחוֹת, "roads ceased," Judg 5:6), which suggests a conflict over the control of trade routes.[30] The four tribes that stay home—Reuben, Gilead, Dan, and Asher—are geographically distant. Reuben and Gilead are בְּעֵבֶר הַיַּרְדֵּן ("across the Jordan," Judg 5:17), and Dan and Asher are לְחוֹף יַמִּים ("at the seacoast," Judg 5:17). These tribes are not dependent on the disrupted trade routes, as they have different locales and economies, dependent either on herding (עֲדָרִים, "flocks," Judg 5:16) or on shipping (אֳנִיּוֹת, "ships," Judg 5:17). Geographically and economically, the tribes are not a unity, hence the Song's anguish at the tribes who stayed home.[31]

In sum, far from a political-cultic unity, Israel is a diffuse network of autonomous tribes who may or may not join together for common interests against a common enemy. The deeper import of the poem reflects the social *imaginaire* of a weakly affiliated tribal society, prior to the rise of a centralized state. The Song itself is a discursive vehicle for creating sociopolitical unity against this backdrop, extolling the victories of the "people of Yahweh" in the face of countervailing forces both outside (Canaanite armies) and inside (tribal disunity). In some respects, the Song aims to fashion a common identity; it sings into being a cultural memory that overcomes internal fissures, situating them in a larger theological-political field: צִדְקוֹת יְהוָה / צִדְקֹת פִּרְזֹנוֹ בְּיִשְׂרָאֵל ("the righteous deeds of Yahweh / the righteous deeds of his villagers in Israel," Judg 5:11).[32]

The archaic nature of the Song of Deborah is granted by most scholars. Among others, Konrad Schmid comments that the Song of Deborah "feature[s] unusually archaic language and may preserve ancient Northern traditions relatively intact."[33] The consilience of the linguistic and historical data indicate that this is a very early text, composed in the premonarchical or early monarchical period. It belongs to the oldest age of biblical literature.

The Philistine Pentapolis

The סַרְנֵי פְלִשְׁתִּים ("rulers of the Philistines") figure prominently in three biblical narratives: the Samson story (seven times in Judges 16), the

Ark narrative (seven times in 1 Sam 5–6), and a portion of the David story (three times in 1 Sam 29). The use of the Philistine loanword סֶרֶן* ("ruler") lends a flavor of authenticity and antiquity to these narratives.[34] It also arguably reflects genuine historical memories of the floruit of the Philistine pentapolis, circa twelfth to ninth centuries BCE. The old Philistine title is consilient with the archaeological evidence in establishing the antiquity of these Philistine memories. The further away from this period that one dates the stories, the less plausible the dating becomes.[35]

These three CBH narratives are examples of the second age of biblical literature. They are typologically later than the archaic poetry (e.g., Song of Deborah) and typologically earlier than TBH texts. Because they serve as source materials for the Deuteronomistic History, they predate the time of this composition (late seventh to early sixth centuries BCE).[36]

The five cities of the Philistine pentapolis were Gaza, Ashdod, Ashkelon, Gath, and Ekron (see Josh 13:3). The archaeological and epigraphic evidence illuminates the history of these five polities. As Assaf Yasur-Landau observes, "The political division of Philistia emerged in the late twelfth century and remained stable for the next two centuries or so."[37] From the late eleventh to the mid-ninth centuries BCE, Gath was the largest of the Philistine cities and probably the largest city in Palestine.[38] Gath was destroyed in the latter part of the ninth century BCE, probably by the Aramean king Hazael (see 2 Kgs 12:18), after which the site was minimally resettled.

Amos 6:2 reflects on the destruction of Gath and other formerly great polities:

> רְדוּ גַת־פְּלִשְׁתִּים / הֲטוֹבִים מִן־הַמַּמְלָכוֹת הָאֵלֶּה / אִם־רַב גְּבוּלָם מִגְּבֻלְכֶם
> Go down to Gath of the Philistines;
> Are you better than these kingdoms?
> Are their boundaries greater than yours?

This text from an eighth-century prophet is testimony to the destruction of Gath, which occurred a generation or two earlier.[39] The oracle against the nations in Amos 1:6–8 condemns the remaining cities of the pentapolis: Gaza, Ashdod, Ashkelon, and Ekron. Gath is absent. At the time of this prophetic oracle, the pentapolis has been reduced to a tetrapolis.

As Israel Finkelstein observes, the inclusion of Gath in the biblical narratives reflects a "genuine memory that in the not-so-distant past, Gath . . . was a major Philistine centre."[40] This memory is prominent in two of the stories that feature the rulers of the pentapolis. When the Philistines capture the Ark, they bring it to three of their five cities—including Gath—and at each the "hand of God" devastates the Philistines (1 Sam 5). David and his mercenary band serve the king of Gath until the death of Saul (1 Sam 27–29). Only the Samson story does not feature Gath. In two of the three stories, the memory of Gath correlates with the use of the old Philistine title, סַרְנֵי פְלִשְׁתִּים, and conjures the fierce glory of the Philistine pentapolis.

The same quality of historical memory applies to the prominence of Shiloh in the Ark narrative and in the preceding story of Hannah and Samuel (1 Sam 1–4). Shiloh was destroyed in the eleventh or early tenth century BCE. Finkelstein writes, "The biblical memory on the prominence of Shiloh in early Israelite history must echo the importance of the site in the Iron I, no later than the tenth century BCE."[41] The memory of Philistine hegemony is linked with the prominence of Gath and Shiloh. These traces of history are consilient with the linguistic evidence of Philistine loanwords.[42] The consilience of these different bodies of evidence shows the imprint of premonarchical and early monarchical memories in classical Hebrew literature.[43] The explicit and implicit setting of these CBH texts is the Iron Age.

Kings and Chronology

There are many details from extrabiblical sources that are consilient with the political history of Israel sketched in Kings and the classical prophets, particularly from the ninth century onward, when monumental inscriptions and royal annals become established genres of political discourse in the ancient Near East.[44] Many Israelite and Judean kings are mentioned in Aramaic, Moabite, Neo-Assyrian, and Neo-Babylonian royal inscriptions and annals. The linguistic details are interesting but are relegated to our notes. Here we focus on the implications for the Bible's literary history. The following are the extrabiblical attestations of Israelite and Judean dynasties and kings:[45]

Royal Dynasties

Davidic	ביתדוד ("house of David"), Tel Dan stele, late ninth century BCE[46]
	בת[ ]וד ("house [of Da]vid"), Mesha stele, mid-ninth century BCE[47]
Omride	*bīt Ḫumrî* ("house of Omri"), many times in Assyrian annals of the ninth to eighth centuries BCE[48]

Northern Kingdom of Israel

Omri	עמרי מלך ישראל ("Omri [was] king of Israel"), Mesha stele[49]
Ahab	*Aḫabu Sir'ilāya* ("two thousand chariots [and] ten thousand troops of Ahab of Israel"), annals of Shalmaneser III[50]
Joram	[יו]רם בר [...] מלך ישראל ("[Jo]ram son of . . . king of Israel"), Tel Dan stele[51]
Jehu	*Yaua* [var.: *Yau*] *mār Ḫumrî* ("the tribute of Jehu, son of Omri"), annals of Shalmaneser III[52]
Joash	*Ya'asu Samerināya* ("the tribute of Joash of Samaria"), annals of Adad-Nirari III[53]
Menahem	*Meniḫime Samerināya* ("Menahem of Samaria"), annals of Tiglath-Pileser III[54]
Pekah	*Paqaḫa* ("[I/they] killed Pekah, their king"), annals of Tiglath-Pileser III[55]
Hoshea	*Ausi'i* ("I placed Hoshea [as king o]ver them"), annals of Tiglath-Pileser III[56]

Southern Kingdom of Judah

Ahaziah	[אחז]יהו בר [... מל]ך ביתדוד ("[Ahaz]yahu, son of [. . . kin]g of the house of David"), Tel Dan stele[57]
Azariah?	*Azriau* ("Azariah"), annals of Tiglath-Pileser III[58]
Ahaz	*Yauḫazi Yaudāya* ("Jehoahaz of Judah"), annals of Tiglath-Pileser III[59]
Hezekiah	*Ḫazaqiyau Yaudāya* ("Hezekiah of Judah"), annals of Sennacherib[60]
Manasseh	*Menasī* [var.: *Minsī*] *šar Yaudi* ("Manasseh, king of Judah"), annals of Esarhaddon, annals of Ashurbanipal[61]
Jehoiachin	[*Ya*]'*ukīnu* and *Yakūkīnu* ("Jehoiachin"), annals of Nebuchadnezzar II[62]

The extrabiblical attestations of Israelite and Judean kings and dynasties—all at the right times and in the right order—show that the book of Kings relies on accurate archival material and historical memories reaching back to the time of these kings.[63] This case is analogous to the accurate representation of details about Philistine history and culture. These royal details attest to the Iron Age context of the political history in Kings. After the destruction of the monarchy and its institutions, including the palace archives, in 586 BCE, many of these details would have been lost or forgotten.

Peripheral details—such as the thirty talents of gold that Hezekiah paid as ransom to Sennacherib (listed in 2 Kgs 18:14 and in Sennacherib's annals)—clearly rely on royal archival texts. Although there is much ideological shaping of events and bursts of legendary material,[64] the details of political history in Kings and the prophetic books are consilient with the other evidence in situating CBH in the monarchical period.

Nimrod and the Deuteronomic Curses: The Neo-Assyrian Empire

The Neo-Assyrian period, from the late ninth to the late seventh centuries BCE, was the floruit of CBH. Some CBH texts explicitly situate themselves in this context, from First Isaiah (e.g., the Isaiah memoir in Isa 6–9, referring to the era of Tiglath-Pilesar III) and portions of Kings to Nahum, which celebrates the fall of Nineveh in 612 BCE. Others texts more obliquely reflect details of Neo-Assyrian cultural history. We address two examples from the Pentateuch, one an explicit case, the account of Nimrod in Gen 10:8–11, and the other an inadvertent case, the curses of Deut 28.

The Nimrod pericope has two distinctive linguistic features of CBH. It uses the *qal* of ילד with a male subject, וְכוּשׁ יָלַד אֶת־נִמְרֹד ("Now Cush begat Nimrod," Gen 10:8), rather than the *hiphil*,[65] and it uses מַמְלָכָה for "kingdom" (Gen 10:10), not מַלְכוּת.[66] It is usually identified as part of the J version of the Table of Nations, which is excerpted in Gen 10:8–19, 21, 24–30 (the Hamite and Shemite branches). There are many local puzzles in the Nimrod pericope;[67] here we focus on the text as an Israelite cultural reflection on Mesopotamian history.

The name "Nimrod" is found once elsewhere. In Micah 5:5, אֶרֶץ נִמְרֹד ("the land of Nimrod") is parallel to אֶרֶץ אַשּׁוּר ("the land of Assyria"). Nimrod seems to be a well-known name for the royal founder and culture hero of the Assyrian empire. The saying cited in Gen 10:9, "Like Nimrod, a mighty hunter before Yahweh," attests his renown in Israelite lore. Nimrod is described as a great hunter and a builder of royal cities. These are two main features of Mesopotamian royal ideology, in which the king's greatness as a military hero is celebrated in his ritualized hunts, and his greatness as a sustainer of culture is celebrated in his urban architectural achievements. In this brief portrait, Nimrod is the Mesopotamian king par excellence.

The name Nimrod is most plausibly an Israelite borrowing and adaptation of the divine name Ninurta, the patron-god of the Neo-Assyrian kings.[68] The name would have been adapted as follows: *ninurt-* → **nimurd* (dissimilation of liquids: *n* → *m*; and voicing of dental: *t* → *d*) → **nimrud* (metathesis: *ur* → *ru*) → *nimrōd* (tonic lengthening). The resulting Hebrew form, נִמְרֹד, literally means "we will rebel" or "let us rebel." It is possible that this is a deliberate deformation of the name of Ninurta, an ironic mimicry of the Assyrian imperial god.

The political context of the text is specified by the sequence of Mesopotamian cities that Nimrod built. The text moves from the royal cities "in the land of Sumer" (e.g., Babylon, Uruk, Akkad) to the royal cities in Assyria:

> מִן־הָאָרֶץ הַהִוא יָצָא אַשּׁוּר וַיִּבֶן אֶת־נִינְוֵה וְאֶת־רְחֹבֹת עִיר וְאֶת־כָּלַח׃ וְאֶת־רֶסֶן
> בֵּין נִינְוֵה וּבֵין כָּלַח הִוא הָעִיר הַגְּדֹלָה׃
>
> From that land, he went out (to) Assyria, and he built Nineveh and Rehovot-Ir, and Calah, and Resen, between Nineveh and Calah, which is the great city. (Gen 10:11–12)

The names Rehovot-Ir and Resen are obscure—it is possible that Rehovot-Ir (lit. "the squares of the city") refers to a part of Nineveh, and it is possible that Resen is from Assyrian *rēš ēni* (lit. "head of the well"), which is the name of a suburb of Sargon II's capital city, Dūr-Šarrukīn ("Fortress of Sargon").[69] The attribute of "the great city" (הָעִיר הַגְּדֹלָה) seems to be applied to Calah, not Nineveh. This would point to a time before circa 700 BCE, during which time Calah was the greatest city of the Neo-Assyrian Empire.

Nineveh, which had long been an important Assyrian city, became the preeminent city of the empire from circa 700 BCE until its destruction in 612 BCE. After his accession in 704 BCE, Sennacherib made Nineveh his administrative center and built there his "Palace with No Rival." The new walls of Nineveh extended for roughly seven miles. The magnificence of Nineveh is recalled in the book of Jonah, where Nineveh is "the great city" (הָעִיר הַגְּדֹלָה, Jon 1:2; 3:2). If "the great city" in the Nimrod pericope is Calah, which is what the grammar says, then it reflects the Neo-Assyrian Empire prior to 700 BCE. Some scholars propose that the epithet ought to refer to Nineveh. If one prefers this approach, then it reflects the period between 700 and 612 BCE. In either case, the historical details cohere with the linguistic evidence in dating this CBH composition to the Neo-Assyrian period. If the Nimrod pericope is a part of the J source, which we think likely, then this local conclusion has wider implications for the compositional history of the Pentateuch.

The core of Deuteronomy shows more indirectly the fingerprints of the Neo-Assyrian Empire. This is most discernible in the covenant curses in Deut 28, which seem to be adaptations of the curses in Esarhaddon's Succession Treaty (EST), promulgated in 672 BCE.[70] This imprint is also discernible in the laws of religious loyalty in Deut 13.[71] On the basis of the recent discovery of a copy of EST at the temple in Tell Tayinat, it seems likely that EST was displayed in the administrative centers of Assyrian provinces and vassal states from the time of its propagation through the reign of Esarhaddon's son, Ashurbanipal (d. 627 BCE). This would include Jerusalem during the reigns of Manasseh and Josiah.[72]

The covenant curses in Deut 28:20–44 appear to be directly adapted from the curses in EST. As Hans Ulrich Steymans has recently argued, "The sequence of motifs [in the main curse section] is identical. In only two cases does a topic appear at a slightly different position, and in both these cases one can explain the difference as a deliberate scribal arrangement."[73] The clearest adaptations are the following curses by all the gods (EST 528–30) and by Sin, Shamash, and Venus (EST 419–29):[74]

Iron Earth and Bronze Heaven

> May they make your ground like iron (so that) nothing can sprout from it. Just as rain does not fall from a bronze heaven, so may rain and dew not come upon your fields and meadows; instead of dew may burning coals rain on your land. (EST 528–33)
>
> The heavens above your head shall be bronze, and the earth beneath you iron. Yahweh will turn the rain of your land into dust, and dirt from the heavens will fall on you until you are destroyed. (Deut 28:23–24)

Skin Disease

> May Sin, the brightness of heaven and earth, clothe you with leprosy. (EST 419)
>
> Yahweh will smite you with Egyptian boils, ulcers, scabs, and itch, from which you cannot be healed. (Deut 28: 27)

Blindness

> May Šamaš, the light of heaven and earth, not judge you justly. May he remove your eyesight. Walk about in darkness! (EST 422–24)
>
> Yahweh will smite you with madness, blindness, and confusion of mind, and you will grope about at noon, like a blind man gropes in the darkness. (Deut 28:28–29)

Violation of Wife and Home

> May Venus, the brightest of the stars, before your eyes make your wives lie in the lap of your enemy; may your sons not take possession of your house. (EST 428–29)

> You shall be engaged to a woman, but another man shall violate her. You shall build a house, but you shall not dwell in it. (Deut 28:30)

In each of these adaptations, the Israelite composer intensified the Assyrian curse, using a variety of literary strategies. In the first curse, the author collapsed the Assyrian simile ("like iron," "just as . . . from a bronze heaven") into a direct transformation ("shall be bronze . . . iron"). He also inverts the order from "ground . . . heaven" to "heaven . . . earth," creating a more cosmic orientation. The Assyrian transformation of rain and dew into burning coals is altered in the Hebrew into a transformation into "dust" and "dirt." These words in Hebrew have an association with death and the underworld.[75] The Hebrew curse has a terse parallelism, compared with the looser construction of the Assyrian curse. This stylistic compression in the Hebrew version yields a high stylistic register and resonance.

The Hebrew adaptation of the curse of skin disease and blindness also uses a strategy of intensification. Assyrian "leprosy," or, more precisely, "scaly skin disease" (*saḫaršubbû*), is expanded into a sequence of skin ailments, approximately translated as "Egyptian boils, ulcers, scabs, and itch." This piling up of skin conditions creates a more global effect, a Jobian panoply of skin ailments. Similarly, the curse of blindness expands the single Assyrian action, "may he remove your eyesight," into a smiting with "madness, blindness, and confusion of mind." The imprecation "Walk about in darkness!" is made more concrete by the specification of the time of day, and by the stark contrast of noon and darkness: "You will grope about at noon, like a blind man gropes in the darkness." The Hebrew adaptation turns the characteristic diseases of the moon god Sin (leprosy) and the sun god Shamash (blindness) into devastating acts of "smiting" by Yahweh.

The curse of violation of wife and home, which are the domain of Ishtar/Venus (Dilbat in EST), is heightened in Hebrew by making the violation of the wife occur before marriage. The man has not yet consummated the marriage when the "betrothed" is violated.[76] This change of marital status may explain why the Hebrew lacks "sons" (as in the Assyrian) to inherit the house, so the Hebrew resolves into "you shall not dwell in it." The repetition of "you" (three times in this sequence) contrasts with "another man" (אִ֣ישׁ אַחֵ֗ר, v. 30) and later, "another people" (עַ֣ם אַחֵ֔ר, v. 32). The Hebrew curse also intensifies the Assyrian curse of Venus by piling up other violations of the domestic domain in the verses that follow (vineyard, ox, sons and daughters, and agricultural produce, vv. 30–33).

Interestingly, this section, adapted from the Assyrian curses of Sin, Shamash, and Ishtar/Venus, ends with a repetition of the curses of madness and skin disease (vv. 34–35), but varying the terms of the previous curses:

> You shall go mad from the sight of what your eyes shall see; and Yahweh shall smite you with evil boils on your knees and thighs from which you cannot be healed, from the soles of your foot to your head. (Deut 28:34–35)

This section of curses is a remarkable adaptation and intensification of the Assyrian sequence, arrogating to Yahweh all the powers of Sin, Šamaš, and Ishtar/Venus.

As Moshe Weinfeld observed, "Though the order of curses in Deuteronomy seems to have no plausible explanation, the sequence in the VTE [= EST] is based on the hierarchy within the Assyrian pantheon."[77] This perception illuminates the historical priority of the Assyrian sequence. Since the discovery of EST at Tell Tayinat, we have a clearer idea of how EST could have been a textual influence on the composition of Deuteronomy.

Rintje Frankena's reflections on the political and religious background of this textual relationship seem even more compelling now than when he wrote them:

> After the death of Ashurbanipal, the empire of Assyria was politically on its decline .... Consequently he [King Josiah] and his people had no longer to serve the Assyrian king as their lord .... [I]t is therefore tempting to regard the renewed Covenant with Yahweh as a substitution of the former treaty with the king of Assyria. Judah, being no more a vassal of Assyria, becomes a vassal of Yahweh again. ... That the text of this Covenant should betray knowledge of the Assyrian treaties which it seems to replace seems only natural to me. The dating of Deuteronomy, moreover, would in that case find corroboration in a rather unexpected way.[78]

This unexpected corroboration—a consilience—regarding the date of the core of Deuteronomy also suits the inferences above regarding Nimrod's kingdom in the J source. If we grant that J and E (including the core of the Covenant Code)—or some analogous construction of non-P texts—were sources of Deuteronomy, then the relative chronology of these textual relationships yields a larger consilience.

These examples of traces of Neo-Assyrian cultural history in J and D also corroborate the general views of Julius Wellhausen regarding these two Pentateuchal sources. In the introduction to his *Prolegomena*, he presents his position on the ages of these sources: "The assumptions I make will find an ever-recurring justification in the course of the investigation; the two principal are, that the work of the Jehovist, so far as the nucleus of it is concerned, belongs to the course of the Assyrian period, and that of Deuteronomy belongs to its close."[79] It is currently not fashionable to agree with Wellhausen, but the consilience between different domains of inference and evidence—some unknown in his time—here support his position.[80]

The consilience of linguistic and historical evidence shows that writers were producing biblical literature in CBH during the Neo-Assyrian period. As we have shown in chapter 5, the inscriptional evidence provides another layer of consilience. The greatest density of ancient Hebrew inscriptions is in the eighth to seventh centuries BCE, including monumental inscriptions from Jerusalem and Samaria.[81] A relatively high degree of literacy was arguably the norm among educated Israelites and Judeans.[82] These and other historical traces confirm that the Neo-Assyrian period (ca. 880 to 612 BCE) was the golden age of CBH.

Babylonians in Jerusalem and Ezekiel in Tel Aviv

The Neo-Babylonian and early Persian period (late seventh to early fifth centuries BCE) is the historical context of TBH. As the books of Jeremiah and Ezekiel are touchstones for TBH, we consider representative cases where details of Neo-Babylonian culture are present in the texts. These include the names of Neo-Babylonian officials in Jer 39, and the traces of Neo-Babylonian science and scholarship in Ezek 1.

In 586 BCE the Babylonian army of Nebuchadnezzar II conquered Jerusalem. According to Jer 39:3, after breaching the city walls, the Babylonian high command set up headquarters at one of the gates of Jerusalem. According to the reading tradition of MT, these Babylonian officials were

> נֵרְגַל שַׂר־אֶצֶר סַמְגַּר־נְבוּ שַׂר־סְכִים רַב־סָרִיס נֵרְגַל שַׂר־אֶצֶר רַב־מָג וְכָל־
> שְׁאֵרִית שָׂרֵי מֶלֶךְ בָּבֶל
>
> Nergal-sar-eṣer, Samgar-nebo, Sar-sechim, the Rab-saris, Nergal-sar-ezer, the Rab-mag, and all the rest of the officials of the king of Babylon. (Jer 39:3)

Four officials are named here, two with official titles. We now know that the list is garbled, because the Hebrew reading tradition lost the correct division of the names and titles. As we have already seen, the terms רַב־סָרִיס, סַמְגַּר, and רַב־מָג are loanwords for titles of Neo-Babylonian officials.[83] The reading tradition linked סַמְגַּר with the beginning of the following name and created a new (imaginary) name. The publication of two Neo-Babylonian texts allows us to correct the MT and to identify two of the officials.[84] By correcting the division of names and titles, we recover three (not four) Babylonian officials, each with a title:

> נֵרְגַל שַׂר־אֶצֶר סַמְגַּר נְבוּ שַׂר־סְכִים רַב־סָרִיס נֵרְגַל שַׂר־אֶצֶר רַב־מָג
> Nergal-sar-ezer, the Samgar, Nebo-sar-sechim, the Rab-saris, Nergal-sar-ezer, the Rab-mag

The first of these is identifiable in Neo-Babylonian texts as Nergal-šarru-uṣur, the *simmagir*, in a list of Babylonian officials from the seventh year of Nebuchadnezzar II (598/597 BCE).[85] He was still *simmagir* in Nebuchadnezzar's court a decade later when he participated in the capture of Jerusalem. As Paul-Alain Beaulieu observes, it is generally accepted that this official is the future king Nergal-šarru-uṣur, who married Nebuchadnezzar's daughter and gained the throne circa 559 BCE by assassinating his brother-in-law, Amel-Marduk, Nebuchadnezzar's son and heir.[86] The text of Jer 39:3, though long misunderstood, is a link in this Babylonian royal drama.

The second official, less notorious, has been identified in a recently published Babylonian text from the reign of Nebuchadnezzar II.[87] His name is Nabû-šarrūssu-ūkin and his title is *rab ša rēši* (= Hebrew רַב־סָרִיס). David Vanderhooft had conjectured that נְבוּ שַׂר־סְכִים in Jer 39:3 "could reflect an Akkadian name such as *Nabû-šarrūssu-ūkin*."[88] His conjecture is confirmed by the Akkadian text. In sum, Jer 39:3, when read correctly, reveals the actual names and ranks of Babylonian officials present at the fall of Jerusalem. It is a chilling glimpse of history at a disastrous time.

The third official, who has the same name as the first, is unknown. His name may be a scribal error, an accidental repetition of the first name. In the parallel list in Jer 39:13, from the second edition of Jeremiah (Jer 39:4–12 is lacking in LXX), the name of Nebuzaradan, the Rab-ṭabbaḥim, has been added from Jer 52:12 (= 2 Kgs 25:8), the two identifiable Babylonians are missing (a different Rab-saris appears), and the third (unknown) official is the same. This is a revised memory of the officials present at the fall of Jerusalem.

At the time that these officials—including a future king—were in Jerusalem, Ezekiel was living with his fellow exiles of the first expulsion (597 BCE) in the Babylonian town of Tel Aviv (Ezek 3:15; from Akkadian *Til Abūbi*). Tel Aviv was in the same district as later communities of Judean exiles, including *āl-Yāhūdu* ("Judah-town") and *Bīt Abīrām* ("House of Abraham"). The Judean exiles were broadly exposed to Babylonian language and culture.[89] Not surprisingly, the book of Ezekiel has a large number of Babylonian loanwords, particularly in the domain of economic and cultural realia.[90] As Vanderhooft observes, "One is struck by how many of the Akkadian loans in the book pertain to what we may broadly term mercantile, juridical, industrial, professional and architectural realms."[91] Neo-Babylonian loanwords like אֶשְׁכָּרִים (< *iškaru*, "work materials," Ezek 27:15), נְדָנִים* (< *nudunnû*, "dowry," Ezek 16:33), סְגוֹר* (< *šigāru*, "neckstock," Ezek 19:9), מַלָּחִים (< *malāḫu*, "boatman," Ezek 27:29), and בְּרֹמִים (< *burrumu*, "multicolored," Ezek 27:24) populate the book.[92]

At a conceptual level, as Abraham Winitzer notes, "the book shows intimate familiarity with key tenets of the Babylonian worldview."[93] Some of the details of Ezekiel's initiatory prophetic vision (Ezek 1–2) are explicable as interpretive transformations of Babylonian cosmology and astronomy, combined with older Hebrew traditions (e.g., Isaiah's initiatory vision in Isa 6). As Christoph Uehlinger and Susanne Trufaut have convincingly argued, "The compound of *raqia'* (firmament), *ḥayyôt* [creatures] and wheels strongly recalls the Babylonian concept of the lower heaven as a solid sphere rotating according to a totally coordinated circular principle."[94] Against this cosmological backdrop, "the four *ḥayyôt* . . . stand for the four horizons as they hold up the heavenly firmament."[95]

Several Mesopotamian cylinder seal impressions, including those in figure 2 and figure 3 from the Neo-Assyrian and Achaemenid periods, illustrate this cluster of cosmological motifs. The first, from the Neo-Assyrian period, shows bull-men (*kusarrikkū*) holding up the firmament of heaven, depicted as a flat sheet, above which appears the sun-god Shamash, who is standing on a horse. Astral symbols of stars and the moon are above the firmament. The second, from the Persian period, shows bull-men with four wings holding up the high-god Ahura Mazda. The image of Ahura Mazda, inside the crescent-circle, is that of an astral god.

Figure 2. *Neo-Assyrian seal impression*
Source: Jeremy Black and Anthony Green, *Gods, Demons and Symbols of Ancient Mesopotamia: An Illustrated Dictionary* (London: British Museum; Austin: University of Texas Press, 1992), 103, fig. 82 (drawing by Tessa Rickards).

Uehlinger and Trufaut suggest that Ezekiel's vision is a projection of the cosmic realities represented in the seals. The four *ḥayyôt*, representing the four horizons, hold up the firmament of heaven, with Yahweh enthroned above it. Their complex motions, along with the parallel motions of the wheels and lights, evoke the inner movements of the celestial cosmos.

Similar mixed creatures decorated the walls and gateways of Babylonian temples, which Ezekiel and his fellow exiles would have been able to view.[96] The Hellenistic Babylonian priest Berossus describes these hybrid creatures as born from the waters of Tiamat (cf. *Enūma Eliš* 3.31–36):

> In this water, strange beings with peculiar forms came to life. For men were born with two wings and some with four wings and two faces; these had one body and two heads, and they were both masculine and feminine. . . . Other men were also born, some with the legs and horns of goats, and some with the feet of horses and the foreparts of men. . . . Bulls were also born with human heads and four-bodied dogs with fish tails . . . and still other creatures with the forms of all sorts of beasts. . . . Images of these also are set up in the temple of Bel.[97]

Figure 3. *Achaemenid seal impression*

Source: Othmar Keel, *Jahwe-Visionen und Siegelkunst: Eine neue Deutung der Majestätsschilderungen in Jes 6, Ez 1 und 10 und Sach 4*, SBS 84/85 (Stuttgart: Katholisches Bibelwerk, 1977), 214, fig. 166 (drawing by Hildi Keel, © Foundation BIBLE+ORIENT, Fribourg Switzerland). See also Uehlinger and Trufaut, "Ezekiel," 167, figs. 1–2.

This description illuminates the sacred zoology of Ezekiel's *ḥayyôt*.

The cosmic imagery of Ezekiel's vision is further elucidated by a Neo-Assyrian text, KAR 307, which describes the multiple layers of heaven and earth.[98] In the middle heaven, whose surface is made of blue stone, Marduk is enthroned in a lapis lazuli sanctuary surrounded by radiant light:

> The middle heavens are *saggilmud* stone [a blue stone]. They belong to the Igigi [the gods of heaven]. Bel [= Marduk] sat on the high dais inside, in the lapis lazuli sanctuary. He made a lamp[?] of *elmešu* stone shine inside.[99]

As Winitzer observes, "This image relates indisputably to the one appearing in the end of Ezekiel's early chariot vision."[100] The Ezekiel text is as follows, from the earlier edition of the book preserved in the LXX:[101]

> Like the appearance of lapis lazuli was the likeness of a throne upon it [the *raqia'*], and above the likeness of the throne was the likeness of the appearance of a man. And I saw something that looked like *ḥašmal* stone from the appearance of his loins upward, and from the appearance of his loins downward I saw something like the appearance of fire, and its radiance surrounded him. Like the appearance of the rainbow in the clouds on a rainy day, so was the appearance of the radiance all around. (Ezek 1:26–28)

The colors, the throne-dais, and the radiance connect these two images of the divine presence above the firmament of heaven. The celestial blue colors of *saggilmud* stone and lapis lazuli are prominent. The radiance of the *ḥašmal* stone is probably equivalent to (and lexically cognate with) the Babylonian *elmešu* stone, which is "a quasi-mythical precious stone of great brilliancy."[102] Both texts convey the dazzling aura of divine mysteries. In sum, Ezekiel's vision gains clarity when seen against its Neo-Babylonian context.

As these texts and images document, Ezekiel drew generously on his Babylonian surroundings, including its scholarly culture. From his exilic locale, he learned from the prestige culture of his time and marshaled its words, images, and concepts in his strangely innovative prophetic visions. From these examples in Jeremiah and Ezekiel, spanning Judean life from Jerusalem to Tel Aviv, we see the consilience of language and cultural history in the age of TBH literature.

Darics and Demographics

At the close of King David's fund-raising speech for the temple in 1 Chr 29:1–5, he asks the assembled officials and people, "Who will willingly bring an offering today to Yahweh?" The response is generous: "They contributed for the service of the house of God: five thousand talents of gold, ten thousand darics, ten thousand talents of silver, eighteen thousand talents of bronze, and one hundred thousand talents of iron" (1 Chr 29:6–7). This is a massive amount, far beyond the ransom of thirty talents of gold that Hezekiah paid to Sennacherib during the Assyrian invasion (2 Kgs 18:14). The king was gratified by the generosity of his people: "David the king rejoiced with great rejoicing" (1 Chr 29:9).

This passage includes a notable pseudoclassicism, לְמַלֹּאות יָדוֹ (lit. "to fill his hand"), meaning "to bring an offering," which is a literalizing reanalysis of the CBH expression, "to ordain to a sacred office."[103] Here we are interested in an inadvertent detail of the offering. The list of contributions includes not only precious metals (gold, silver, bronze, and iron) but also the most expensive coinage of the Persian era, the daric. As we saw in chapter 2, this gold coin was first minted in the late sixth century BCE, during the reign of the Persian king Darius. The mention of darics at the time of King David is an anachronism that indicates the Persian-era composition of this passage.[104]

But the use of this Persian loanword is not merely an accidental anachronism. It also has rhetorical and ideological purpose. The use of foreign words from a prestige language lends cultural authority to the narrated scene. It adds a touch of international wealth, like the mention of Deutsche Bank bonds in one's portfolio. The addition of gold darics to the list of bullion is a stylistic nuance that affirms the prestige of the first temple and its imagined wealth. The legendary prosperity of the Davidic-Solomonic era, expressed by the mention of the most valuable currency of the day, is here a feature of the Jerusalem temple and extends by analogy to the Second Temple of the Chronicler's day. As Gary Knoppers comments, "The use of late terminology [e.g., darics] . . . blurs the distinction between the First and Second Temples."[105] The prestige of the Jerusalem temple—then and now—and the importance of generous contributions are expressed by the vast sums of gold darics.

The story is, as commentators have noted, an invention of the Chronicler. In the book of Kings, David dies well before the preparations for the temple construction (as related in 1 Kgs 5–8). In Chronicles, David is the nation's founding father who initiates all the major royal and religious institutions.[106]

The historical context of Chronicles clarifies the resonance of the darics in David's Jerusalem. During the Persian era, Judah and Jerusalem were massively depopulated and impoverished. As Oded Lipschits observes, "Between the Iron Age and the Persian Period there was a sharp decline—more than 90%—in occupation in the environs of Jerusalem."[107] It was a demographic disaster zone. Israel Finkelstein estimates that during the Persian period "the population of Jerusalem . . . numbered no more than a few hundred people," and Jerusalem was nothing more than "a small Temple village."[108] Not until the Hellenistic period did Jerusalem fully recover from its demographic disaster.

For the Chronicler, writing during this period of decline, the appeal to the glorious past of the first temple was a way to gloss over the poor reality of contemporary Jerusalem and its temple. The glorious memory of the first temple is, in a sense, an ideological compensation for the relative poverty of the second. The massive wealth in darics, freely given by Israel's upper class, is an imagined treasure, masking the poverty of Jerusalem in the Persian era.

As William Schniedewind has emphasized, this demographic decline correlates with the gap between TBH and LBH. Because of the collapse of the infrastructure that supported scribal schools, he posits a virtual "gap in the Hebrew scribal tradition" in Judah from the late sixth to the early fourth centuries BCE.[109] This institutional and scribal decline created the conditions for a new literary dialect—LBH—as the vehicle for the revival of Hebrew writing. The darics and the LBH features in Chronicles are the tracks of this correlation between linguistic and cultural decline and revival in the Persian period.

As Finkelstein observes, the demographic evidence "challenge[s] the notion that much of the historical material in the Bible was written in Persian period Yehud."[110] The core of religious scribal activity during this period seems to have consisted of conserving and expanding existing books, and occasionally writing books in new or transformed genres (e.g., Chronicles, Ezra-Nehemiah, Esther, Ecclesiastes, Song of Songs). LBH scribes were crucial links in the chain of textual tradition that began centuries earlier. They were partners and innovators in the ages-long production of the Hebrew Bible.

A Hellenistic Orchestra

Like the mention of darics in Chronicles, the burst of Greek loanwords in the Aramaic of Dan 3:5 is a hybrid emulation of the dominant culture. In the wake of Alexander's conquest of the Persian empire in 333 BCE, Greek became the prestige language. In Dan 3, when the herald (כָּרוֹזָא, a Persian loanword) describes the royal orchestra next to the gold statue of Nebuchadnezzar, he uses a sequence of Greek loanwords:[111]

קַתְרוֹס	lyre (Greek *kithara*)
סַבְּכָא	small harp (Greek *sambuke*)
פְּסַנְתֵּרִין	large harp (Greek *psalterion*)
סוּמְפֹּנְיָה	bagpipe or double-flute (Greek *sumfonia*)

There are perfectly good Aramaic words for these kinds of instruments, but the author used Greek words to provide an aura of prestige and foreign elegance for the Babylonian royal orchestra. This is a technique of style switching, which inadvertently betrays the Hellenistic context of the last works of biblical literature. This example, from Aramaic, not Hebrew, clearly shows the imprint of the Greek age.[112]

Conclusions

We have shown in the textual samples in this chapter that a variety of historical evidence—from the early Iron Age to the Greek era—is consilient with the linguistic model that we have advanced. The most illuminating consiliences are in the realm of cultural history, the glimpses of political institutions, foreign affairs, high culture, and ideology that are conveyed by casual details. From Canaanite duals to Greek instruments, the traces of cultural history correspond to the linguistic phases of Biblical Hebrew. They confirm that the typologically distinctive phases of CBH, TBH, and LBH are chronolects, not contemporary dialects or registers.

There are, as we have shown, complexities within each of these chronolects; for example, there are earlier and later elements in CBH, and there are linguistic differences among the LBH books. A book that is predominantly CBH can also have insets of TBH or LBH text, as distinct literary layers exist side by side. A further complexity is the gradual nature of the transition from one chronolect to another. Each phase consists of a congeries of changes that occur at different speeds and locations, progressing in waves rather than immediate steps. Nonetheless, we can specify the historical range for each of these major phases of the language. The poetic dialect of archaic Biblical Hebrew is found in premonarchical and early monarchical poetry. CBH is at home in the monarchical period, with its floruit in the period of the Neo-Assyrian empire.[113] TBH is at home in the Neo-Babylonian and early Persian periods. LBH is at home in the mid-Persian period through the Greek age.[114] The Hebrew Bible is a multi-age book whose history can, in many cases, be traced with a strong degree of probability. The historical linguistics of Biblical Hebrew is a vital instrument in this task.

The consilience between the linguistic and historical evidence and the complementarity of warranted inferences from different fields of inquiry show the viability of this model. One wants a model that successfully accommodates as many different classes of data as possible. The examples presented here are far from comprehensive, but we believe that they are salient samples, bridging linguistic, historical, cultural, epigraphic, and archaeological scholarship.

We emphasize that there are many gaps in our knowledge in each of these areas. The extant data are piecemeal and incomplete. Some of the inferences we have drawn are stronger than others. But even relatively weak inferences are valuable when they are consilient with stronger ones. The consilience of multiple independent inferences is the best confirmation of a theory. We have shown how, in Gould's formulation, "many independent sources 'conspire' to indicate a particular historical pattern." The inferences that we have drawn from different classes of data are consilient with each other.

We also emphasize that this historical model is incomplete and will require revision based on future discoveries and inferences. This is the normal condition of scholarship. Whewell's primary example of consilience—Newton's laws of nature—has undergone modification in the wake of subsequent discoveries. These laws are now regarded as valid only within certain parameters of size and motion (i.e., they break down at the quantum level and near the speed of light). Nonetheless, they are still a useful approximation within these parameters. Similarly, the historical model we have presented will undergo further refinements.

Consilience is not the same as absolute certainty, which is a misleading standard for scholarship. As we have insisted previously, the criterion of certainty—the reflex of a naïve positivism—is not available in historical inquiry. The past is discernible only through the traces that we gather and the inferences that we derive. We work with expectations of warranted knowledge, which is marked by coherence, precision, and scope. Consilience in our scholarly models is the best we can achieve, and it is enough.

The standard of consilience includes the ability of a model to accommodate future discoveries. In our case, such discoveries include inscriptions and other archaeological evidence. For true theories, Whewell argues: "The system becomes more coherent as it is further extended. The elements which we require for explaining a new class of facts are already contained in our system. Different members of the theory run together, and we have thus a constant convergence to unity. In false theories, the contrary is the case."[115] A true theory can explain new data, which were unknown when the theory was formulated. This expansion of the theory makes it more coherent. In our case, we can show that the model of the linguistic history of Biblical Hebrew that has been refined since Gesenius's time has a high degree of consilience with newly discovered data. Several of our examples in this chapter illustrate that new data—including the Mesha stele, the

Tel Dan inscription, Assyrian annals and treaties, Babylonian texts, details of Ugaritic and other previously unknown languages, plastic arts, and the archaeology of the Neo-Babylonian and Persian periods—are successfully accommodated by this model.

A relatively recent epigraphic find that confirms and expands the consilience of this model is the Ketef Hinnom silver amulets, found in a burial cave outside Jerusalem in 1979 and fully deciphered only recently.[116] The archaeological and paleographical evidence agree in dating these inscriptions to the late seventh or early sixth century BCE. These tiny amulets contain prayers that are closely related to Priestly and Deuteronomic texts.

The first amulet begins:

> יהו[. . .] גד[. . .] הברית ו[. . .]חסד לאהב[. . .] ושמרי [. . .]ד העלם
> Yahwe[h . . .] grea[t . . .] the covenant and [. . .] steadfast love for those who love [. . .] and keep [. . . f]or ever

This sequence is close to the language of Deut 7:9:

> יְהוָה . . . שֹׁמֵר הַבְּרִית וְהַחֶסֶד לְאֹהֲבָיו וּלְשֹׁמְרֵי מִצְוֹתָיו לְאֶלֶף דּוֹר
> Yahweh . . . who keeps the covenant, and steadfast love for those who love him and who keep his commandments, to the thousandth generation

The Deuteronomy passage is, in turn, related to—and perhaps an allusion to—the Deuteronomic language in the First Commandment (Exod 20:6 = Deut 5:10). Close echoes of the language of Deuteronomy and the Decalogue are here found in a preexilic inscription. This does not mean that the amulet itself is necessarily quoting or alluding to the book of Deuteronomy, but it does show that Deuteronomic formulations were current in the late preexilic period.[117] This amulet echoes the CBH language of Deuteronomy and is consilient with the preexilic context of the core of Deuteronomy. If one holds that Deuteronomy and the Deuteronomic movement were products of the Persian period or later, then this parallel language is a problem.

This condition also holds for the near-verbatim quotation of the Priestly Benediction in both amulets. We infer that this prayer, found in Num 6:24–26, must have been current in late seventh-century or early sixth-century Jerusalem. An historical model that places the composition of D and P in the Persian or Hellenistic period lacks consilience with these data and inferences. For this reason, some scholars who date the composition of the Hebrew Bible to these later periods also hold that the Ketef Hinnom inscriptions date to the Hellenistic period.[118] But the late dating of these inscriptions does not withstand scrutiny. By extension, the same criticism holds for the late-dating model as a whole.

Some scholars maintain that scribes in the Persian and Hellenistic-Roman periods could have written flawless CBH, in which case any CBH composition could date to these periods.[119] It is worth considering this argument in the light of our examples in this chapter. It is notable that the Chronicler wrote in LBH, even though he was rewriting CBH books (mostly Samuel-Kings). His language has an abundance of Persian loanwords. The use of such words derives from the prestige of the source language and culture. It was not a colloquial or low style but a high register, reflecting the elite emulation of the dominant culture

The authors of these late biblical books were not writing in CBH. They were continuing the tradition as they understood it, using old features and pseudoclassicisms, mixed with the substrate of spoken Hebrew and Aramaic, and drawing on foreign loanwords for prestige or literary effects. LBH is, in this sense, a pastiche or bricolage, consisting of several overlapping layers of linguistic features from past and present. This is why the linguistic profile of each LBH book differs in some features. The authors were active creators of the postclassical tradition, which was never precisely fixed. They were not slavish imitators but updated the classical language with constructions and words that made sense in their time. Features of CBH that had become strange or unintelligible were discontinued or reanalyzed, but the stylistic resonance of the classical language was conserved, now yoked to LBH vocabulary and syntax. Some authors—as in the sectarian literature of Qumran—eschewed foreign loanwords and postclassical vocabulary. But even in this high classicizing language, the syntax of LBH shines through.

Similarly, in the scribal expansions in biblical books during the postexilic period, the scribes did not slavishly reproduce CBH but used syntax and vocabulary that were intelligible in their time. Indeed, an exegetical motivation in some scribal schools was to modernize obscure CBH language (including legal formulations) in accord with contemporary usage.[120]

Recently Shimon Gesundheit has adduced the example of Lucian and other second-century CE Greek writers who "learned to produce literary works in nearly flawless imitations of fifth-century Attic."[121] These late authors were proficient in classical Greek. However, as we have noted, they had available whole libraries of classical works, a situation that did not obtain in Judea of the Second Temple period.[122] In the only Judean library that has been recovered—from the caves of Qumran—there are no CBH works other than the Pentateuch and the Former Prophets. These works do not cover all areas of life and were too limited to allow a later author to develop full proficiency in the ancient language. Moreover, if late scribes were somehow able to write works in CBH, one would expect some of the new compositions at Qumran to be written in CBH. Instead, all of them are written in a language that, in spite of strong archaizing tendencies, is recognizably late.

In sum, the argument that Persian or Hellenistic-Roman period scribes could write in perfect CBH lacks evidential warrant. It is a thought experiment, a logical possibility, like Borges's conjecture of a French author who successfully composed *Don Quixote* in nineteenth-century Paris.[123] But this is a fictional conjecture, belonging to the genre of magic realism. It lacks consilience with the historical and linguistic data.

In this chapter we have adopted the method of cultural history to test the linguistic model we have advanced. The secrets of language and culture are here, in Burkhardt's terms, disclosed "unconsciously and even, paradoxically, through fictitious elaborations."[124] Many of our examples in this chapter are from texts that are partly or mostly fictitious, whether legendary (Nimrod), visionary (Ezekiel), or fictive elaborations of historical events (e.g., Judges, Samuel). The textual *imaginaire* is, in this sense, a rich source for the consilience of the linguistic and literary history of the Hebrew Bible.

In sum, the linguistic and historical inferences are consilient, indicating the correctness of the theory. There are other possible explanations for the linguistic diversity in the Hebrew Bible—such as contemporary dialects or stylistic preferences—but these possibilities lack consilience. We close with a statement of why the most consilient model—based on the convergence of different bodies of data and inference—is preferable to one that is merely possible:

> We infer the explanations precisely because they would, if true, explain the phenomena. Of course, there is always more than one possible explanation for any phenomenon—the tracks [in the snow] might have instead been caused by a trained monkey on snowshoes, or by the elaborate etchings of an environmental artist—so we cannot infer something simply because it is a possible explanation. It must somehow be the best of competing explanations.[125]

We submit that the best explanation—the most consilient one—is the model we have advanced of the ages of biblical literature.

Appendix 1

Historical Linguistics and the Books of the Hebrew Bible: A Bibliographical Survey

No comprehensive and systematic survey of the biblical corpus from an historical linguistics perspective has been attempted in scholarship.[1] The publication that comes closest to offering such a survey is Samuel R. Driver's *Introduction to the Literature of the Old Testament*.[2] Although that book is more than a century old, it can still profitably be used wherever it addresses the question of language. The present appendix provides bibliographical guidance to more recent studies focusing on the language of specific portions or strata of the Hebrew Bible.

The Pentateuch

As we noted in chapter 3, the classical corpus was from the start delimited in a purely negative way: whatever could not be shown to be late was considered early. Only LBH could be positively characterized. This lopsided approach has dominated research to the present day. It substantially undercuts the extensive study of Richard Wright, *Linguistic Evidence for the Pre-Exilic Date of the Yahwistic Source*.[3] Wright argues for an early date of the J source by showing that this source contains very few LBH elements and is therefore representative of CBH. No positive evidence showing that J's language is preexilic is advanced. This prompted Christoph Levin to state that J might as well be early postexilic as against late postexilic LBH.[4] Throughout our book, we have argued that the preexilic date of CBH is nevertheless basically correct and can be established on positive grounds. A fuller, book-by-book or source-by-source demonstration remains a desideratum.

Although the Hebrew of the Pentateuch can globally be classified as CBH, it is not entirely unified. Poetic portions of the corpus reflect an earlier type of language, Archaic Biblical Hebrew (ABH). The corpus of ABH is usually held to include the poetry in Gen 49, Exod 15, Num 23 and 24, and Deut 32 and 33. Good general surveys are the following:

- Angel Sáenz Badillos, *A History of the Hebrew Language,* trans. John Elwolde (Cambridge: Cambridge University Press, 1993), 56–62.
- Yigal Bloch, "The Prefixed Perfective and the Dating of Early Hebrew Poetry: A Re-Evaluation," *VT* 59 (2009): 34–70.
- Yigal Bloch, "The Third-Person Masculine Plural Suffixed Pronoun *-mw* and Its Implications for Dating Biblical Hebrew Poetry," in *Diachrony in Biblical Hebrew*, ed. Cynthia Miller-Naudé and Ziony Zevit (Winona Lake, IN: Eisenbrauns, 2012), 147–70.
- Agustinus Gianto, "Archaic Biblical Hebrew," in *A Handbook of Biblical Hebrew*, vol. 1, *Periods, Corpora, and Reading Traditions*, ed. W. Randall Garr and Steven E. Fassberg (Winona Lake, IN: Eisenbrauns, 2016), 19–29.
- Alice Mandell, "Biblical Hebrew, Archaic," *Encyclopedia of Hebrew Language and Linguistics*, ed. Geoffrey Khan (Leiden: Brill, 2013), 1:325–29.

See also:

- Na'ama Pat-El and Aren Wilson-Wright, "Features of Archaic Biblical Hebrew and the Linguistic Dating Debate," *HS* 54 (2013): 387–410.

Verbal syntax in the ABH corpus has recently been analyzed in detail:

- Tania Notarius, *The Verb in Archaic Biblical Poetry: A Discursive, Typological, and Historical Investigation of the Tense System*, SSLL 68 (Leiden: Brill, 2013).

The prose of the Pentateuch is much more homogeneous, but several scholars have attempted to show that the language of the Priestly Source (P) differs from that of the other narrative prose and reflects a later period. The most systematic attempt is that of Robert Polzin:

- Robert Polzin, *Late Biblical Hebrew: Toward an Historical Typology of Biblical Hebrew Prose*, HSM 12 (Missoula, MT: Scholars Press, 1976).

See also (focusing on single features):

- Baruch Levine, "Research in the Priestly Source: The Linguistic Factor," *ErIsr* 16 (1982): 124–31 (Hebrew).

- Baruch Levine, "Late Language in the Priestly Source: Some Literary and Historical Observations," *Proceedings of the Eighth World Congress of Jewish Studies: Panel Sessions, Bible Studies and Hebrew Language* (Jerusalem: Magnes, 1983), 69–82.
- Ronald Hendel, "'Begetting' and 'Being Born' in the Pentateuch: Notes on Historical Linguistics and Source Criticism," *VT* 50 (2000): 38–46.

But other scholars have resisted the suggestion of a late date. Polzin's approach has been criticized extensively by Rendsburg:

- Gary Rendsburg, "Late Biblical Hebrew and the Date of 'P,'" *JANESCU* 12 (1980): 65–80.

Avi Hurvitz has shown convincingly that the language of P is systematically earlier than the TBH of Ezekiel:

- Avi Hurvitz, *A Linguistic Study of the Relationship between the Priestly Source and the Book of Ezekiel: A New Approach to an Old Problem*, CahRB 20 (Paris: Gabalda, 1982).

Lina Petersson is preparing an analysis of P's verbal syntax in diachronic perspective. She will argue that P's language is mostly CBH, as can be gathered from a brief article:

- Lina Petersson, "Priestly Source of the Pentateuch," in *Encyclopedia of Hebrew Language and Linguistics*, ed. Geoffrey Khan, 4 vols. (Leiden: Brill, 2013), 3:230–32.

Frank Polak has recently argued that the mixture of styles, derived from oral and scribal-bureaucratic settings, indicates that P is composed of a variety of texts written between the eighth and sixth centuries BCE:

- Frank H. Polak, "Syntactic-Stylistic Aspects of the So-Called 'Priestly' Work in the Torah," in *Le-ma'an Ziony: Essays in Honor of Ziony Zevit*, ed. Frederick E. Greenspahn and Gary A. Rendsburg (Eugene, OR: Wipf and Stock, 2017), 345–82.

Finally, a small number of passages have been subjected to linguistic analysis with a view to arguing for their late date. A good example is Gen 24:

- Alexander Rofé, "An Enquiry into the Betrothal of Rebekah," in *Die Hebräische Bibel und ihre zweifache Nachgeschichte: Festschrift für Rolf Rendtorff zum 65. Geburtstag*, ed. Erhard Blum, Christian Macholz, and

Ekkehard W. Stegemann (Neukirchen: Neukirchener Verlag, 1990), 27–39.

This passage has been discussed in chapters 3 and 6. Another example is Num 36, a priestly chapter that nevertheless exhibits late linguistic features not found elsewhere in P:

- Jan Joosten, "Diachronic Linguistics and the Date of the Pentateuch," in Gertz et al., *Formation of the Pentateuch*, 327–44.

Former Prophets

The situation for the Pentateuch also holds true for the second part of the CBH corpus: most of the Former Prophets reflects the type of prose narrative that must, according to what is argued in this book, have been in use during the monarchic period. The similarity between the Hebrew of the patriarchal narratives in Genesis and the succession history in 2 Sam 11 through 1 Kgs 2 is impressive. Some of the poetry reflects ABH, notably Judg 5 but perhaps also 1 Sam 2:1–10 and 2 Sam 22 and 23:1–7. Literature on ABH has been listed earlier. The Deuteronomistic redactional frame of the books of Joshua through 2 Kings may be expected to reflect TBH, and so also the last chapter of 2 Kgs. However, no systematic diachronic analysis of the language of these texts has been undertaken.

As in the Pentateuch, putatively late language has been detected in some individual passages. Linguistic features pointing to the Persian period have been found in the narrative of the altar built by the Transjordanian tribes:

- Ronnie Goldstein, "Joshua 22:9–34—A Priestly Narrative from the Second Temple Period," *Shnaton* 13 (2002): 43–81 (Hebrew), in particular 51–52.

Possible indications of TBH have been identified in the story of the concubine of the Levite and its aftermath:

- Cynthia Edenburg, *Dismembering the Whole: Composition and Purpose of Judges 19–21*, AIL 24 (Atlanta: SBL Press, 2016), 115–59.

Latter Prophets

Prose chapters in the Latter Prophets usually conform to the type of language that the prima facie historical context would lead one to expect.

Amos, Hosea, and Isaiah are figures of the eighth century BCE; the prose of Am 7, Hos 1, and Isa 7 and 36–39 are duly written in CBH. Jeremiah witnessed the fall of Jerusalem and the end of the monarchy, and unsurprisingly, the prose narratives in his book reflect TBH.

The correspondence of the prima facie date and the language is not an immutable rule, however. Jonah is a prophet of the eighth century (2 Kgs 14:25), but the book is written in TBH:

- Athalia Brenner, "The Language of Jonah as an Index of Its Date," *Beth Mikra* 24 (1979): 396–405 (Hebrew).
- George M. Landes, "Linguistic Criteria and the Date of the Book of Jonah," *ErIsr* 16 (1982): *147–*170.
- Baraq Dan, "The Language of Jonah in the Literature: A Reevaluation and Assessment," *Beth Miqra* 41 (1996): 344–68 (Hebrew).

Similarly, Daniel is a figure of the Babylonian period, but the Hebrew chapters of the book reflect a much later period—of course Daniel is not included in the Latter Prophets according to the Hebrew canon.

The larger part of prophetic books is written in poetry, thus making diachronic analysis of the language harder. As is the case for prose, little research has been done to establish the early date of prophets of the monarchic age. Christopher Hays's article arguing for a monarchic dating of Isa 24–27 is an interesting exception:

- Christopher B. Hays, "The Date and Message of Isaiah 24–27 in Light of Hebrew Diachrony," in *Intertextuality and Formation of Isaiah 24–27*, ed. J. Todd Hibbard and H. C. Paul Kim, AIL 17 (Atlanta: Society of Biblical Literature, 2013), 7–24.

Instead, linguistic acumen has been focused for the most part on TBH and LBH elements in the prophets. As we have seen in more detail in chapter 6, Jeremiah, Ezekiel, Isa 40–66, Haggai, and Zech 1–8 are considered TBH:

- Aaron Hornkohl, *Ancient Hebrew Periodization and the Language of the Book of Jeremiah: The Case for a Sixth-Century Date of Composition*, SSLL 74 (Leiden: Brill, 2013).
- Mark Rooker, *Biblical Hebrew in Transition: The Language of the Book of Ezekiel* (Sheffield: Academic Press, 1990).
- Shalom Paul, "Signs of Late Hebrew in Isaiah 40–66," in *Diachrony in Biblical Hebrew*, ed. Cynthia Miller-Naudé and Ziony Zevit (Winona Lake, IN: Eisenbrauns, 2012), 293–300.

- Gary A. Rendsburg, "Late Biblical Hebrew in the Book of Haggai," in *Language and Nature: Papers Presented to John Huehnergard on the Occasion of His 60th Birthday*, ed. Rebecca Hasselbach and Na'ama Pat-El (Chicago: Oriental Institute, 2012), 329–44.
- Seoung-Yun Shin, "A Diachronic Study of the Language of Haggai, Zechariah, and Malachi," *JBL* 135 (2016): 265–81.

Finally, Malachi seems to represent LBH:

- Andrew E. Hill, "Dating the Book of Malachi: A Linguistic Reexamination," in *The Word of the Lord Shall Go Forth: Essays in Honor of David Noel Freedman*, ed. Carol L. Meyers and Michael O'Connor (Philadelphia: ASOR, 1983), 77–89.

The Writings

All of the books belonging to the LBH corpus are part of the third division of the Hebrew Bible, the Writings (*Ketuvim*). Driver's lists of late features occurring in all these writings are still very helpful: Ezra-Nehemiah and Chronicles (*Introduction*, 535–39), Esther (*Introduction*, 484), Ecclesiastes (*Introduction*, 474–75) and Daniel (*Introduction*, 506–8). See also:

- Choon-Leong Seow, "Linguistic Evidence and the Dating of Qohelet," *JBL* 115 (1996): 643–66.

Although Song of Songs is not part of the core group, Chip Dobbs-Allsopp has recently shown that it should be considered LBH:

- F. W. Dobbs-Allsopp, "Late Linguistic Features in the Song of Songs," in *Perspectives on the Song of Songs / Perspektiven der Hoheliedauslegung*, ed. Anselm C. Hagedorn, BZAW 346 (Berlin: De Gruyter, 2005), 27–77.

It does not follow, however, that the Writings as a whole are late. The book of Psalms may contain some very old poems, although demonstrating their early date on linguistic grounds is difficult. Avi Hurvitz has shown that a relatively small number of Psalms exhibit sufficient late features to be regarded as belonging to the LBH corpus (Pss 103, 117, 119, 124, 125, 133, 144), whereas for a number of others the linguistic evidence is not entirely conclusive but nonetheless suggests a late date (Pss 19B, 28, 33, 40, 45, 63, 75, 104, 106, 107, 109, 111, 112, 113, 116, 126, 128, 135, 137, 143, 146, 147, 148):

- Avi Hurvitz, *The Transition Period in Biblical Hebrew* (Jerusalem: Bialik, 1972; Hebrew).

All other Psalms would seem to be older, although, once again, it is hard to demonstrate that this is so.

No similarly comprehensive research exists for Proverbs, although a recent publication by Nili Samet is promising:

- Nili Samet, "The Lexical Enigma of מָנוֹן and the Problem of Dating the Hezekian Collection," *ZAW* 128 (2016): 419–32.

As the title of this article shows, Proverbs will almost certainly prove to be composed of units whose language testifies to a spread of different dates.

The book of Job has been discussed in chapter 6. The narrative framework would seem to reflect TBH, but the poetry remains to be analyzed in diachronic perspective. Lamentations has been cogently argued to be written in TBH; see again chapter 6:

- Jan Joosten, "Linguistic Clues as to the Date of the Book of Job: A Mediating Position," in *Interested Readers: Essays on the Hebrew Bible in Honor of David J. A. Clines*, ed. James K. Aitken, Jeremy M. S. Clines, and Christl M. Maier (Atlanta: Society of Biblical Literature, 2013), 347–57.
- F. W. Dobbs-Allsopp, "Linguistic Evidence for the Date of Lamentations," *JANESCU* 26 (1998): 1–36.

Finally, the date of the book of Ruth is difficult to determine. However, its language leads us to place it in the TBH corpus. If one disregards the explanatory gloss in Ruth 4:7, whose language is late,[5] there are only a few features that do not tally with CBH: 1:4, נָשָׂא אִשָּׁה ("to take wife," cf. CBH לָקַח אִשָּׁה); 1:13, Aramaizing לָהֵן ("therefore") and שׂבר ("hope"); and a few doubtful pieces of morphology. Against these stand several CBH features that are rare or absent in LBH: paragogic *nun* (2:8, 9, 21; 3:4); passive *qal* (4:7); פֶּן (4:6), אָנֹכִי (3:9; 4:4), and some others:

- Ziony Zevit, "Dating Ruth: Legal, Linguistic, and Historical Observations," *ZAW* 117 (2005): 574–600.

- Robert D. Holmstedt, *Ruth: A Handbook on the Hebrew Text* (Waco, TX: Baylor University Press, 2010), 17–39.

Appendix 2
A Critique of the Revisionist Model

In two major works, Ian Young and Robert Rezetko have advanced a novel explanation for linguistic variation in the Hebrew Bible.[1] In contrast to the standard model, which incorporates synchronic variation (e.g., dialects, style, register) and diachronic change (e.g., phonological shifts, morphosyntactic reanalysis, language contact), they argue that most or all linguistic variation in the Bible is the result of "co-existing styles of literary Hebrew."[2] They develop, in their words, "a new perspective on the language of Biblical Hebrew (BH): not only is the linguistic dating of biblical writings infeasible, but the distribution of linguistic data in the Masoretic Text (MT) of the Hebrew Bible suggests that EBH and LBH are better explained in general by a model of co-existing styles of literary Hebrew throughout the biblical period."[3] In their second book they develop this thesis and add an additional feature: not only is linguistic dating infeasible, so also is historical linguistics of Biblical Hebrew. They state: "it is largely impossible to undertake 'normal' or conventional historical linguistic research on ancient Hebrew simply because the nature of the sources of data does not permit it."[4]

These are two strong claims, which seem to support each other. If historical linguistics of Biblical Hebrew cannot be properly done, then neither can its findings be used to date biblical texts, either relatively or absolutely. So far, so good. But upon closer examination, there are aspects of these two claims that do not cohere, and the methodology on which both claims rest seems to unravel. Let us pull at some of these threads.

Aside from inaccuracies in individual analysis,[5] Young and Rezetko's "non-chronological" model is flawed by three interrelated problems of method:[6]

1. In their first book they rely on what they call an "MT-only approach," which skews their data and results. They later disavow this approach but continue to use it in their statistical analyses.
2. Their construal of the nature and implications of ancient textual variation—on which they base their disavowal of historical linguistics—is incorrect according to the normal procedures of textual criticism.
3. The inferences they draw from their statistics are incorrect according to the normal procedures of historical linguistics.

Let us unpack these problems. We will occasionally refer to the distribution of מַמְלָכָה and מַלְכוּת (alternative morphological patterns of "kingdom"), which is usually seen as an unproblematic example of diachronic change in Biblical Hebrew (see chapter 4).[7] Other cases involve the same issues, so this particular case is illustrative.

Our brief critique of these problems supports the detailed critique from the perspective of historical linguistics by Elan Dresher, a distinguished linguist, who concludes: "The methodology they use to argue against particular diachronic interpretations of variation is overly rigid and would, if applied to other languages, fail to identify even well-attested diachronic variation in texts. Further, their central arguments against diachronic accounts rest on flawed reasoning and unrealistic assumptions about dialects and language change."[8]

MT-Only Approach

Their first book announces a surprising claim: "All biblical books have LBH features."[9] This is the basis for their non-chronological model. If all books—including relatively early ones—have LBH features, then it seems self-evident that LBH features are not necessarily late. They naturally conclude that, according to the linguistic evidence, the biblical books could have been written in any period. This is their main argument.

One problem with this argument is that it ignores the importance of the distribution of features, which inevitably changes over time. It is the distribution of features, not their isolated occurrences, that provides the primary evidence for linguistic change. We discuss this issue later. Here we emphasize that the claim that "all biblical books have LBH features" depends on a flawed methodology, which they call the "MT-only approach."[10]

If one looks only at MT, then one does find LBH features in all biblical books. As they state, there is "no doubt that Persian elements do occur in the current text of EBH books,"[11] such as the Persian loanword דָּת ("law") in the MT of Deut 33:2.[12] Many LBH words occur in the MT of putatively early books. For instance, the LBH form מַלְכוּת occurs once in Numbers, once in Samuel, once in Kings, and three times in Jeremiah.[13] And so on. They conclude, "Therefore, if EBH texts are early, and most LBH features are attested in EBH texts, then LBH features already existed in an early period, and were available to early authors, and thus their use is a matter of style, not chronology."[14]

But these results are tainted, because most of these cases are well-known textual problems in MT. As we have noted, the odd expression אֵשׁ דָּת ("fire of the law") makes no sense in context.[15] Richard Steiner has plausibly analyzed דָּת as a contraction of the feminine singular verb, "flew," from דאה.[16] The meaning "fire flew," accompanying the march of Yahweh and his heavenly host from the southern mountains, makes far better sense in context. On מַלְכוּת in CBH texts, the only instance that is textually unproblematic is Num 24:7, an archaic poem, where the form is probably an instance of style switching, using an Aramaic form to color the foreign speech of an Aramean seer (Balaam).[17] As for the other cases, 4QSam^b of 1 Sam 20:31 reads ממלכה, which is arguably the older reading; the formula in 1 Kgs 2:12 is repeated in 1 Kgs 2:46 with מַמְלָכָה instead of מַלְכוּת, raising suspicion that the former verse originally had ממלכה; and the three cases of מַלְכוּת in Jeremiah are all in late editorial strata of the book, which unsurprisingly use the LBH form.[18]

In sum, these LBH features do not support Young and Rezetko's argument that they "were available to early authors." Most of these are secondary textual readings. Some are scribal modernizations, and one is probably a misconstrual of an obscure form. Features that are textually late do not support Young and Rezetko's contention that these forms were available to early authors.

Why do the authors adopt an MT-only approach? Their rationale is as follows: "We do not give text-critical data . . . [because] an MT-only approach is advocated by most proponents of the chronological model of EBH and LBH. This means, for the purpose of linguistic analysis, that LBH features in EBH books should be taken as original to those texts."[19] This is incorrect in several respects. Most proponents of the chronological model, including Wilhelm Gesenius, Samuel R. Driver, and most current Hebraists, rely on text-critical analysis. The MT approach is, however, advocated by Avi Hurvitz and his students, and this group is the main target of Young and Rezetko's critique. We note that Hurvitz and colleagues adopt this approach with the explicit intent to make their procedure less subjective, and they compensate by focusing on the accumulation of features rather than individual items.[20] In contrast, Young and Rezetko focus on individual items, as shown in our examples.

Robert Holmstedt has pointed to the methodological error of the MT-only approach for linguistic analysis. Drawing on the work of Mark Hale, he observes that "linguistic research on ancient Hebrew texts requires the researcher to be both philologist and linguist."[21] This entails a principled distinction between a "historical artifact" (i.e., a particular object inscribed with linguistic signs) and a "philological text," which has been subjected to philological analysis prior to linguistic generalization. In our case, the historical artifacts are manuscripts such as the Leningrad Codex or 4QSam^{b}, which can be dated to the eleventh century CE and the third century BCE, respectively. As Hale writes: "We have a set of artifacts, attested in some chronological sequence. It is assumed that the source of the linguistic forms on these artifacts is a set of 'texts': philological constructs which abstract away from irrelevant features such as weathering, worm-holes, and scribal errors. These 'texts' may have come into being in a different chronological sequence than the artifacts themselves did."[22] Historical linguistics entails "a rigorous linguistic analysis of the text which was philologically established from a given historical artifact."[23] One cannot simply choose a particular historical artifact (e.g., the Leningrad Codex, or BHS), as do Young and Rezetko, and expect a linguistic analysis to yield sound results. One needs to analyze a philologically responsible text. This requires that one do textual criticism, which Young and Rezetko eschew. The results of this unsound method is precisely their claim that "all biblical books have LBH features." When done properly, linguistic analysis shows that only some biblical books have LBH features, and that they cluster in books and sections that are relatively late.

In their second book, Rezetko and Young admit that the MT-only approach is flawed. They write: "Any historical linguistic research on BH that simplistically assumes the integrity or 'originality' of the MT as a primary source . . . is unsound in theory and ill-conceived in method."[24] Yet, while they include references to non-MT readings, they do not change their procedures or their claim that LBH features are found in every biblical book. They merely restate their conclusion (as quoted earlier): "The distribution of linguistic data *in the Masoretic Text (MT)* of the Hebrew Bible suggests that EBH and LBH are better explained in general by a model of co-existing styles of literary Hebrew throughout the biblical period" (emphasis added). This conclusion is based on the MT-only approach, which they know to be (in their words) "unsound in theory and ill-conceived in method." It is perplexing that they do not revise their claims in light of their rejection of their own method. This lack of self-criticism regarding their method is peculiar. In sum, the "non-chronological" model is based on an uncritical use of MT—in place of a "philological text"—as the basis for their linguistic generalizations.

Textual Variation

In the second book, they claim that historical linguistics of Biblical Hebrew is infeasible "because the nature of the sources of data does not permit it."[25] By this they mean that the proliferation of textual variation in the biblical texts makes it impossible to do cogent historical linguistic analysis. The problem of textual variation, which they mostly avoid with the MT-only approach in the first book, becomes a leitmotif of the second book. They claim that the preparation of what we call a "philological text" for linguistic analysis is impossible because of the extent of textual variation. They write: "The current texts of the biblical books are late, thoroughly revised and reworked versions of earlier texts whose distinctive linguistic features are lost to us."[26] As textual critics of the Hebrew Bible, we find this to be a surprising claim.

The degree of fluidity in the transmission of the biblical texts is not as great as they suggest. Part of the problem is that their non-chronological approach does not allow them to distinguish between earlier and later readings. All variants, in the eyes of their method, are stylistic choices. There is no room for scribal modernizations or secondary readings. For instance, when they compare, in their second book, the different readings for "kingdom" in MT and 4QSam[b] of 1 Sam 20:31 (מַלְכוּת and ממלכה, respectively), they make no text-critical judgments. These are stylistic variants, part of the endless proliferation of fluid texts. Their method has no room for textual criticism of variant readings.

By this non-chronological move, Young and Rezetko deny the possibility or viability of textual criticism of the Hebrew Bible. We would note that the textual variations in biblical manuscripts are not of a different kind or extent than in other fields of philological scholarship. If the textual criticism of Old English texts can proceed (as Young and Rezetko grant), then there is no warranted rationale for denying the possibility of biblical textual criticism. The textual criticism of the Hebrew Bible should not operate by different rules and standards than other fields. Correspondingly, textual criticism can be used to establish a responsible "philological text," which allows for cogent linguistic analysis. Such things are both possible and warranted, as we have demonstrated. Young and Rezetko rely on the works of important textual critics such as Emanuel Tov and Eugene Ulrich to advance their view of maximal textual fluidity. But Tov and Ulrich would certainly join us in maintaining that textual criticism—and by extension, historical linguistics—is a necessary and viable task for critical scholarship and achieves substantial results, according to the normal standards of the discipline.

The authors' rejection of the viability of textual criticism of the Hebrew Bible is also a consequence of their naïve positivist criteria of "certainty" and "objectivity." They write:

> "There is no certainty to any of the results of textual criticism."[27]
>
> "We have no objective basis for determining which of the scribes who copied the various writings were 'copiers,' 'translators,' or 'mixers.'"[28]
>
> "The details of the biblical writings were so fluid in their textual transmission that we have no way of knowing with any degree of certainty what the original of any biblical composition looked like."[29]
>
> "All we can talk about with certainty are the variant linguistic forms of the current texts."[30]

Certainty is their standard for a successful analysis. As we have noted in chapter 1, this position shows a weak grasp of the accepted practices and epistemology of textual criticism, historical linguistics, and other fields of historical inquiry.[31] Historical scholarship does not yield certainty. It is a misunderstanding of these fields to imagine that they could do so. This problem generates an "all-or-nothing" evaluative scale. In the absence of certainty, all we have is ignorance. Therefore, any logically possible model could be true. This is the core epistemology of Young and Rezetko's method.

This condition explains the recurring rhetoric of "certainty" versus "possibility" in their arguments. Because there is no certainty or proof for the chronological model, other models are logical possible. This dialectic provides much of the logical structure for their arguments, as the following statements illustrate. In each, the lack of certainty or proof entails the possibility of the authors' model:

> "Therefore, it is possible that EBH texts *could* have an early provenance, but it is impossible to prove on the basis of language that they *must* be dated early."[32]
>
> "Scholars have not demonstrated on the basis of linguistic analysis alone that LBH must have been written late."[33]
>
> "There is no logical reason why a concentration of them [i.e., LBH features] could not appear in early texts."[34]

Young and Rezetko require objectivity and certainty for the views they contest but only logical possibility for their own. They are correct to assert that their views are logically possible. But there are many logical possibilities. Possibility is the wrong standard for scholarship. We deal in degrees of probability, not in proof or mere possibility.

If Young and Rezetko's standards were correct, then textual criticism, historical linguistics, and other fields of historical inquiry would be infeasible. This is precisely their claim. But this is not the world we live in, and it is certainly not the normal and accepted standard for historical scholarship. Uncertainty is our condition. We must prefer the most probable explanation, the one that best fits the imperfect data of our philological texts. The operational criteria for our models are coherence, simplicity, and scope, along with patient attention to detail. To demand more is beyond the domain of critical scholarship.

Statistics in Historical Linguistics

The inferences that Young and Rezetko draw from their statistics contradict the normal procedures of historical linguistics, as Dresher has shown. This problem is exacerbated by their MT-only approach, which skews their statistics. Consider their graph of the statistical distribution of מַמְלָכָה and מַלְכוּת in the biblical books (see figure 4).[35]

Young and Rezetko grant that the graph seems to indicate a clustering of uses of מַלְכוּת in the later biblical books. But they counter this perception by noting that "'late' writers were not 'obliged' to use מלכות, that is, ממלכה was a possible alternative."[36] They conclude: "Words for 'kingdom' could be 'freely' selected in any period."[37] In their view, lexical variation has solely to do with style. This is also their general conclusion: "'Style' is a common and

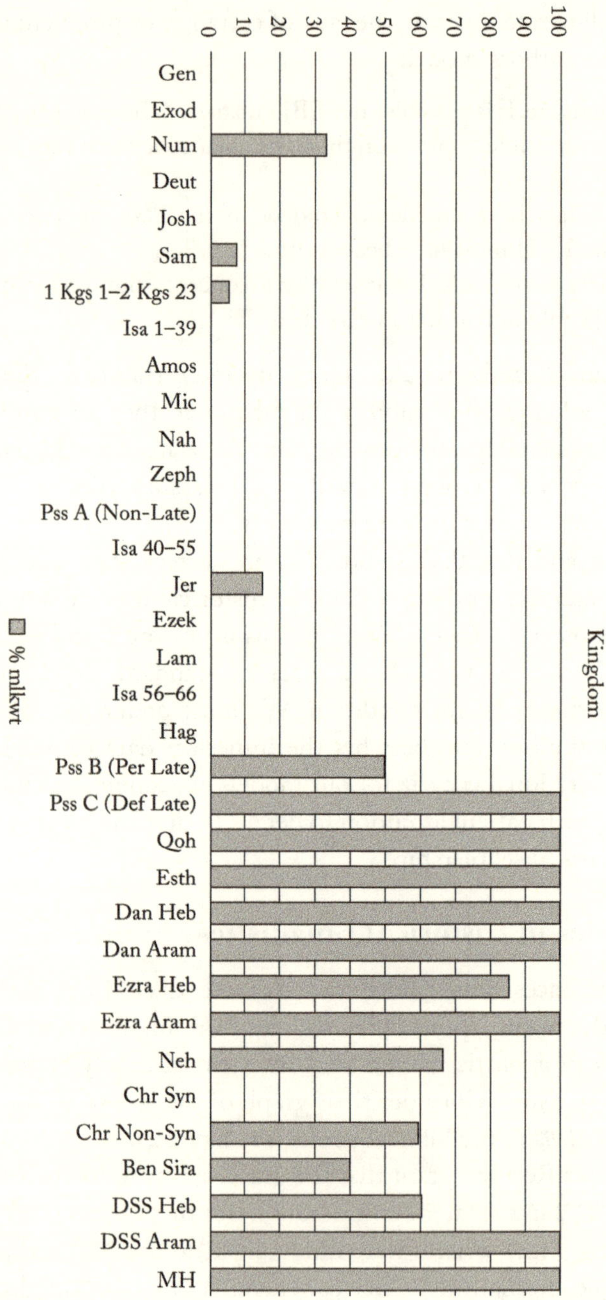
Kingdom
0
10
20
30
40
50
60
70
80
90
100
Gen
Exod
Num
Deut
Josh
Sam
1 Kgs 1–2 Kgs 23
Isa 1–39
Amos
Mic
Nah
Zeph
Pss A (Non-Late)
Isa 40–55
Jer
Ezek
Lam
Isa 56–66
Hag
Pss B (Per Late)
Pss C (Def Late)
Qoh
Esth
Dan Heb
Dan Aram
Ezra Heb
Ezra Aram
Neh
Chr Syn
Chr Non-Syn
Ben Sira
DSS Heb
DSS Aram
MH
% mlkwt

Figure 4.

applicable, though not comprehensive, explanation for language variation in BH."[38]

But the idea that both terms were generally available in all periods depends on the sparse attestations that they list in the MT of Numbers, Samuel, Kings, and Jeremiah, which we have criticized earlier.[39] With the exception of the stylistic choice of an Aramaic form (for an Aramean seer) in Num 24:7, all these other forms are text-critically dubious. It is more warranted to say that only one Hebrew form was available prior to the Persian period, at which time bilingual Hebrew-Aramaic speakers domesticated the Aramaic form מַלְכוּת into the Hebrew lexicon. The authors' MT-only approach obscures the clarity of this chronological scenario.

Moreover, as Dresher observes, their own statistics belie their conclusion. What is important for historical linguistics is not the availability but the distribution of features over time. He writes: "This notion of 'availability' is contrary to findings in historical linguistics that much synchronic variation has a diachronic trajectory."[40] That trajectory is shown, as in figure 4, by how the distribution of features changes over time: "The proportion in which the forms occur has a characteristic signature in a given time and place and can have considerable predictive value in dating a text."[41] A distribution of מַמְלָכָה ~ מַלְכוּת in which מַלְכוּת occurs hardly at all is characteristic of CBH, whereas a spread of 40 to 100 percent is characteristic of LBH. The different distributions among the LBH writings may well be a matter of style. Presumably the older form would seem more archaic, and therefore have a more formal or "biblical" register, in the late period. This may account for the mixture of forms in the nonsynoptic parts of Chronicles and in Ben Sira and Qumran Hebrew.

In sum, the inferences that Young and Rezetko draw from their statistical distributions are unwarranted. Dresher rightly criticizes their linguistic method: "It is a well-attested fact in many languages that competing forms may coexist over a period of time, and thus a late form may occur sporadically in early texts, and an early form may survive in late texts. It is an empirical question, in any given case, whether the distribution of forms has a diachronic dimension or not; there is no basis for ruling out chronology as part of the story."[42]

A final consideration is a recurring tendency in the revisionist model to cherry-pick the statistical data in a manner that misrepresents their true import. This propensity is illustrated by the following claim about the distribution of directive *he*: "While in inscriptions the directive *hê* is always (100%) used with the motion verbs בוא and עלה to express movement to a destination, MT Samuel uses it in similar contexts only once, i.e., 3% of the time."[43] This statistical contrast—100 percent versus 3 percent—supports the claim that "all the biblical manuscripts in our possession reflect major linguistic developments away from Hebrew of the monarchic era."[44] A fuller consideration of the data, however, belies these statistics and the conclusions drawn from them.

The problem is that the data are presented partially, in both senses of the word: incompletely and tendentiously. The assertion that "directive *he* is always (100%) used" fails to note that there are only four such occurrences in the inscriptions. This is a statistically insignificant sample. If one expands the data set to include all verbs of motion, the results are different. One finds that that the inscriptions use four constructions for directionality:

- directive *he* (three times with בוא, Arad 17 obv. 1–2, Arad 24 rev. 9, Lachish 3 obv. 15–16; once with עלה, Lachish 4 obv. 7)
- אל + definite noun (once with הלך, Siloam 4–5)
- ל + geographical noun (once with שלח, Arad 17 obv. 5).
- Ø (unmarked, once with שלח, Arad 24 rev. 2)

These are the same four constructions used in CBH. This is consonant with the inference that the inscriptions and the CBH corpus stem from the monarchic period.[45] There is a difference of proportions, but the sample size in the inscriptions is too small to draw any valid inferences from the statistical spread. In sum, the conclusions based on the partial data are disconfirmed by conclusions based on the fuller evidential picture. One is left with a sense that the use of statistical arguments in the revisionist model is driven more by rhetorical aims than philological precision.

Accordingly, we conclude that Young and Rezetko's methodology is infelicitous. For all these reasons, the revisionist model of Biblical Hebrew cannot be regarded as a viable proposal. It is put forward with considerable erudition, but its logical structure is riven with flaws. When one pulls at the threads, the garment swiftly unravels.

Notes

Chapter 1. All Things Change

1. Quoted or paraphrased in Plato, *Cratylus* 402a; see Geoffrey S. Kirk, John E. Raven, and Malcolm Schofield, *The Presocratic Philosophers*, 2nd ed. (Cambridge: Cambridge University Press, 1983), 195–97.
2. Ibn Ḥayyuj, Ibn Gikatilla, and Ibn Janaḥ in the tenth and eleventh centuries CE, and Friedrich Böttcher and Jakob Barth in the nineteenth century; see recently Steven E. Fassberg, "The Movement from *Qal* to *Pi'el* in Hebrew and the Disappearance of the *Qal* Internal Passive," *HS* 42 (2001): 243–55; and Eric D. Reymond, "The Passive *Qal* in the Hebrew of the Second Temple Period, Especially as Found in the Wisdom of Ben Sira," in *Sibyls, Scriptures, and Scrolls: John Collins at Seventy*, ed. Joel Baden, Hindy Najman, and Eibert Tigchelaar (Leiden: Brill, 2017), 1110–27.
3. H. L. Ginsberg, "Studies on the Biblical Hebrew Verb: Masoretically Misconstrued Internal Passives," *AJSL* 46 (1929): 53–56; Ginsberg, "Behind the *Masoret*," *Tarbiz* 5 (1934–35): 208–15 (Hebrew).
4. Often the passive *qal* prefix conjugation was reanalyzed as a *hophal*, which would not require the additional *waw*.
5. See Shmuel Aḥituv, *Echoes from the Past: Hebrew and Cognate Inscriptions from the Biblical Period*, trans. Anson F. Rainey (Jerusalem: Carta, 2008), 467–72 (line 9).
6. Ibid., 392, 417 (line 31).
7. Joel S. Baden, *The Composition of the Pentateuch: Renewing the Documentary Hypothesis* (New Haven, CT: Yale University Press, 2012); David M. Carr, *The Formation of the Hebrew Bible: A New Reconstruction* (New York: Oxford University Press, 2011); Reinhard G. Kratz, *The Composition of the Narrative Books of the Old Testament*, trans. John Bowden (London: Clark, 2005); Konrad Schmid, *The Old Testament: A Literary History*, trans. Linda M. Maloney (Minneapolis: Fortress, 2012). Baden (*Composition*, 30–31) holds that the issue of relative or absolute dates is irrelevant for source criticism. However, because source criticism is an

inquiry into literary history, it is unwarranted to exclude historical linguistic criteria and arguments.

8. Alexander Rofé, *Introduction to the Literature of the Hebrew Bible*, JBS 9 (Jerusalem: Simor, 2009).
9. Carr, *Formation*, 131–32.
10. Carr, *Formation*, 446, following Ian M. Young, *Diversity in Pre-Exilic Hebrew*, FAT 5 (Tübingen: Mohr Siebeck, 1993), 157–65. See appendix 2.
11. Benjamin D. Sommer, "Dating Pentateuchal Texts and the Perils of Pseudo-Historicism," in *The Pentateuch: International Perspectives on Current Research*, ed. Thomas B. Dozeman, Konrad Schmid, and Baruch J. Schwartz, FAT 78 (Tübingen: Mohr Siebeck, 2011), 85–108.
12. Carr, *Formation*, 442.
13. See F. W. Dobbs-Allsopp, "Late Linguistic Features in the Song of Songs," in *Perspectives on the Song of Songs / Perspektiven der Hoheliedauslegung*, ed. Anselm C. Hagedorn, BZAW 346 (Berlin: De Gruyter, 2005), 27–77; Michael V. Fox, *The Song of Songs and the Ancient Egyptian Love Songs* (Madison: University of Wisconsin Press, 1985), 186–90. These features are identified as dialectal (Israelian Hebrew) and the book dated to circa 900 BCE by Scott B. Noegel and Gary A. Rendsburg, in *Solomon's Vineyard: Literary and Linguistic Studies in the Song of Songs*, AIL 1 (Atlanta: Society of Biblical Literature, 2009), 3–55, 174–84; see our discussion of dialects in chapter 3.
14. On the following, see Peter Lipton, *Inference to the Best Explanation*, 2nd ed. (London: Routledge, 2004); and Ronald Hendel, *Steps to a New Edition of the Hebrew Bible*, TCS 10 (Atlanta: SBL Press, 2016), 127–47.
15. Marc Bloch, *The Historian's Craft*, trans. Peter Putnam (New York: Vintage, 1953), 129.
16. Ibid., 133.
17. However, the book's distinctive and consistent poetic style complements its linguistic profile, making it difficult to postulate a lengthy compositional history; see Fox, *Song of Songs*, 190: "*This* song is, to judge from its linguistic characteristics, post-exilic and probably Hellenistic, and we have no way of even speculating reasonably about the earlier forms from which it supposedly evolved."
18. E.g., Niels Peter Lemche, *The Israelites in History and Tradition* (Louisville, KY: Westminster John Knox, 1998), 130: "[Hellenistic Jews] constructed their own origin myth as a program for taking over a country which they reclaimed for themselves in spite of the inhabitants who already lived there." In this construal, the Hebrew Bible is Zionist propaganda avant la lettre. We note that the ideological reward of ignoring the historical linguistic evidence is shared equally by "minimalist" and "maximalist" scholars.
19. E.g., Philip Davies, "Biblical Hebrew and the History of Ancient Judah: Typology, Chronology and Common Sense," in *Biblical Hebrew: Studies in Chronol-*

ogy and Typology, ed. Ian Young, JSOTSup 369 (London: T&T Clark, 2003), 154: "The argument is completely circular."

20. Nelson Goodman, *Fact, Fiction, and Forecast* (Cambridge, MA: Harvard University Press, 1983), 64.
21. A. E. Housman, "The Application of Thought to Textual Criticism," in *Selected Prose*, ed. John Carter (Cambridge: Cambridge University Press, 1961), 145.
22. Bloch, *Historian's Craft*, 122.
23. Hugo Grotius, *Annotata ad Vetus Testamentum*, 3 vols. (Paris: Cramoisy, 1644), 1:521.
24. Wilhelm Gesenius, *Geschichte der hebräischen Sprache und Schrift* (Leipzig: Vogel, 1815), 19–20.
25. See Jan Joosten, "Wilhelm Gesenius and the History of Hebrew in the Biblical Period," *in Biblische Exegese und hebräische Lexikographie: Das "Hebräisch-deutsch Handwörterbuch" von Wilhelm Gesenius als Spiegel und Quelle alttestamentlicher und hebräischer Forschung, 200 Jahre nach seiner ersten Auflage*, ed. Stefan Schorch and Ernst-Joachim Waschke, BZAW 427 (Berlin: de Gruyter, 2013), 94–106; Joosten, "Diachronic Linguistics and the Date of the Pentateuch," in *The Formation of the Pentateuch: Bridging the Academic Cultures of Europe, Israel, and North America*, ed. Jan C. Gertz et al., FAT 111 (Tübingen: Mohr Siebeck, 2016), 327–29.

Chapter 2. Kinds and Causes of Linguistic Change

1. Lyle Campbell, *Historical Linguistics: An Introduction*, 2nd ed. (Cambridge, MA: MIT Press, 2004), 325.
2. Mark Hale, *Historical Linguistics: Theory and Method* (Oxford: Blackwell, 2007), 171.
3. Campbell, *Historical Linguistics*, 284.
4. On compensatory "therapy" as an explanation for linguistic innovation, see ibid., 319–29.
5. This means we do not generally address the changes that produced Hebrew as a distinct Northwest Semitic language (viz. proto-Hebrew) but later phases in its history.
6. Edgar Schneider, "Shakespeare in the Coves and Hollows? Toward a History of Southern English," in *English in the Southern United States*, ed. Stephen J Nagle and Sara L. Sanders (Cambridge: Cambridge University Press, 2003), 17–35.
7. See W. Randall Garr, *Dialect Geography of Syria-Palestine, 1000–586 B.C.E.* (Philadelphia: University of Pennsylvania Press, 1985), 61–63; Aren M. Wilson-Wright, "A Reevaluation of the Semitic Direct Object Markers," *HS* 57 (2016): 7–15.
8. See Scott C. Layton, *Archaic Features of Canaanite Personal Names in the Hebrew Bible*, HSS 47 (Atlanta: Scholars Press, 1990), 50–87.

9. This archaic form has a stylistic effect, marking God's speech as a high (archaic and poetic) register. Compare the narrator's speech in the following verse, which uses the normal (stylistically unmarked) form: חַיַּת הָאָרֶץ. On poetry and register, see chapter 3.
10. See Hans R. Bosker, "Sibilant Consonants," in *Encyclopedia of Hebrew Language and Linguistics*, ed. Geoffrey Khan (Leiden: Brill, 2013), 3:557–61.
11. See Benjamin Sass, *The Alphabet at the Turn of the Millennium: The West Semitic Alphabet ca. 1150–850 BCE, The Antiquity of the Arabian, Greek and Phrygian Alphabets* (Tel Aviv: Institute of Archaeology, 2005), 134–52.
12. Richard C. Steiner, *The Case for Fricative-Laterals in Proto-Semitic* (New Haven, CT: American Oriental Society, 1977). This sound (written "ll" in Welsh) occurs in Modern South Arabian dialects (ibid., 12–21).
13. This is indicated by the Egyptian and Akkadian transcriptions of Northwest Semitic *shin* and by the merger of the phoneme /ṯ/ with /š/ in all Iron Age Canaanite languages; see Yigal Bloch, "On Some Alleged Developments of the Proto-Semitic Phoneme /ṯ/ in Iron Age Canaanite Dialects," *JSS* 53 (2008): 1–28. Cf. Arabic pronunciation of /š/ as [s], which arguably preserves the Proto-Semitic articulation; see recently Leonid Kogan, "Proto-Semitic Phonetics and Phonology," in *The Semitic Languages: An International Handbook*, ed. Stefan Weninger (Berlin: de Gruyter, 2011), 69–70.
14. On the following, see Ronald Hendel, "Sibilants and *šibbōlet* (Judges 12:6)," *BASOR* 301 (1996): 69–75; and the alternative arguments in Robert Woodhouse, "The Biblical Shibboleth Story in the Light of Late Egyptian Perceptions of Semitic Sibilants: Reconciling Divergent Views," *JAOS* 123 (2003): 271–89.
15. John A. Emerton, "Some Comments on the Shibboleth Incident (Judges XII 6)," in *Mélanges bibliques et orientaux en l'honneur de M. Mathias Delcor*, ed. A. Caquot et al. (Neukirchen-Vluyn: Neukirchener, 1985), 153.
16. A similar phonetic relationship arguably obtains in the correspondence between *shin* in the royal name בעלישע (probably *Baʿlīša*) on an early sixth-century Ammonite seal, and the *samek* in this king's Hebrew name in Jer 40:14, written בַּעֲלִיס in MT and Βελισα in the LXX (note the final *–a*). In both cases, the Cisjordanian *samek* approximates the pronunciation of the Transjordanian *shin*; see Hendel, "Sibilants," 71–72.
17. Steiner, *Fricative-Laterals*, 123–29, 137–43.
18. Ibid., 141.
19. GKC §6i; note also Franz Rosenthal's comment (*A Grammar of Biblical Aramaic* [Wiesbaden: Harrassowitz, 1974], 16) about this change in Aramaic: "In BA times, this process was in its incipient stages. שׂ, in Aramaic words, is as a rule used correctly. Exceptions are סַתְרֵהּ 'he tore down' E 5:12 and, possibly, יִסְבַּר 'he intends' D 7:25."
20. Compare the older (historically correct) form in Eccl 2:12–13 (twice) סִכְלוּת ("folly").

21. Elisha Qimron, *The Hebrew of the Dead Sea Scrolls*, HSS 29 (Atlanta: Scholars Press, 1986), 28–30.
22. Ze'ev Ben-Ḥayyim, *A Grammar of Samaritan Hebrew* (Jerusalem: Magnes Press, 2000), 35–37.
23. See John Huehnergard, *An Introduction to Ugaritic* (Peabody, MA: Hendrickson, 2012), 63–64.
24. Garr, *Dialect Geography*, 119–21; Fassberg, "Movement from *Qal* to *Pi'el*," 252–53.
25. Ronald Hendel, "'Begetting' and 'Being Born' in the Pentateuch: Notes on Historical Linguistics and Source Criticism," *VT* 50 (2000): 38–46; Hendel, *Remembering Abraham: Culture, Memory, and History in the Hebrew Bible* (New York: Oxford University Press, 2005), 115–16.
26. The *nuphal* is a late analogical formation, with the initial *u* of the passive stems (*pual* and *hophal*). This verse rewrites 2 Sam 21:22, which uses the passive *qal*.
27. In place of the source siglum "J" (here and throughout), some scholars might prefer a looser reference, e.g., "the aggregate of non-P texts formerly known as J."
28. The form ויולד in Gen 4:18 (J) is reanalyzed as *niphal*, but in context it is better construed as a *qal* passive; cf. Gen 4:26.
29. Gen 35:26; 36:5; 46:22, 27.
30. Arad 111.4 (ילקח); F. W. Dobbs-Allsopp, J. J. M. Roberts, C. L. Seow, and R. E. Whitaker, *Hebrew Inscriptions: Texts from the Biblical Period of the Monarchy with Concordance* (New Haven, CT: Yale University Press, 2005), 106–7. The ל indicates that the form is *yillāqaḥ* (*niphal*) not **yulqaḥ* > *yuqqaḥ* (passive *qal*).
31. See the catalog of probable passive *qal*s in *IBHS*, 374–75nn29–36.
32. Huehnergard, *Ugaritic*, 31.
33. Garr, *Dialect Geography*, 79–80. Samalian also preserves the long form, one of its unusual features, see ibid., 230–31.
34. Several phonological changes are behind the proto-Hebrew development **ʾanākū* → *ʾānōkī*: (1) **ā* → *ō* by the Canaanite shift; (2) *ū* → *ī* by dissimilation from the previous *ō* (both are back rounded vowels); and (3) *a* → *ā* for unknown reasons, perhaps dissimilating from the (ultra)short *a* of the short pronoun. See Na'ama Pat-El and Aren Wilson Wright, "The Features of Canaanite: A Reevaluation," *ZDMG* 166 (2016): 42–43.
35. See Robert Polzin, *Late Biblical Hebrew: Toward an Historical Typology of Biblical Hebrew Prose*, HSM 12 (Missoula, MT: Scholars Press, 1976), 126–27; K. Gunther, "אֲנִי," in *TLOT*, 162–66.
36. But see E. John Revell, "The Two Forms of First Person Singular Pronoun in Biblical Hebrew: Redundancy or Expressive Contrast?" *JSS* 40 (1995): 199–217, where Revell argues for a status distinction, with אֲנִי connoting a higher status or degree of "responsibility" than אָנֹכִי. Cf. *IBHS*, 292: "There is no functional difference between them."
37. BDB, 59.

38. See Samuel R. Driver, ("On Some Alleged Affinities of the Elohist," *Journal of Philology* 11 [1882]: 222–27), who considers factors of prosody and formulaic usage (e.g., אֲנִי יהוה); see also appendix 1.
39. From Driver, "Alleged Affinities," and Richard M. Wright, *Linguistic Evidence for the Pre-Exilic Date of the Yahwistic Source*, LHBOTS 419 (London: T&T Clark, 2005), 80.
40. This chapter has some H features; see Israel Knohl, *The Sanctuary of Silence: The Priestly Torah and the Holiness School* (Minneapolis: Fortress, 1995), 103. On the linguistic profiles of P and H, see above, pages 128–29.
41. This is a late stratum of Ezekiel, lacking in the Greek manuscript p967, which is probably the best exemplar of the Old Greek, as noted by Ian Young and Robert Rezetko, with the assistance of Martin Ehrensvärd, *Linguistic Dating of Biblical Texts*, 2 vols. (London: Equinox, 2008), 1:352. This passage derives from Jer 11:4, 30:22.
42. From 2 Sam 7:2.
43. Qimron, *Scrolls*, 57.
44. Hendel, "Begetting," 38–46. This feature is consistent in the J source and relatively rare elsewhere; see BDB, 408 (§2).
45. Note that the J usage is typologically earlier than the P usage.
46. This may be a late supplement; see the commentaries.
47. The LBH exception is Dan 11:6, which uses a *qal* participle, הַיֹּלְדָהּ ("he who fathered her").
48. Qumran Hebrew consistently uses the masculine form, with three exceptions; see Qimron, *Scrolls*, 45.
49. On the following, see Avi Hurvitz, "The Origins and Development of the Expression מְגִלַּת־סֵפֶר: A Study in the History of Writing-Related Terminology in Biblical Times," in *Texts, Temples, and Traditions: A Tribute to Menahem Haran*, ed. Michael V. Fox et al. (Winona Lake, IN: Eisenbrauns, 1996), 37*–46* (Hebrew).
50. Dobbs-Allsopp et al., *Inscriptions*, 309.
51. There are seven LBH instances of the older meaning of סֵפֶר as "letter": 2 Chr 32:17; Esth 1:22; 3:13; 8:5, 10; 9:20, 25, 30; and see chapter 5.
52. Hurvitz, "Origins," 407.
53. See Jan Joosten, *The Verbal System of Biblical Hebrew: A New Synthesis Elaborated on the Basis of Classical Prose*, JBS 10 (Jerusalem: Simor, 2012), 377–410.
54. Huehnergard, *Ugaritic*, 53.
55. John A. Cook, "Detecting Development in Biblical Hebrew Using Diachronic Typology," in *Diachrony in Biblical Hebrew*, ed. Cynthia Miller-Naudé and Ziony Zevit (Winona Lake, IN: Eisenbrauns, 2012), 86–93.
56. Verbs of perception are a subcategory of stative verbs; see *IBHS*, 364. In some uses ידע is a dynamic (fientive) verb, as in וְהָאָדָם יָדַע אֶת־חַוָּה אִשְׁתּוֹ ("the man knew Eve, his wife," Gen 4:1). Such uses are excluded from this analysis.

57. Cook, "Development," 91. The graph in figure 1 is reprinted with the permission of Eisenbrauns.
58. See also the S curve of the replacement of the relative particle אשר by ש in Robert D. Holmstedt, *The Relative Clause in Biblical Hebrew* (Winona Lake, IN: Eisenbrauns, 2016), 241–44.
59. Campbell, *Historical Linguistics*, 64.
60. Mats Eskhult, "The Importance of Loanwords for Dating Biblical Hebrew Texts," in *Biblical Hebrew: Studies in Chronology and Typology*, ed. Ian Young (London: T&T Clark, 2003), 23.
61. Sarah G. Thomason, *Language Contact: An Introduction* (Edinburgh: Edinburgh University Press, 2001), 139.
62. Ibid., 139.
63. See the previous section "Complication of Categories of Writing," for Aramaic loanwords in the field of scribal administration.
64. Na'ama Pat-El, "Syntactic Aramaisms as a Tool for the Internal Chronology of Biblical Hebrew," in Miller-Naudé and Zevit, *Diachrony*, 251.
65. Frank H. Polak, "Sociolinguistics and the Judean Speech Community in the Achaemenid Empire," in *Judah and Judeans in the Persian Period*, ed. Oded Lipschits and Manfred Oeming (Winona Lake, IN: Eisenbrauns, 2006), 592.
66. David S. Vanderhooft, "'el-mĕdînâ ûmĕdînâ kiktābāh: Scribes and Scripts in Yehud and in Achaemenid Transeuphratene," in *Judah and Judeans in the Achaemenid Period: Negotiating Identity in an International Context*, ed. Oded Lipschits, Gary Knoppers, and Manfred Oeming (Winona Lake, IN: Eisenbrauns, 2011), 537: "Judean chancery scribes adopted the Aramaic lapidary script for use in the provincial system of administration already in the sixth century."
67. See William M. Schniedewind, *A Social History of Hebrew: Its Origins through the Rabbinic Period* (New Haven, CT: Yale University Press, 2013), 165–172. Because the Pentateuchal manuscripts are found at Qumran in paleo-Hebrew script, it is possible that the Pentateuch continued to be copied in some circles in the paleo-Hebrew script; see Gordon J. Hamilton, "Paleo-Hebrew Texts and Scripts of the Persian Period," in *"An Eye for Form": Epigraphic Essays in Honor of Frank Moore Cross*, ed. Jo Ann Hackett and Walter E. Aufrecht (Winona Lake, IN: Eisenbrauns, 2014), 283–86.
68. Schniedewind, *Social History*, 141.
69. E.g., דְּיוֹ ("ink"), גֹּמֶא ("papyrus"), and the measures אֵיפָה ("ephah"), הִין ("hin"), and קַב ("kab"); see Aaron D. Rubin, "Egyptian Loanwords in Hebrew," in *Encyclopedia of Hebrew Language and Linguistics*, ed. Geoffrey Khan (Leiden: Brill, 2013), 1:794.
70. Eskhult, "Loanwords," 23.
71. The singular form may be a segholate, סֶרֶן*, or a *qāṭāl* form, סָרָן*; see Hendel, *Remembering Abraham*, 110–11.

72. See Federico Giusfredi, "The Problem of the Luwian Title *Tarwanis*," *Altorientalische Forschungen* 36 (2009): 140–45. He documents that "*tarwanis* is attested from the 10th to the 8th century BCE, from the Tabal to Syria" (140); see also Franco Pintori, "Seren, Tarwanis, Turannos," in *Studi orientalistici in ricordo di Franco Pintore*, ed. Mario Liverani et al. (Pavia: GJES Edizione, 1983), 285–322.
73. It is possible that the word טר̊ן (= Hebrew סרן?) occurs in a seventh-century neo-Philistine ostracon; however, the third letter is difficult to decipher; see Frank M. Cross, "Inscriptions in Phoenician and Other Scripts," in *Ashkelon I: Introduction and Overview (1985–2006)*, ed. Lawrence E. Stager, J. David Schloen, and Daniel M. Master (Winona Lake, IN: Eisenbrauns, 2008), 339.
74. Aḥituv, *Echoes from the Past*, 335–38.
75. Assaf Yasur-Landau, *The Philistines and Aegean Migration at the End of the Late Bronze Age* (Cambridge: Cambridge University Press, 2010), 313; cf. Alexander Zukerman, "Titles of 7th Century BCE Philistine Rulers and Their Historical-Cultural Background," *BO* 68 (2011): 465–71.
76. See chapter 8 for further traces of Philistine contact.
77. Paul V. Mankowski, *Akkadian Loanwords in Hebrew*, HSS 47 (Winona Lake, IN: Eisenbrauns, 2000). The following details are culled from this work.
78. The cognate Hebrew word סֹכֵן, "steward," (Isa 22:15; 1 Kgs 1:2, 4) is Northwest Semitic, attested in Ugaritic, Phoenician, and Old Aramaic; Mankowski, *Akkadian*, 112–14.
79. On this Babylonian official and his colleague, the רַב־מָג, see chapter 8.
80. On the following, see Aren Wilson-Wright, "From Persepolis to Jerusalem: A Reevaluation of Old-Persian-Hebrew Contact in the Achaemenid Period," *VT* 65 (2015): 152–67. The only (nonadministrative) Persian loanword that may predate this period is the architectural term פַּרְוָר ("forecourt," 2 Kgs 23:11) < Old Persian **paribāra-*; cf. the variant phonology of פַּרְבָּר ("forecourt," 1 Chr 26:18); see ibid., 158–59.
81. Ibid., 157.
82. On the strange phrase אֵשׁ דָּת ("fire of the law")" in Deut 33:2, see chapter 4.
83. The only other possible case in Hebrew is אַפִּרְיוֹן, "canopied bed" < Greek φορεῖον, "sedan chair" (Cant 3:9); see F. W. Dobbs-Allsopp, "Late Linguistic Features in Song of Songs," in *Perspectives on the Song of Songs / Perspektiven der Hoheliedauslegung*, ed. Anselm C. Hagedorn, BZAW 346 (Berlin: De Gruyter, 2005), 67–71. For the Greek loanwords in the Aramaic of Dan 3:5–7 (musical instruments), see later in this chapter.
84. Michael Alram, "The Coinage of the Persian Empire," in *The Oxford Handbook of Greek and Roman Coinage*, ed. William E. Metcalf (New York: Oxford University Press, 2012), 64. Prosthetic *'aleph* is found in several Persian loanwords. The final *nun* indicates the Greek form; see H. G. M. Williamson, "Eschatology in Chronicles," in *Studies in Persian Period History and Historiography* (Tübingen: Mohr Siebeck, 2004), 170.

85. There seems to be mixing of "daric" and "drachma" in the Hebrew form.
86. Haim Gitler and Oren Tal, *The Coinage of Philistia of the Fifth and Fourth Centuries BC: A Study of the Earliest Coins of Palestine* (Milan: Ennere, 2006), 13–22.
87. Alram, "Coinage," 69: "The daric . . . was desirable for anyone who wanted to accumulate wealth. . . . [T]he tetradrachms of Athens . . . had developed in the course of the fifth century to a kind of world trade currency."
88. See further in chapter 8.
89. On the following, see Pat-El, "Syntactic Aramaisms," 253–54; Polzin, *Late Biblical Hebrew*, 64–66; and Peter Bekins, "The Difficulty with Diagnosing *Lamed Objecti*," *JNSL* 42, no. 2 (2016): 1–22.
90. This verse is lacking in the Old Greek; it belongs to the second edition of Jeremiah.
91. Pat-El, "Syntactic Aramaisms," 254.
92. On the following, see Pat-El, "Syntactic Aramaisms," 256–59; Max Wagner, *Die lexikalischen und grammatikalischen Aramaismen im alttestamentlichen Hebräisch* (Berlin: Töpelmann: 1966), 110–11; and BDB, 83 (§8).
93. Pat-El, "Syntactic Aramaisms," 256–59; Na'ama Pat-El, "Traces of Aramaic Dialectal Variation in Late Biblical Hebrew," *VT* 58 (2008): 650–55.

Chapter 3. How to Handle Linguistic Variation

1. See, e.g., the statement by David Carr quoted in chapter 1, as well as publications by Ian Young and Robert Rezetko, where much is made of this theoretical point; see appendix 2.
2. See Gary A. Rendsburg, "The Strata of Biblical Hebrew," *JNSL* 17 (1991): 81–99.
3. For dialectal variety in Hebrew inscriptions, see chapter 5.
4. The textual attestations of the form are Jud 5:7 (twice); Ezek 16:18; 22, 31 (2x), 43 (2x), 47, 51, 59; Jer 2:20; 2:33; 3:4, 5; 4:19; 46:11; Mic 4:13; Ruth 3:3, 4; see Hans Bauer and Pontus Leander, *Historische Grammatik der hebräischen Sprache des Alten Testaments* (Halle: Niemeyer, 1922; reprint, Hildesheim: Olms, 1962), 310, §42k9. In Jer 2:20 and Mic 4:13, the form is pointed with *hireq*, probably intended as first-person singular. Similar forms ending in *–i* are attested for independent and suffixed personal 3fs pronouns: -אתי, כי.
5. See, notably, many publications by Rendsburg, e.g., Gary A. Rendsburg, "A Comprehensive Guide to Israelian Hebrew: Grammar and Lexicon," *Orient* 38 (2003): 5–35. For criticisms, see William Schniedewind and Daniel Sivan, "The Dialect of the Elisha-Elijah Narratives: A Case Study in *Northern* Hebrew," *JQR* 87 (1997): 303–37; Na'ama Pat-El, "Israelian Hebrew: A Re-Evaluation," *VT* 67 (2017): 227–63.
6. Rendsburg, "Comprehensive Guide," 29.
7. See Gary A. Rendsburg, "Style Switching," in *Encyclopedia of Hebrew Language and Linguistics*, ed. Geoffrey Khan, 4 vols. (Leiden: Brill, 2013), 3:633–36.

8. See Jonas Greenfield, "Aramaic Studies and the Bible," in *Congress Volume Vienna 1980*, ed. John Emerton, VTSup 32 (Leiden: Brill, 1980), 110–30, in particular 129–30.
9. See Gary A. Rendsburg, "Some False Leads in the Identification of Late Biblical Hebrew Texts: The Cases of Genesis 24 and 1 Samuel 2:27–36," *JBL* 121 (2002): 23–46.
10. "Code switching" would be more exact: what the author does is not to exchange one style for another but to pepper his text with elements from another "code"—a different dialect or another language.
11. Rendsburg, "Comprehensive Guide," 31.
12. See Alfred Bloch, *Vers und Sprache im Altarabischen* (Basel: Verlag für Recht und Gesellschaft, 1946), 31–35; Raphael Sappan, *The Typical Features of the Syntax of Biblical Poetry in Its Classical Period* (Jerusalem: Kiryat Sefer, 1981) (Hebrew).
13. See also Mattitiahu Tsevat, *A Study of the Language of the Biblical Psalms* (Philadelphia: Society of Biblical Literature, 1955).
14. On differences in register between early and late biblical texts, see Frank Polak, "Sociolinguistics: A Key to the Typology and the Social Background of Biblical Hebrew," *HS* 47 (2006): 115–62.
15. John MacDonald, "Some Distinctive Characteristics of Israelite Spoken Hebrew," *BO* 32 (1975): 162–75; Gary A. Rendsburg, *Diglossia in Ancient Hebrew*, AOS 72 (New Haven, CT: American Oriental Society, 1990).
16. See BDB, 585, §5.
17. See BDB, 585, §4.
18. Note also Jer 34:9,14.
19. Originally the word may have had a distinct meaning. Note that in 1 Sam 14:21 "Hebrews" are distinguished from Israelites. In Exodus and Deuteronomy the word always refers to Israelites.
20. See Samuel R. Driver, *Deuteronomy*, ICC (Edinburgh: T&T Clark, 1895), 181–83; Benjamin Kilchör, *Mosetora und Jahwetora: Das Verhältnis von Deuteronomium 12–26 zu Exodus, Levitikus und Numeri*, BZABR 21 (Wiesbaden: Harrasowitz, 2015), 137–53.
21. The word בָּרִחַ occurs also in Job 26:13, probably alluding to the same myth.
22. See, most recently, Edward J. Bridge, "Female Slave vs Female Slave: אָמָה and שִׁפְחָה in the Hebrew Bible," *JHS* 12 (2012): https://doi.org/5508/jhs.2012.v12.a2.
23. Alexander Rofé, "An Enquiry into the Betrothal of Rebekah," in *Die Hebräische Bibel und ihre zweifache Nachgeschichte: Festschrift für Rolf Rendtorff zum 65. Geburtstag*, ed. Erhard Blum, Christian Macholz, and Ekkehard W. Stegemann (Neukirchen: Neukirchener Verlag, 1990), 30; Rendsburg, "False Leads," 28–29.
24. For Aramaic, see, e.g., Noam Mizrahi, "A Matter of Choice: A Sociolinguistic Perspective on the Contact between Hebrew and Aramaic, with Special Attention to Jeremiah 10," in *Discourse, Dialogue and Debate in the Bible Essays in Honour of Frank H. Polak*, ed. Athalya Brenner-Idan (Sheffield: Phoenix Press,

2014), 107–24; for Persian, see Wilson-Wright, "From Persepolis to Jerusalem," 152–67.

25. Initially Jonah was included in the LBH corpus, but it may be better to regard the book as transitional (see chapter 6). Recently, Dobbs-Allsopp has argued extensively that Song of Songs is written in LBH; see Dobbs-Allsopp, "Late Linguistic Features."
26. See Choon-Leong Seow, "Linguistic Evidence and the Dating of Qohelet," *JBL* 115 (1996): 643–66.
27. See Eskhult, "Loanwords," 8–23.
28. This hypothesis was first developed by Philip Davies, *In Search of "Ancient Israel,"* JSOTSup 148 (Sheffield: JSOT Press, 1992), 102–5. It was then argued extensively by Ian Young and Robert Rezetko in several publications; see appendix 2.
29. Syntactic features have always been included in the discussion. Important contributions are Rebecca Corwin, *The Verb and the Sentence in Chronicles, Ezra and Nehemiah* (Borna: Noske, 1909); Arno Kropat, *Die Syntax des Autor der Chronik*, BZAW 16 (Giessen: Töpelman, 1909); A. R. Guenther, "A Diachronic Study of Biblical Hebrew Prose Syntax: An Analysis of the Verbal Clause in Jeremiah 37–45 and Esther 1–10" (PhD diss., University of Toronto, 1977); Mats Eskhult, *Studies in Verbal Aspect and Narrative Technique in Biblical Hebrew Prose* (Uppsala: Almqvist & Wiksell, 1990); Eskhult, "Verbal Syntax in Late Biblical Hebrew," in *Diggers at the Well: Proceedings of a Third International Symposium on the Hebrew of the Dead Sea Scrolls and Ben Sira*, ed. Takamitsu Muraoka and John. F. Elwolde (Leiden: Brill, 2000), 84–93. See further Jan Joosten, "The Distinction between Classical and Late Biblical Hebrew as Reflected in Syntax," *IIS* 46 (2005): 327–39; Joosten, *Verbal System*, 377–409.
30. See Kropat, *Syntax*, 23; Eskhult, "Verbal Syntax," 90. The usage is found in Jer 32:14; 35:2; Zech 6:10, but there are no certain examples of it in the LBH corpus or in postbiblical Hebrew.
31. See Gary A. Rendsburg, "Late Biblical Hebrew in the Book of Haggai," in *Language and Nature: Papers Presented to John Huehnergard on the Occasion of His 60th Birthday*, ed. Rebecca Hasselbach and Na'ama Pat-El (Chicago: Oriental Institute, 2012), 329–44, in particular 331–32.
32. Incidentally, the complexity and subtlety of syntax also explains why it has taken longer for scholars to discover the syntactic markers of language evolution.
33. The particle is found 271 times in the CBH corpus but only 18 times in LBH. The LBH corpus is only one-third the size of the CBH corpus, but the absolute difference is significant nevertheless. See Steven E. Fassberg, *Studies in Biblical Syntax* (Jerusalem: Magnes, 1994), 51–52 (Hebrew).
34. See Guenther, *Diachronic Study*, 212; E. John Revell, "Conditional Sentences in Biblical Hebrew Prose," in *Semitic Studies in Honor of Wolf Leslau*, ed. Alan S. Kaye (Wiesbaden: Harrassowitz, 1991), 1278–90.
35. *Ketiv*: ביהודיים.

36. For the different forms of these words, see Wilson-Wright, "From Persepolis to Jerusalem," 160–61.
37. On the alleged occurrence of דת in Deut 33:2, see chapter 4.
38. See Aaron Hornkohl, *Ancient Hebrew Periodization and the Language of the Book of Jeremiah: The Case for a Sixth-Century Date of Composition*, SSLL 74 (Leiden: Brill, 2013), 152–56.
39. It is found once in Ezekiel (13:9), which is transitional; see chapter 6.
40. See Avi Hurvitz, *A Concise Lexicon of Late Biblical Hebrew: Linguistic Innovations in the Writings of the Second Temple Period*, VTSup 160 (Brill: Leiden, 2014), 76–77.
41. Hurvitz, *Lexicon,* 201–3.
42. The syntagm is attested in the MT of 1 Kgs 18:29 but not in the Old Greek.
43. Hurvitz, *Lexicon,* 36.
44. Joosten, *Verbal System,* 391–96.
45. Hurvitz, *Lexicon*, passim.
46. See *supra* note 29.
47. Occasionally a feature characteristic of LBH may be typologically earlier; for example, the demonstrative pronoun זֹה attested many times in Ecclesiastes (and in Mishnaic Hebrew) is an older form than CBH זֹאת.
48. Quoted from the *Jewish Chronicle* in Moshe Weinfeld, "Julius Wellhausen's Understanding of the Law of Ancient Israel and Its Fallacies," *Shnaton* 4 (1980): 62–93 (Hebrew).
49. See Young and Rezetko, *Linguistic Dating,* 1.65.
50. The only exception is 1 Chr 1:19 (quoting Gen 10:25).
51. See Hurvitz, *Lexicon,* 9–11. The four criteria are late biblical distribution, linguistic contrast with classical equivalents, extrabiblical corroboration, and accumulation.
52. See John Huehnergard, "On the Etymology of the Hebrew Relative *šɛ*," in *Biblical Hebrew in Its Northwest Semitic Setting: Typological and Historical Perspectives*, ed. Steven E. Fassberg and Avi Hurvitz (Winona Lake, IN: Eisenbrauns, 2006), 103–25.
53. It is found in Gen 6:3, twice in the Song of Deborah, three times in the Gideon story, and once in Kings (however, the text of 2 Kgs 6:11 may not be in order).
54. Outside the CBH corpus, סֵפֶר occurs in Jer 29:1, 25, 29; Esth 1:22; 3:12; 8:5, 10; 9:20, 25, 30; 2 Chr 32:17.
55. Some old features resurface in Qumran Hebrew, where imitation of Biblical Hebrew became much more systematic; see chapter 7.
56. See *supra* note 30.
57. See Jan Joosten, "The Disappearance of Iterative WEQATAL in the Biblical Hebrew Verbal System," in *Biblical Hebrew in Its Northwest Semitic Setting: Typological and Historical Perspectives*, ed. Steven E. Fassberg and Avi Hurvitz (Winona Lake, IN: Eisenbrauns, 2006), 135–47.

58. Jan Joosten, "Diachronic Aspects of Narrative *Wayhi* in Biblical Hebrew," *JNSL* 35 (2009): 43–61.
59. Joosten, "Distinction," 337–38.
60. See Angel Sáenz Badillos, *A History of the Hebrew Language*, trans. John Elwolde (Cambridge: Cambridge University Press, 1993), 56–62.

Chapter 4. Textual History and Linguistic History

1. Roman Jakobson, *On Language*, ed. Linda R. Waugh and Monique Monville-Burston (Cambridge, MA: Harvard University Press, 1990), 64, 148.
2. The traditional interpretation is not the only possible one. Steiner has argued that דָּת is not a Persian loanword, nor even a noun, but a verb in the feminine; Richard C. Steiner, "דָּת and עֵין: Two Verbs Masquerading as Nouns in Moses' Blessing (Deuteronomy 33:2, 28)," *JBL* 115 (1996): 693–98.
3. See, for instance, Young and Rezetko, *Linguistic Dating*, 1:303–4, 2:93–94.
4. E.g., Esth 4:8; Ezra 8:36. The word also occurs several times in Biblical Aramaic and Qumran Aramaic, and in Mishnaic Hebrew. Its Persian origin is not in doubt. It may have come to Hebrew through Aramaic.
5. Admittedly the *ketiv* is hard to understand.
6. See the discussion in Carmel McCarthy, *Deuteronomy*, BHQ (Stuttgart: Deutsche Bibelgesellschaft, 2007), 155*–156*.
7. See Jan Joosten, "The Tiberian Vocalization and the Edition of the Hebrew Bible Text," in *Making the Biblical Text: Textual Studies in the Hebrew and Greek Bible*, ed. Innocent Himbaza, OBO 275 (Fribourg: Academic Press; Göttingen: Vandenhoeck & Ruprecht, 2015), 19–32.
8. See, e.g., Stefan Schorch, *Die Vokale des Gesetzes*, vol. 1, *Genesis*, BZAW 339 (Berlin: de Gruyter, 2004).
9. The *qal* is not attested, but it is reflected in the Peshitta; see Dominique Barthélemy, *Critique textuelle de l'Ancien Testament*, vol. 2, *Isaïe, Jérémie, Lamentations*, OBO 50, no. 2 (Fribourg: Éditions Universitaires; Göttingen: Vandenhoeck & Ruprecht, 1986), 4.
10. See the discussion in ibid., 3–5.
11. The change in the oral reading tradition may have been made relatively early, as it is attested already in the Septuagint. Williamson, although he does not comment on the oral nature of the change, speculates that it may have been made by "the compiler of the chapter itself"; see H. G. M. Williamson, *Isaiah 1–5*, ICC (London: T&T Clark, 2006), 91.
12. The particle is followed by the perfect in Gen 24:15. On the date of Gen 24, see Rofé, "An Enquiry," 27–39.
13. Samuel R. Driver, *Notes on the Hebrew Text of the Books of Samuel* (Oxford: Clarendon, 1890), 42–43. Note that in this case the proposed variant is not attested in any textual witness. It is a conjecture, although a very strong one.

14. See CD II, 7; 1QH[a] V, 14; VII, 17; IX, 10; 4QTanḥ (4Q176) 22, 3; 4QAgesCreatA (4Q180) I, 2; II, 10; 11QPs[a] (11Q5) XXI, 11.
15. See Joosten, "Tiberian Vocalization."
16. See, further, Jan Joosten, "Textual Developments and Historical Linguistics," in *After Qumran: Old and Modern Editions of the Biblical Texts—The Historical Books*, ed. Hans Ausloos, Bénédicte Lemmelijn, and Julio Trebolle Barrera, BETL 246 (Leuven: Peeters 2012), 21–31.
17. See Driver, *Notes*, 305, and more fully, Rendsburg, "Late Biblical Hebrew in the Book of Haggai," 334–35.
18. Note that the order "PN the king" is the normal one in Imperial Aramaic (דריוש מלכא).
19. Julius Wellhausen, *Der Text der Bücher Samuelis* (Göttingen: Vandenhoeck & Ruprecht, 1871), 190–91, 223.
20. See Ps 143:7 and compare Ps 84:3 with נֶפֶשׁ instead of רוּחַ.
21. Only the *ḥet* is legible, but it suffices to show that 4QSam[a] read רוח and not דוד.
22. See Barthélemy, *Critique textuelle de l'Ancien Testament*, vol. 1, *Josué, Juges, Ruth, Samuel, Rois, Chroniques, Esdras, Néhemie, Esther*, OBO 50, no. 1 (Fribourg: Éditions Universitaires; Göttingen: Vandenhoeck & Ruprecht, 1982), 267.
23. See 1 Sam 13:13; 2 Sam 7:12, 13; 1 Kgs 2:12, 46.
24. See Gen 21:8; Exod 21:28; Num 7:10, 84, 88; 26:55; Deut 12:22; 20:8; 2 Kgs 18:30; Neh 6:13; 14:48.
25. See Hurvitz, *Lexicon*, 169–74.
26. The Samaritan versions for the most part render the verb as if it were a form of כון, and Ben-Ḥayyim parses the oral pronunciation of the form (*takk[e]n*) in the same way. See Ze'ev Ben-Ḥayyim, *The Literary and Oral Tradition of Hebrew and Aramaic amongst the Samaritans*, vol. 4, *The Words of the Pentateuch* (Jerusalem: Academy of the Hebrew Language, 1977), 136 (Hebrew). The oral pronunciation of the form fits the infinitive *piel* of the root תכן, however, and a variant in the Samaritan Targum renders it תמצה ("set in the middle"), reflecting the root תכן.
27. See Moshe Weinfeld, *Deuteronomy and the Deuteronomic School* (Oxford: Clarendon, 1972), 237n5. Weinfeld argues for the meaning "to measure" on the basis of the root כון and the MT.
28. Joosten, *Verbal System*, 265–66.
29. While it is possible that a text written in CBH could pick up late features in textual transmission (see the section "Linguistic Modernization"), the reverse is hard to imagine and unattested in scribal practices of the Second Temple period.
30. See chapter 3.
31. Hurvitz, *Lexicon*, 13.
32. Other Aramaisms are the adjective צְנֻמוֹת ("hard," 41:23) and the verb טען ("load," 45:17); late syntax is found in the use of the participle in 39:22–23 (Joosten, *Verbal System*, 393).

33. Hurvitz, *Lexicon*, 48–51.
34. See BDB, 6.
35. Joosten, "Distinction," 337–38.
36. Eduard Yechezkel Kutscher, *The Language and Linguistic Background of the Isaiah Scroll (1QIsa^{a})* (Leiden: Brill, 1974), 41.
37. Eskhult, "Verbal Syntax," 86–87.
38. Note that מָזוֹן in Gen 45:23 is not represented in the Septuagint; similarly, the Aramaizing adjective צְנֻמוֹת in Gen 41:23 is not attested in the Septuagint.
39. See Kutscher, *Linguistic Background.*
40. Note that in 1QpHab XII, 15, דומם is changed into דומה.
41. See Ze'ev Ben-Ḥayyim, *A Grammar of Samaritan Hebrew* (Jerusalem: Magnes, 2000); Schorch, *Vokale des Gesetzes.*
42. See Reinhard Müller, Juha Pakkala, and Bas ter Haar Romeny, *Evidence of Editing: Growth and Change of Texts in the Hebrew Bible*, RBS 75 (Atlanta: Society of Biblical Literature, 2014).
43. See, e.g., J. Gerald Janzen, *Studies in the Text of Jeremiah*, HSM 6 (Cambridge, MA: Harvard University, 1973); Emanuel Tov, *Textual Criticism of the Hebrew Bible*, 3rd ed. (Minneapolis: Fortress, 2012), 286–94.
44. See Jan Joosten, "L'excédent massorétique du livre de Jérémie et l'hébreu post-classique," in *Conservatism and Innovation in the Hebrew Language of the Hellenistic Period: Proceedings of a Fourth International Symposium on the Hebrew of the Dead Sea Scrolls and Ben Sira,* ed. Jan Joosten and Jean-Sébastien Rey, STDJ 73 (Leiden: Brill, 2008), 93–108.
45. See, however, the remarks on the language of Jeremiah in chapter 6.
46. See Joosten, "Textual Developments," 27–30. Pluses in non-Masoretic sources also at times exhibit postclassical features (e.g., the plus in 4QSam^{a} at 1 Sam 10:27), but the point is particularly relevant with regard to the MT, which is often followed indiscriminately in biblical scholarship.
47. See Juha Pakkala, *God's Word Omitted: Omissions in the Transmission of the Hebrew Bible*, FRLANT 251 (Göttingen: Vandenhoeck & Ruprecht, 2013).
48. See Choon-Leong Seow, *Job 1–21: Interpretation and Commentary* (Grand Rapids, MI: Eerdmans, 2013), 6–8.
49. Eugene Ulrich, "The Developmental Composition of the Book of Isaiah: Light from 1QIsa^{a} on Additions in the MT," *DSD* 8 (2001): 288–305.
50. See H. G. M. Williamson, "Scribe and Scroll: Revisiting the Great Isaiah Scroll from Qumran," in *Making a Difference: Essays on the Bible and Judaism in Honor of Tamara Cohn Eskenazi*, ed. David J. A. Clines, Kent Harold Richards, and Jacob L. Wright (Sheffield Phoenix Press, 2012), 329–42; Drew Longacre, "Developmental Stage, Scribal Lapse, or Physical Defect? 1QIsa^{a}'s Damaged Exemplar for Isaiah Chapters 34–66," *DSD 20* (2013): 17–50.
51. Full literature is contained in Robert Rezetko, "The Qumran Scrolls of the Book of Judges: Literary Formation, Textual Criticism, and Historical Linguistics," *JHS* 13 (2013): https://doi.org/10.5508/jhs.2013.a2.

52. Alexander Rofé, "Studying the Biblical Text in the Light of Historico-Literary Criticism: The Reproach of the Prophet in Judg 6:7–10 and 4QJudg[a]," in *The Dead Sea Scrolls in Context: Integrating the Dead Sea Scrolls in the Study of Ancient Texts, Languages, and Cultures*, ed. Armin Lange et al., VTSup 140 (Leiden: Brill, 2011), 111–23, in particular 121–22.
53. The root זעק is not a diagnostic feature, as it is found many times in CBH. The "pseudo-cohortative" forms וָאֶתְּנָה (v. 9) and וָאֹמְרָה (v. 10) are characteristic of LBH, where they are attested sixty times, but they occur also in CBH (Gen 32:6; 41:11; 43:21; Num 8:19; Josh 24:8; Jud 10:12; 12:3; 1 Sam 2:28; 28:15; 2 Sam 4:10; 7:9; 12:8; 22:24).
54. In LBH the only attestations are Dan 10:11, Neh 1:6, and 1 Chr 17:1 (parallel 2 Sam 7:2); see chapter 2.
55. See chapter 3.

Chapter 5. Inscriptions and Preexilic Hebrew Literature

1. See Sandra Landis Gogel, *A Grammar of Epigraphic Hebrew*, RBS 23 (Atlanta: Scholars Press, 1998); Shmuel Aḥituv, W. Randall Garr, and Steven E. Fassberg, "Epigraphic Hebrew," in *A Handbook of Biblical Hebrew*, ed. Steven E. Fassberg and W. Randall Garr (Winona Lake, IN: Eisenbrauns, 2016), 55–68. See also Ian Young, "Late Biblical Hebrew and Hebrew Inscriptions," in *Biblical Hebrew: Studies in Chronology and Typology* (London: T&T Clark, 2003), 276–311 (Young's article offers rich material but is marred by a tendentious approach).
2. A few Phoenician inscriptions were known; see Reinhard G. Lehmann, "Wilhelm Gesenius and the Rise of Phoenician Philology," in *Biblische Exegese und hebräische Lexikographie: Das "Hebräisch-deutsche Handwörterbuch" von Wilhelm Gesenius als Spiegel und Quelle alttestamentlicher und hebräischer Forschung, 200 Jahre nach seiner ersten Auflage*, ed. Stefan Schorch and Ernst-Joachim Waschke, BZAW 427 (Berlin: De Gruyter, 2013), 209–66.
3. See Gesenius, *Geschichte,* 32.
4. For some Hebrew inscriptions discovered earlier, though not clearly identified as such, see André Lemaire, "A History of Northwest Semitic Epigraphy," in *"An Eye for Form": Epigraphic Essays in Honor of Frank Moore Cross*, ed. Jo Ann Hackett and Walter E. Aufrecht (Winona Lake, IN: Eisenbrauns, 2014), 5–29, in particular 6.
5. For a recent collection, see Aḥituv, *Echoes from the Past.* More complete collections can be found in the following publications: Graham I. Davies, *Ancient Hebrew Inscriptions: Corpus and Concordance*, 2 vols. (Cambridge: Cambridge University Press, 1991–2004); Johannes Renz and Wolfgang Röllig, *Handbuch der althebraïschen Epigraphik*, 3 vols. (Darmstadt: Wissenschaftliche Buchgesellschaft, 1995); Dobbs-Allsopp et al., *Hebrew Inscriptions.*
6. For שנה, see Nahman Avigad, "Two Hebrew 'Fiscal' Bullae," *IEJ* 40 (1990): 262–65; Aḥituv, *Echoes from the Past,* 180.

7. For details, see Jacob Hoftijzer and Karel Jongeling, *Dictionary of the North-West Semitic Inscriptions*, HdO 1, no. 21, 2 vols. (Leiden: Brill, 1995).
8. Although parts of the Hebrew Bible almost certainly originated in the territory of the Northern Kingdom, preexilic material contained in the biblical corpus was, after 721 BCE, transmitted exclusively via Judean channels, as far as we know. Similarity of Biblical Hebrew to Judean inscriptions is therefore hardly due to accident. It may even suggest that northern texts were at some point edited to agree with the Judean dialect (see, however, chapter 3 on the possible traces of early dialects).
9. The date of many inscriptions can be approximately determined on the basis of their archeological context and on the evolution of the form of their Hebrew letters.
10. See George A. Cooke, *A Text-Book of North-Semitic Inscriptions: Moabite, Hebrew, Phoenician, Aramaic, Nabataean, Palmyrene, Jewish* (Oxford: Clarendon, 1903), 16.
11. See, e.g., Avi Hurvitz, "The Historical Quest for 'Ancient Israel' and the Linguistic Evidence of the Hebrew Bible," *VT* 47 (1997): 301–15, in particular 307–10 ("External Controls for the Classical Phase of BH"), where Hurvitz reviews much earlier literature. Rainey, review of *A Grammar of Epigraphic Hebrew*, by Sandra Landis Gogel, *JQR* 91 (2001): 419–27.
12. Thus Ernst Axel Knauf, "War 'Biblisch-Hebräisch' eine Sprache? Empirische Gesichtspunkte zur linguistischen Annäherung an die Sprache der althebräischen Literatur," *ZAH* 3 (1990): 11–23; Andreas Schüle, *Die Syntax der althebräischen Inschriften: Ein Beitrag zur historischen Grammatik des Hebräischen*, AOAT 270 (Münster: Ugarit-Verlag, 2000); Young, "Hebrew Inscriptions."
13. Knauf, "Biblisch-Hebräisch," 11: "Biblisch-Hebräisch ist als Sprache der biblischen Literatur in exilisch-nachexilischer Zeit entstanden und als 'Bildungssprache' tradiert und benutz worden."
14. For the use of the square script in biblical texts, see Joseph Naveh, *Early History of the Alphabet* (Jerusalem: Magnes, 1997), 112–23. For the later history of the paleo-Hebrew script, see Hamilton, "Paleo-Hebrew Texts," 253–90.
15. See, e.g., Shemeryahu Talmon, "The Paleo-Hebrew Alphabet and Biblical Text Criticism," in *Text and Canon in the Hebrew Bible: Collected Studies* (Winona Lake, IN: Eisenbrauns, 2010), 125–70.
16. On the *–he* suffix, see Ian Young, "Observations on the Third Person Masculine Singular Pronominal Suffix *–h* in Hebrew Biblical Texts," *HS* 42 (2001): 225–42. A similar distribution is found with regard to the 3ms suffix on plural nouns: אנשו in Lach 3:18 is the earlier and expected form, but the later form פניו (with *–yw*) is found in Ketef Hinnom 2:9. In the Bible, the later form is the normal one, but the earlier form is found occasionally (e.g., 1 Sam 18:22, עֲבָדָו, "his servants").
17. See, e.g., Kutscher, *Linguistic Background*.

18. As was indicated in the preceding chapter, the modernization in the Qumran scroll did not stop at the orthography but affected more substantial matters as well. Occasional modernization of vocabulary or grammar may have happened earlier in the textual history of the Hebrew Bible as well; see chapter 4.
19. The word is attested in Qumran Hebrew: 4QpapPrQuot (4Q503) 1-3, 9: תסובות כלי אור ("rotations of the luminaries").
20. See Jan Joosten, "The Operation of a Syntactic Rule in Classical Biblical Hebrew and in Hebrew Inscriptions of the Monarchic Period," in *On Stone and Scroll: Essays in Honour of Graham Ivor Davies*, ed. James K. Aitken, Katherine J. Dell, and Brian A Mastin, BZAW 420 (Berlin: de Gruyter, 2011), 493–505.
21. Meindert Dijkstra, "'He Pours the Sweet Wine Off, Only the Dregs Are for the Wicked': An Epigraphic Note on *Mizzæh* in Psalm 75, 9," *ZAW* 107 (1995): 296–300.
22. See also *supra* note 15.
23. See Aḥituv, Garr, and Fassberg, "Epigraphic Hebrew," 60 (postvocalic voicing in a closed syllable).
24. See also the peculiar case discussed by William M. Schniedewind, "Sociological Reflections on the Letter of a 'Literate' Soldier (Lachish 3)," *ZAH* 13 (2000): 157–67.
25. See Young, "Hebrew Inscriptions," 297–98, and the literature cited there.
26. The same phenomenon occurs in lines 1–3.
27. See Andreas Schüle, "Zur Bedeutung der Formel *wajjehi* in Übergang zum mittelhebräischen Tempussystem," in *Studien zur hebräischen Grammatik*, ed. Andreas Wagner, OBO 156 (Fribourg: Presses Universitaires; Göttingen: Vandenhoeck & Ruprecht, 1997), 115–25; Schüle, *Syntax*, 182–86.
28. See Joosten, "Diachronic Aspects," 43–61.
29. As Adolf Deissmann argued at the end of the nineteenth century, New Testament Greek is much closer to the language of documentary papyri than to literary Greek of the first century CE. For the debate, see Stanley E. Porter, ed., *The Language of the New Testament: Classic Essays*, JSNTSup 60 (Sheffield: Academic Press, 1991).
30. For example, הית in Siloam 1.3 may be an archaic form of the 3fs *qatal* (*hāyāt*), but it may also be the "normal" BH form *hāyᵉtā* written defectively.
31. For cases in which the Tiberian Hebrew may have been partly overlaid with later forms due to the later reading tradition, see chapter 4.
32. See Gogel, *Grammar*, passim.
33. See Martin Ehrensvärd, "Once Again: The Problem of Dating Biblical Hebrew," *SJOT* 11 (1997): 29–40.
34. Job is TBH; see chapter 6.
35. The word resurfaces in Mishnaic Hebrew.
36. See Gen 30:33; Num 35:30; 1 Sam 12:3; 2 Sam 1:16; Isa 3:9; 59:12; Mic 6:3; Jer 14:7; Job 15:6; Ruth 1:21. The construction in Meṣad Ḥashavyahu is not exactly the same as in BH, however.

37. See Hurvitz, *Lexicon*, 24–26, and chapter 2 of this volume.
38. 2 Chr 32:17; Esth 1:22; 3:13; 8:5, 10; 9:20, 25, 30.
39. See 1 Kgs 16:9; 18:3; 2 Kgs 10:5; 18:18, 37; 19:2; Isa 22:15; 36:3, 22; 37:2.
40. See also 2 Chr 19:11, which also uses נָגִיד.
41. For the analysis of the formula, see Moshe Greenberg, "The Hebrew Oath Particle *ḥay/ḥē*," *JBL* 76 (1957): 34–39. The orthography of the inscriptions differs at times from that of the Bible: for example, in Lachish 3.9 the expression is written as one word with a single *yod*, חיהוה. But the syntax and the meaning are the same.
42. See, e.g., Esther Eshel, "A Late Iron Age Ostracon Featuring the Term לערכך," *IEJ* 53 (2003): 151–63; Shmuel Aḥituv and Ada Yardeni, "Silver, Pistachio and Wheat: Two Letters of the Seventh-Sixth Centuries BCE," in *Zaphenath-Paneah: Linguistic Studies Presented to Elisha Qimron on the Occasion of his Sixty-Fifth Birthday*, ed. Daniel Sivan, David Talshir, and Chaim Cohen (Beer Sheva: Ben Gurion University Press, 2009), 15–28.
43. For this example, see in more detail, Joosten, "Distinction," 327–39, in particular 337–38.
44. Eccl 4:17; 12:5; Esth 2:3, 8, 14, 16; 4:2, 6; 6:12; 7:7; Ezra 3:7, 8; 10:6; Neh 2:13, 14; 6:10; 1 Chr 11:15; 13:13; 19:2; 2 Chr 7:2; 20:28. This construction is frequent also in CBH.
45. See Qimron, *Scrolls*, 69.
46. See Takamitsu Muraoka, "An Approach to the Morphosyntax and Syntax of Qumran Hebrew," in *Diggers at the Well: Proceedings of a Third International Symposium on the Hebrew of the Dead Sea Scrolls and Ben Sira*, ed. Takamitsu Muraoka and John F. Elwolde (Leiden: Brill, 2000), 193–214, in particular 194–95 (with reference to earlier publications by Kutscher and Qimron).
47. For the interpretation of the clause, see Aḥituv, *Echoes*, 67–68.
48. See 1 Sam 16:18; 1 Kgs 3:7; Isa 8:4; and in poetry, Isa 47:11; 56:11; Jer 1:6; Amos 3:10.
49. With ידע: Eccl 4:13, 17; 6:8; 10:15; 2 Chr 2:6, 7, 13.
50. Gen 25:31, 33; 1 Sam 2:16; 9:27; 1 Kgs 1:51; 22:5. See Driver, *Notes*, 31.
51. Ehrensvärd, "Problem of Dating."
52. See 1 Chr 12:18; 14:8; 19:14; 2 Chr 14:9; 15:2; 20:17; 28:9. This feature was pointed out in a different connection by Zecharias Frankel, *Über den Einfluss der palästinensischen Exegese auf die alexandrinische Hermeneutik* (Leipzig: Barth, 1851), 20.
53. The same form also occurs in the second letter published in Aḥituv and Yardeni, "Silver, Pistachio and Wheat," 17 (line 3). See also Kuntillet ʿAjrud 18.1; 19.5, which are not Judean.
54. See Joosten, *Verbal System*, 120–21, 202–4.
55. With ברך ("to bless"): Pss 118:26; 129:8.
56. See Eskhult, "Verbal Syntax," 84–93, in particular 86. Note that in 2 Chr 1:12, a different construction is used where the parallel, 1 Kgs 3:12, has a performative *qatal*.

57. Joüon, 429–30, §123u–v.
58. See Kropat, *Syntax,* 23; Eskhult, "Verbal Syntax," 90.
59. See Eskhult, "Verbal Syntax," 90.
60. See ibid., 87.
61. See Young's article quoted in note 1, *supra.* Young lists twenty-seven features, but practically all of them are inconclusive (as Young himself signals in some instances) or dissolve upon closer examination. Some items are based on reconstructions and are therefore uncertain, others are in fact attested in CBH, and three are from the Moussaieff Ostraca 1 and 2, today widely regarded as forgeries.
62. See, e.g., Dong-Hyuk Kim, *Early Biblical Hebrew, Late Biblical Hebrew and Linguistic Variability. A Sociolinguistic Evaluation of the Linguistic Dating of Biblical Texts*, VTSup 156 (Leiden: Brill, 2013), 89–91 and the literature discussed there.
63. See, e.g., André Lemaire, "Edom and the Edomites," in *The Book of Kings. Sources, Composition, Historiography, and Reception*, ed. André Lemaire and Baruch Halpern, VTSup 129 (Leiden: Brill, 2010), 236.
64. A full bibliographical review of the question can be found in Jason C. Dykehouse, "An Historical Reconstruction of Edomite Treaty Betrayal in the Sixth Century B.C.E. Based on Biblical, Epigraphic, and Archaeological Data" (PhD diss., Baylor University, 2008), 136.
65. For the very meager remains, see Hamilton, "Paleo-Hebrew Texts," 253–90; Schniedewind, *Social History*, 148–61.

Chapter 6. Transitional Biblical Hebrew

1. For indications of possible developments within CBH, see chapter 2.
2. See the bibliographical references in appendix 1. Ruth may also be assigned to TBH.
3. See, e.g., Hag 1:12–14; 2:10–13; and many passages in Zech 1–8.
4. Avi Hurvitz, "The Date of the Prose-Tale of Job Linguistically Reconsidered," *HTR* 67 (1974): 17–34.
5. See Jan Joosten, "Linguistic Clues as to the Date of the Book of Job: A Mediating Position," in *Interested Readers: Essays on the Hebrew Bible in Honor of David J. A. Clines*, ed. James K. Aitken, Jeremy M. S. Clines, and Christl M. Maier (Atlanta: Society of Biblical Literature, 2013), 347–57.
6. See the bibliographical references in appendix 1.
7. See the review of the debate in Wolf-Dieter Syring, *Hiob und sein Anwalt: Die Prosatexte des Hiobbuches und ihre Rolle in seiner Redaktions- und Rezeptionsgchichte*, BZAW 336 (Berlin: de Gruyter, 2003), 25–41.
8. Frank Polak, "On Prose and Poetry in the Book of Job," *JANESCU* 24 (1996): 61–97.
9. F. W. Dobbs-Allsopp, "Linguistic Evidence for the Date of Lamentations," *JANESCU* 26 (1998): 13.

10. See Mark Rooker, *Biblical Hebrew in Transition: The Language of the Book of Ezekiel* (Sheffield: Academic Press, 1990); Shalom Paul, "Signs of Late Hebrew in Isaiah 40–66," in *Diachrony in Biblical Hebrew*, ed. Cynthia Miller-Naudé and Ziony Zevit (Winona Lake, IN: Eisenbrauns, 2012), 293–300.
11. See chapter 4.
12. See Ernst Jenni, "Miszellen zu Einzeltexten: Jer 3,17 'nach Jerusalem': Ein Aramaismus," *ZAH* 1 (1988): 107–11. See also BDB, 511a, §1g; Hornkohl, *Periodization*, 231, n. 1114.
13. See Driver, *Notes*, 177.
14. The word is found in Ezek 22:25; Zec 11:13; Ps 49:13, 21; Job 28:10; Prov 20:15; and eight times in Esther.
15. See Joosten, "L'excédent," 93–108.
16. Hornkohl, *Periodization.*
17. Ibid., 298–300.
18. This usage is found also in Jer 44:28 (where the Septuagint may indicate the existence of a variant reading).
19. Paul, "Signs of Late Hebrew in Isaiah 40–66."
20. See Christopher B. Hays, "The Date and Message of Isaiah 24–27 in Light of Hebrew Diachrony," in *Intertextuality and Formation of Isaiah 24–27: Ancient Israel and Its Literature*, ed. J. Todd Hibbard and Paul Kim, AIL 17 (Atlanta: Society of Biblical Literature, 2013), 7–24.
21. The meaning of אֵי־זֶה changes over the biblical period from "where" to "which"; see BDB, 32a, §1b, 2a.
22. Daniel, unlike Ezekiel, is thick with LBH elements. Note from the first chapter: v. 1, מַלְכוּת; v. 2, מִקְצָת; v. 3, אמר followed by indirect speech; v. 4, מַדָּע; v. 5, מנה *piel* ("to appoint"); v. 10, אֲשֶׁר לָמָּה ("lest"), and גִּיל ("age"); *piel* of hollow roots; and the Persian words פַּרְתְּמִים ("nobles") and פַּתְבַּג ("delicacies").
23. Nevertheless, the fact that the linguistic data line up with the prima facie evidence remains striking. It is very unlikely that authors of the Persian period invented a special "mixed" style for use in writings situated in the intermediary period.
24. Gesenius, *Geschichte*, 35.
25. See Avi Hurvitz, *A Linguistic Study of the Relationship between the Priestly Source and the Book of Ezekiel*, CahRB 20 (Paris: Gabalda, 1982); Rooker, *Biblical Hebrew.*
26. CBH uses מַחְתָּה ("censer") and רחץ ("to wash") instead.
27. See, e.g., Ezek 6:6; 12:12, 25, 28; 13:15; 14:7; 24:27; 26:21; 27:30; 32:28; 33:31; 40:42; 47:9. The usage is well established in LBH; CBH uses *weqatal* instead. See Joosten, *Verbal System*, 397–99.
28. See ibid., 394.
29. See Daniel Bodi, *The Book of Ezekiel and the Poem of Erra*, OBO 104 (Fribourg: Universitätsverlag; Gottingen: Vandenhoeck & Ruprecht, 1991); David S.

Vanderhooft, "Ezekiel in and on Babylon," *Transeuphratène* 46 (2014): 99–119; and Abraham Winitzer, "Assyriology and Jewish Studies in Tel Aviv: Ezekiel among the Babylonian *Literati*," in *Encounters by the Rivers of Babylon: Scholarly Conversations between Jews, Iranians, and Babylonians in Antiquity*, ed. Uri Gabbay and Shai Secunda (Tübingen: Mohr Siebeck, 2014), 163–216.

30. Winitzer, "Assyriology," 166.
31. Ibid., 166–67.
32. For these words and many more, see Mankowski, *Akkadian*; and Hayim ben Yosef Tawil, *An Akkadian Lexical Companion for Biblical Hebrew: Etymological-Semantic and Idiomatic Equivalents with Supplement on Biblical Aramaic* (Jersey City, NJ: KTAV, 2009).
33. More examples are given below in chapter 8.
34. See particularly Vanderhooft, "Ezekiel in and on Babylon."
35. For this and other Babylonianisms in Second Isaiah, see H. G. M. Williamson, "The Setting of Deutero-Isaiah: Some Linguistic Considerations," in *Exile and Return: The Babylonian Context,* ed. Jonathan Stökl and Caroline Waerzeggers, BZAW 478 (Berlin: de Gruyter, 2015), 253–67.
36. Alexander Rofé, "An Enquiry into the Betrothal of Rebekah," in *Die hebräische Bibel und ihre zweifache Nachgeschichte: Festschrift für Rolf Rendtorff zum 65. Geburtstag*, ed. Erhard Blum, Christian Macholz, and Ekkehard W. Stegemann (Neukirchen: Neukirchener Verlag, 1990), 27–39.
37. Otherwise attested only in Jonah 1:9; Ezra 1:2; Neh 1:4, 5; 2:4, 20; 2 Chr 36:23.
38. The form is otherwise attested only in Ezra 1:6; 2 Chr 21:3; 32:23.
39. See chapter 3; and Rendsburg, "False Leads," 23–46.
40. E.g., for the expression אִם־לֹא ("but"); see chapter 3.
41. Some of the evidence marshaled by Rendsburg is weak, as he himself realizes. For instance, Gen 24 uses the CBH expression לָקַח אִשָּׁה ("to take a wife," vv. 37, 38, 40, 48, 67) and not the usual LBH equivalent נָשָׂא אִשָּׁה. But the probative force of this argument is low, for the CBH expression is found three times in Chronicles, including two nonparallel passages (1 Chr 7:15; 2 Chr 11:18).
42. See Stefan Schorch, "'Vielleicht wird der Herr doch gnädig sein!' Das Konzept der Unverfügbarkeit *Jhwhs* in der alttestamentlichen Prophetie," in *Ex oriente Lux: Studien zur Theologie des Alten Testaments: Festschrift für Rüdiger Lux zum 65. Geburtstag*, ed. Angelika Berlejung and Raik Heckl (Leipzig: Evangelische Verlagsanstalt, 2012), 457–68, in particular 462.
43. This form of the pronoun is found three times in LBH: Dan 10:11; Neh 1:6; 1 Chr 17:1 (a parallel passage), but LBH otherwise uses only the shorter form אֲנִי (more than one hundred times).
44. Ruth, too, may reflect TBH; see appendix 1.
45. Some of the features occur only in part of the corpus: linguistic change did not affect all authors in the same way.
46. There may be a Persian word in 2 Kgs 23:11, פַּרְוָרִים; see chapter 2.

47. Instead, TBH continues to use the classical word עֵת ("time," seventy-one times).
48. Note that Ezek 43:25 uses classical שָׂעִיר ("he goat") instead.
49. This verb is attested in LBH and the late Psalm, Ps 119:133; TBH always uses classical משל ("to rule") instead.
50. See Neh 9:27–28; 2 Chr 24:11; Joosten, *Verbal System*, 398–99.

Chapter 7. Pseudoclassicism

1. See, e.g., Carr, *Formation*, 73–78, with discussion of recent literature.
2. See, e.g., Hannah K. Harrington, "The Use of Leviticus in Ezra-Nehemiah," *JHS* 13 (2013): https://doi.org/10.5508/jhs.2013.v13.a3, with references to earlier literature.
3. See, e.g., the seminal article by H. L. Ginsberg, "The Oldest Interpretation of the Suffering Servant," *VT* 3 (1953): 400–404.
4. See, e.g., Sandra B. Berg, *The Book of Esther: Motifs, Themes and Structure* (Missoula, MT: Scholars Press, 1979), 124–28.
5. But see Jenny Barbour, *The Story of Israel in the Book of Qohelet: Ecclesiastes as Cultural Memory* (Oxford: Oxford University Press, 2012).
6. Apart from Neh 4:1, it is found only in Neh 3:33 and 5:6, and 1 Chr 13:11 (where it was simply borrowed from 2 Sam 6:8).
7. Other examples from Nehemiah include the expressions יוֹמָם וָלַיְלָה ("day and night," 4:3); וְאֵין לְאֵל יָדֵנוּ ("we were powerless," 5:5; cf. Deut 28:32); רַחֲבַת יָדַיִם ("spread out," 7:4; cf. Gen 34:21); וַיִּשְׁתַּחֲוּ לַיהוָה אַפַּיִם אָרְצָה ("they prostrated themselves before YHWH," 8:6; cf. Gen 19:1); צְבָא הַשָּׁמַיִם ("the host of heaven," 9:6; cf. Deut 17:3).
8. See Yohanan Aharoni, *The Land of the Bible: A Historical Geography*, trans. and ed. Anson F. Rainey, 2nd ed. (Philadelphia: Westminster, 1979), 72.
9. The only exception seems to be Judg 3:3, where the entire name is transliterated in the Septuagint (both B and A texts).
10. The original discovery was made by Karl Elliger; see Aharoni, *Land of the Bible*, 80.
11. Note that the expression לְבוֹא חֲמָת occurs in 1 Chr 13:5; 2 Chr 7:8. From the context it is impossible to know whether the Chronicler understood this as a composite geographical noun or, as seems more likely, as an expression meaning "to the border of Hamath."
12. See also 1 Chr 5:9, לְבוֹא מִדְבָּרָה.
13. See Jan Joosten, "Pseudo-Classicisms in Late Biblical Hebrew, in Ben Sira, and in Qumran Hebrew," in *Sirach, Scrolls and Sages: Proceedings of a Second International Symposium on the Hebrew of the Dead Sea Scrolls, Ben Sira, and the Mishnah, held at Leiden University, 15–17 December 1997*, ed. Takamitsu Muraoka and John F. Elwolde (Leiden: Brill, 1999), 146–59.

14. The expression recurs in 2 Chr 13:9; 29:31.
15. See also Exod 28:41; 29:9, 29, 33, 35; Lev 8:33; 16:32; 21:10; Num 3:3; Jud 17:5, 12; 1 Kgs 13:33. In Ezek 43:26 the expression refers to the consecration of an altar.
16. The expression is correctly interpreted as referring to consecration in the Septuagint. It is used with the same meaning in the Temple Scroll (e.g., 11QT XXXV, 6) and in Ben Sira 45:15—both writings are dependent on biblical models.
17. See, notably, Deut 15:3, וַאֲשֶׁר יִהְיֶה לְךָ אֶת־אָחִיךָ תַּשְׁמֵט יָדֶךָ ("but you must remit your claim on whatever any member of your community owes you").
18. Cf. Moshe Weinfeld, "Sabbatical Year and Jubilee in the Pentateuchal Laws," in *The Law in the Bible and in Its Environment*, ed. Timo Veijola (Göttingen: Vandenhoeck & Ruprecht, 1990), 39–62, in particular 48.
19. Targum Neofiti parses the clause correctly, against the Masoretic vowels. The Septuagint rendering is too free to ascertain how the translator analyzed the syntax.
20. See Fassberg, *Studies*, 13–35; Fassberg, "The Lengthened Imperative קָטְלָה in Biblical Hebrew," *HS* 40 (1999): 7–13; Ahouva Shulman, "The Use of Modal Verb Forms in Biblical Hebrew Prose" (PhD diss., University of Toronto, 1996), 65–84; see also Jan Joosten, "The Lengthened Imperative with Accusative Suffix in Biblical Hebrew," *ZAW* 111 (1999): 423–26.
21. Fassberg, *Studies*, 34–35.
22. A concordance search shows that the lengthened imperative is found 130 times in CBH and 22 times in LBH. The LBH corpus is only around a third the length of the CBH corpus, yet these statistics are still meaningful.
23. In the Qumran corpus, the form is used often in prayers, but not exclusively; see, e.g., 1QM X, 3; 4Q88 (4QApocryphalPs[f]) X, 7–8.
24. See, notably, 1 Chr 29:18; Neh 6:14; 13:29.
25. See the passages quoted in *supra* note 23 as well as 4Q416 (4QInstruction[b]) 4, 3, and 4Q508 (4QFestival Prayers[b]) 2, 2. In Sir 31:15 the form used is dependent on Prov 24:14.
26. For other examples, see Joosten, *Verbal System*, 405.
27. Emily Brontë's novel *Wuthering Heights* was written more than 150 years ago, but reading it today does not necessitate any particular expertise in nineteenth-century English.
28. See, e.g., Kutscher's note on words in Qumran Hebrew "whose meaning changed owing to a certain interpretation of their original meaning which had been forgotten." Eduard Yechezkel Kutscher, "Hebrew Language: The Dead Sea Scrolls," in *Encyclopedia Judaica*, vol. 16, ed. Cecil Roth (Jerusalem: Keter, 1972), columns 1583–90, in particular 1589. See also the quote from James Barr in *infra* note 31.
29. See Solomon Schechter, *Fragments of a Zadokite Work*, Documents of Jewish Sectaries 2 (Cambridge: Cambridge University Press, 1910), xi.

30. Ian Young, "Late Biblical Hebrew and the Qumran Pesher Habakkuk," *JHS* 8 (2008): https://doi.org/10.5508/jhs.2008.v8.a25; criticisms of Young can be found in Gary A. Rendsburg, "Late Biblical Hebrew and the Qumran Pesher Habakkuk," in *Hebrew of the Late Second Temple Period: Proceedings of a Sixth International Symposium on the Hebrew of the Dead Sea Scrolls and Ben Sira*, ed. Eibert Tigchelaar and Pierre Van Hecke, STDJ 114 (Leiden: Brill, 2015), 132–59.
31. See James Barr, "Hebrew, Aramaic, and Greek in the Hellenistic Age," in *The Cambridge History of Judaism*, ed. W. D. Davies and Louis Finkelstein (Cambridge: Cambridge University Press, 1990), 79–114, in particular 90: "[In Qumran Hebrew] we find old words of the Bible, probably long archaic, reused with senses which have come to be attached to them through exegetical tradition. Thus the Hodayot use no less than four times the word *ḥelka'im*, which occurs thrice in the difficult Ps. 10 and is obscure already there. It is hardly to be supposed that this word was still current in conversational Hebrew; rather, its very obscurity lent it to exegetical speculation and reuse in the sense attained by such study."
32. See Jan Joosten, "Sectarian Terminology and Biblical Interpretation: The Meaning of the Verb אות in the Qumran Scrolls," *Meghillot* 1 (2003): 219–26 (Hebrew).
33. Joosten, "Pseudo-Classicisms in Late Biblical Hebrew, Ben Sira," 150–51.
34. Note also the spelling אפע in Isa 59:5 according to 1QIsa[a].
35. See the detailed discussion in Jean Carmignac, "Précisions apportées au vocabulaire de l'Hébreu biblique par la guerre des fils de lumière contre les fils de ténèbres," *VT* 5 (1955): 345–65, in particular 355–57.
36. See Qimron, *Scrolls*, 98.
37. Ibid., 109.
38. See Noam Mizrahi, "The Linguistic History of מדהבה: From Textual Corruption to Lexical Innovation," *RevQ* 26 (2013): 93–116, with references to earlier literature.
39. See Jan Joosten, "The Knowledge and Use of Hebrew in the Hellenistic Period: Qumran and the Septuagint," in *Diggers at the Well: Proceedings of a Third International Symposium on the Hebrew of the Dead Sea Scrolls and Ben Sira*, ed. Takamitsu Muraoka and John F. Elwolde (Leiden: Brill, 2000), 115–30, in particular 127–28.
40. Qimron, *Scrolls*, 114.
41. Jan Joosten, "Pseudo-Classicisms in Late Biblical Hebrew," *ZAW* 128 (2016): 16–29, in particular 22–23.
42. Other examples are given in Menahem Kister, "Some Lexical Features of the Writings from Qumran," in *The Qumran Scrolls and Their World*, 2 vols. (Jerusalem: Yad Izhak Ben-Zvi, 2009), 2:561–69 (Hebrew).
43. Michael Wise has aptly compared Qumran Hebrew to Atticism, the return to classical models that marks much literary Greek from the middle of the first

century BCE or so; see Michael O. Wise, *Language and Literacy in Roman Judaea: A Study of the Bar Kokhba Documents* (New Haven, CT: Yale University Press, 2015), 285. However, while Atticists of the Roman period had extensive libraries of works written in authentic fifth-century Attic Greek at their disposal, writers of the LBH and Qumran Hebrew periods had little more than the Torah and Former Prophets. The extant CBH works were too limited to allow scribes to master the ancient language. See further note 124 in chapter 8.

44. See Steven Weitzman, "Why did the Qumran Community Write in Hebrew?" *JAOS* 119 (1999): 35–45.

Chapter 8. Consilience and Cultural History

1. Alexander Rofé, "Not by Language Alone: The Dating of Biblical Sources," in *Houses Full of All Good Things: Essays in Memory of Timo Veijola*, ed. Juha Pakkala and Martti Nissinen (Helsinki: Finnish Exegetical Society; Göttingen: Vandenhoeck & Ruprecht, 2008), 656–65.
2. Erhard Blum, "The Linguistic Dating of Biblical Texts: An Approach with Methodological Limitations," in Gertz et al., *Formation of the Pentateuch*, 305.
3. See Clifford Geertz, "Thick Description: Toward an Interpretive Theory of Culture," in *The Interpretation of Cultures: Selected Essays* (New York: Basic Books, 1973), 3–30.
4. Blum, "Linguistic Dating," 304.
5. William Whewell, *Novum Organon renovatum: Being the Second Part of the Philosophy of the Inductive Sciences*, 3rd ed. (London: Parker, 1858), 70–71; see Laura J. Snyder, *Reforming Philosophy: A Victorian Debate on Science and Society* (Chicago: University of Chicago Press, 2006), 173–85; and Edward O. Wilson, *Consilience: The Unity of Knowledge* (New York: Knopf, 1998).
6. Stephen J. Gould, *Wonderful Life: The Burgess Shale and the Nature of History* (New York: Norton, 1989), 282, quoted in Aviezer Tucker, *Our Knowledge of the Past: A Philosophy of Historiography* (Cambridge: Cambridge University Press, 2004), 148.
7. Bloch, *Historian's Craft*, 55.
8. See Peter Burke, *What Is Cultural History?*, 2nd ed. (Cambridge: Polity, 2008).
9. Bloch, *Historian's Craft*, 64.
10. Jacob Burckhardt, *The Greeks and Greek Civilization*, ed. Oswyn Murray, trans. Sheila Stern (New York: St. Martin's, 1998), 5. See also Murray's introduction (xxxi): "It does not matter whether the stories which it uses are true, as long as they are believed to be true."
11. R. G. Collingwood, *The Idea of History*, rev. ed. (Oxford: Oxford University Press, 1994), 263.
12. Ibid., 265.
13. Sommer, "Dating Pentateuchal Texts," 85–108.

14. Ibid., 85.
15. Ibid., 85, 96, 100.
16. Ibid., 101.
17. On this poem, see recently Mark S. Smith, *Poetic Heroes: Literary Commemorations of Warriors and Warrior Culture in the Early Biblical World* (Grand Rapids, MI: Eerdmans, 2014), 220–66, with bibliography.
18. In the construct phrase, צַוְּארֵי שָׁלָל ("necks of the spoil"), we prefer vocalizing the second noun as the agentive form, שַׁלָּל ("despoiler"); for other proposals, see Jack M. Sasson, *Judges 1–12*, AB 6D (New Haven, CT: Yale University Press, 2014), 279, 310.
19. This term does not have a pejorative sense, as is sometimes assumed; compare the plural רחמת ("young women, maidens") in the Mesha inscription (line 17), and the parallel epithets of the goddess Anat in Ugaritic: *rḥm ʿnt* ("maiden Anat") and *btlt ʿnt* ("virgin Anat"); see Aḥituv, *Echoes from the Past*, 392–93, 409.
20. On the gendered activity of weaving in the ancient Near East, see Susan Ackerman, "Asherah, the West Semitic Goddess of Spinning and Weaving?" *JNES* 67 (2008): 1–29.
21. These gendered ironies also have sexual content, as Sisera falls "between her feet" (Judg 5:27), in contrast to the spoil of young women that Sisera and his men fail to take. In a sense, Sisera is Jael's spoil.
22. Huehnergard, *Ugaritic*, 38.
23. Our thanks to Mark Smith for bringing this example to our attention.
24. Gary A. Rendsburg, "Style-Switching," in *Encyclopedia of Hebrew Language and Linguistics*, ed. Geoffrey Khan, 4 vols. (Leiden: Brill, 2013), 3:633; and see chapter 3.
25. Tania Notarius, "The Archaic System of Verbal Tenses in 'Archaic' Biblical Poetry," in *Diachrony in Biblical Hebrew*, ed. Cynthia. L. Miller-Naudé and Ziony Zevit (Winona Lake, IN: Eisenbrauns, 2012), 195–98.
26. Ibid., 198.
27. See Smith, *Poetic Heroes*, 220–27 and references cited there.
28. In CBH texts Manasseh is the father of Machir (e.g., Gen 50:23; Num 26:29), and Machir is the father of Gilead (Num 26:29). Gilead is primarily a territorial term.
29. Smith, *Poetic Heroes*, 249.
30. J. David Schloen, "Caravans, Kenites, and *Casus Belli*: Enmity and Alliance in the Song of Deborah," *CBQ* 55 (1993): 18–38.
31. See Lawrence E. Stager, "Archaeology, Ecology, and Social History: Background Themes to the Song of Deborah," in *Congress Volume: Jerusalem 1986*, ed. John A. Emerton, VTSup 40 (Leiden: Brill, 1988), 221–34.
32. See similarly, Jacob L. Wright, "Deborah's War Memorial: The Composition of Judges 4–5 and the Politics of War Commemoration," *ZAW* 123 (2011): 529:

"Belonging in ancient Israel was negotiated in some circles via memories of wartime contributions and sacrifice."

33. Konrad Schmid, *The Old Testament: A Literary History*, trans. Linda M. Maloney (Minneapolis: Fortress, 2012), 480.
34. See chapter 2.
35. See Lawrence E. Stager, "Biblical Philistines: A Hellenistic Literary Creation?" in *"I Will Speak the Riddles of Ancient Times": Archaeological and Historical Studies in Honor of Amihai Mazar*, ed. Aren M. Maeir and Pierre de Miroschedji (Winona Lake, IN: Eisenbrauns, 2006), 375–84.
36. See later in this chapter on the Neo-Assyrian milieu of the curses of Deuteronomy.
37. Yasur-Landau, *Philistines*, 330; see also Israel Finkelstein, "The Philistine Countryside," *IEJ* 46 (1996), 225–42.
38. On the history of Gath, see Aren M. Maeir, "Introduction, Overview and Synopsis of Results," in *Tell es-Safi/Gath I: The 1996–2005 Seasons* (Wiesbaden: Harrassowitz, 2012), 19–65; William M. Schniedewind, "The Geopolitical History of Philistine Gath," *BASOR* 309 (1998): 69–77.
39. Aren M. Maeir, "The Historical Background and Dating of Amos VI 2: An Archaeological Perspective from Tell es-Safi/Gath," *VT* 54 (2004): 319–34.
40. Israel Finkelstein, "The Philistines in the Bible: A Late-Monarchic Perspective," *JSOT* 27 (2002): 142.
41. Ibid., 155.
42. Besides סרן, another possible Philistine loanword in Hebrew is כּוֹבַע/קוֹבַע ("helmet"), cognate with Hittite *kupaḫi*, Hurrian *kuwaḫi*, and Greek κύμβαχος; see *HALOT*, 463. The variation of word-initial כ/ק in Hebrew indicates a foreign loanword: it is written both ways in 1 Sam 17:5, 38, describing the armor of Goliath and Saul.
43. For additional archaeological and historical considerations, see Stager, "Biblical Philistines"; Avraham Faust, "The Bible, Archaeology, and the Practice of Circumcision in Israelite and Philistine Societies," *JBL* 134 (2015): 273–90.
44. On the political motives and effects of ninth-century royal annals and monumental inscriptions, see Seth Sanders, *The Invention of Hebrew* (Urbana: University of Illinois Press, 2009), 113–22.
45. On the following, see Mordechai Cogan and Hayim Tadmor, *II Kings*, AB 11 (New York: Doubleday, 1988), 333–40, and their notes on the royal names, *ad loc.*; and Alan R. Millard, "Israelite and Aramean History in the Light of Inscriptions," in *Israel's Past in Present Research: Essays on Ancient Israelite Historiography*, ed. V. Philips Long (Winona Lake, IN: Eisenbrauns, 1999), 137–39; Baruch Halpern, "Erasing History: The Minimalist Assault on Ancient Israel," in Long, *Israel's Past*, 418–19. Our normalization of Akkadian generally follows Cogan and Tadmor.
46. Aḥituv, *Echoes from the Past*, 467–68 (line 9). In Iron Age inscriptions a word divider is optional in construct chains with a proclitic noun (like *bêt or ben*) + PN.

47. Ibid., 392–93 (line 31).
48. Alan K. Grayson, *Assyrian Rulers of the Early First Millennium BC: II (858–754 BC)* (Toronto: University of Toronto Press, 1996), 149 (102.88 and parallels); Hayim Tadmor and Shigeo Yamada, *The Royal Inscriptions of Tiglath-pileser III (744–727 BC) and Shalmaneser V (726–722 BC), Kings of Assyria* (Winona Lake, IN: Eisenbrauns, 2011), 201 (eight times).
49. Aḥituv, *Echoes from the Past*, 392–93 (lines 4–5).
50. Grayson, *Assyrian Rulers*, 23 (Kurkh Monolith 102.2 ii.91–92). There is some simplification and vowel harmony in the Assyrian borrowing: **(yi)śra('il)* → *sir('il)*. However, the second vowel in the Akkadian normalization (*sir-'-la-a-a* = *Sir'ilāya*) is uncertain, as the glottal stop (') sign can represent *'aleph* + any vowel.
51. Aḥituv, *Echoes from the Past*, 467–68 (lines 7–8).
52. Grayson, *Assyrian Rulers*, 149 (Black Obelisk epigraph, 102.88), 48, 54, 60 (other annalistic texts, 102.8, 102.10, 102.12). The phonology is presumably **Yawhū'* → *Yayhū'* → *Yêhū'* (= יֵהוּא), with the Akkadian reflecting the older, uncontracted form; see Cogan and Tadmor, *II Kings*, 106.
53. Grayson, *Assyrian Rulers*, 211 (Tell al-Rimah stele, 104.7, line 8).
54. Tadmor and Yamada, *Tiglath-pileser*, 46 (e.g., 14.10). Samaria has the determinative "city" (URU = *āl*); compare "land" (KUR = *māt*) in the previous instance (Joash). The use of determinatives is often inconsistent, but Samaria does have both meanings.
55. Ibid., 106 (42.17).
56. Ibid., 106 (42.17–18).
57. Aḥituv, *Echoes from the Past*, 467–68 (lines 8–9).
58. Tadmor and Yamada, *Tiglath-Pileser*, 42–43 (13.2, 10); on the uncertain identification, see Cogan and Tadmor, *II Kings*, 165–66.
59. Tadmor and Yamada, *Tiglath-Pileser*, 122–23 (47 rev. 11). Notably, the Akkadian reflects the full name יְהוֹאָחָז (Jehoahaz), whereas the Bible has only the short version אָחָז (Ahaz).
60. Alan K. Grayson and Jamie Novotny, *The Royal Inscriptions of Sennacherib, King of Assyria (704–681 BC), Part 1* (Winona Lake, IN: Eisenbrauns, 2012), 64–65 (e.g., 4.42, 49, 55)
61. Erle Leichty, *The Royal Inscriptions of Esarhaddon, King of Assyria (680–669 BC)* (Winona Lake, IN: Eisenbrauns, 2011), 23 (1.v.55), 46 (5.vi.7).
62. Cogan and Tadmor, *II Kings*, 311.
63. On the nature of these archival materials, see Mark Leuchter, "The Sociolinguistic and Rhetorical Implications of the Source Citations in Kings," in *Soundings in Kings: Perspectives and Methods in Contemporary Scholarship*, ed. Leuchter and Klaus-Peter Adam (Minneapolis: Fortress, 2010), 119–34; Nadav Na'aman, "The Temple Library of Jerusalem and the Composition of the Book of Kings," in *Congress Volume: Leiden 2004*, ed. André Lemaire, VTSup 109 (Leiden: Brill,

2006), 129–52; Menahem Haran, "The Books of the Chronicles 'Of the Kings of Judah' and 'Of the Kings of Israel': What Sort of Books Were They?" *VT* 49 (1999): 156–64.

64. For example, the legendary tales of Solomon's wisdom and wealth, the prophetic narratives of Elijah and Elisha; see Rofé, *Introduction*, 1–41.
65. See chapter 2.
66. See Hurvitz, *Lexicon*, 165–70; see also chapter 4.
67. See recently Arie van der Kooij, "The City of Babel and Assyrian Imperialism: Genesis 11:1–9 Interpreted in the Light of Mesopotamian Sources," in *Congress Volume: Leiden 2004*, ed. André Lemaire, 1–17; David S. Vanderhooft, "Biblical Perspectives on Nineveh and Babylon: Views from the Endangered Periphery," *Canadian Society for Mesopotamian Studies Journal* 3 (2008): 83–85; Ronald Hendel, "Genesis 1–11 and Its Mesopotamian Problem," in *Cultural Borrowings and Ethnic Appropriations in Antiquity*, ed. Erich Gruen (Stuttgart: Steiner, 2005), 29–31.
68. See Christoph Uehlinger, "Nimrod," *DDD*, 627–30 and references cited there.
69. Victor A. Hurowitz, "In Search of Resen (Genesis 10:12): Dūr-Šarrukīn?" in *Birkat Shalom: Studies in the Bible, Ancient Near Eastern Literature, and Postbiblical Judaism Presented to Shalom M. Paul*, ed. Chaim Cohen et al. (Winona Lake, IN: Eisenbrauns, 2008), 511–24.
70. The classic studies are Rintje Frankena, "The Vassal-Treaties of Esarhaddon and the Dating of Deuteronomy," *OtSt* 14 (1965), 122–54; and Moshe Weinfeld, "Traces of Assyrian Treaty Formulae in Deuteronomy," *Bib* 36 (1965), 417–47; revised in *Deuteronomy and the Deuteronomic School* (Oxford: Clarendon Press, 1972), 116–29; and see the comprehensive study of Hans Ulrich Steymans, *Deuteronomium 28 und die adê zur Thronfolgeregelung Asarhaddons: Segen und Fluch im Alten Orient und in Israel*, OBO 145 (Freiburg: Universitätsverlag; Göttingen: Vandenhoeck & Ruprecht, 1995). On the criticisms of textual dependence by Carly L. Crouch, *Israel and the Assyrians: Deuteronomy, the Succession Treaty of Esarhadon, and the Nature of Subversion*, ANEM 8 (Atlanta: SBL Press, 2014), see Laura Quick, *Deuteronomy 28 and the Aramaic Curse Tradition* (Oxford: Oxford University Press, 2017), 37–40 and passim.
71. Weinfeld, *Deuteronomy*, 91–100; Paul E. Dion, "Deuteronomy 13: The Suppression of Alien Religious Propaganda in Israel during the Late Monarchical Era," in *Law and Ideology in Monarchic Israel*, ed. Baruch Halpern and Deborah W. Hobson (Sheffield: JSOT Press, 1991), 147–216; Bernard M. Levinson, "Esarhaddon's Succession Treaty as the Source for the Canon Formula in Deuteronomy 13:1," *JAOS* 130 (2010): 337–47.
72. See Jacob Lauinger, "Esarhaddon's Succession Treaty at Tell Tayinat: Text and Commentary," *JCS* 64 (2012): 87–123; Bernard M. Levinson and Jeffrey Stackert, "Between the Covenant Code and Esarhaddon's Succession Treaty: Deuteronomy 13 and the Composition of Deuteronomy," *JSJ* 3 (2012): 123–40; Hans

Ulrich Steymans, "Deuteronomy 28 and Tell Tayinat," *Verbum et Ecclesia* 34 (2013): https://doi.org/10.4102/ve.v34i2.870.

73. Steymans, "Deuteronomy 28"; see Steymans, *Deuteronomium*, 300–12.
74. Numeration and translation (slightly adapted) from Simo Parpola and Kazuko Watanabe, *Neo-Assyrian Treaties and Loyalty Oaths* (Helsinki: Helsinki University Press, 1988), 28–58.
75. See Delbert Hillers, "Dust: Some Aspects of Old Testament Imagery," in *Love and Death in the Ancient Near East: Essays in Honor of Marvin H. Pope*, ed. John H. Marks and Robert M. Good (Guilford, CT: Four Quarters, 1987), 105–9.
76. The Hebrew *ketiv* יִשְׁגָּלֶנָּה ("he shall violate her") is stronger than the euphemistic "lie with" in the Assyrian and in the Hebrew *qere*.
77. Weinfeld, "Traces," 420.
78. Frankena, "Vassal-Treaties," 152–53.
79. Julius Wellhausen, *Prolegomena to the History of Israel*, trans. John S. Black and Allan Menzies (Edinburgh: Black, 1885), 13 (translation slightly altered).
80. Compare the return to some Wellhausenian positions in Thomas Römer, "How to Date Pentateuchal Texts: Some Case Studies," in Gertz et al., *Formation of the Pentateuch*, 357–70. Römer grants the Neo-Assyrian context of the early edition of Deuteronomy and situates some other non-P Pentateuchal texts to this era based on affinities with extrabiblical texts and names.
81. Aḥituv, *Echoes from the Past*, 19–26 (Siloam Inscription), 25–26 (stela from the City of David), 257 (royal stela from Samaria).
82. Note that two fragmentary Hebrew literary texts from the Neo-Assyrian period have been found on plaster at Kuntillet 'Ajrud (ca. 800 BCE); compare the Balaam text from Deir Alla (ca. 700 BCE), written in a dialect close to Hebrew; Aḥituv, *Echoes from the Past*, 324–28; 433–65. See also Schniedewind, *Social History*, 99–124.
83. See chapter 2.
84. See Paul-Alain Beaulieu, "Arameans, Chaldeans, and Arabs in Cuneiform Sources from the Late Babylonian Period," in *Aramaeans, Chaldaeans, and Arabs in Babylonia and Palestine in the First Millennium B.C.*, ed. Angelika Berlejung and Michael P. Streck (Wiesbaden: Harrassowitz, 2013), 33–35; Vanderhooft, "Nineveh and Babylon," 87.
85. The *Hofkalender* of Nebuchadnezzar; reedited in Beaulieu, "Arameans," 33–34.
86. Ibid., 35.
87. Michael Jursa, "Nabû-šarrūssu-ūkin, *rab ša-rēši*, und 'Nebusarsekim' (Jer. 39:3)," *NABU* 5 (2008): 9–10; Bob Becking, "The Identity of Nabu-sharrussu-ukin, the Chamberlain: An Epigraphic Note on Jeremiah 39,3, with an Appendix on the Nebusarsekim Tablet," *BN* 140 (2009): 35–46.
88. David S. Vanderhooft, *The Neo-Babylonian Empire and Babylon in the Latter Prophets*, HSM 59 (Atlanta: Scholars Press, 1999), 151.

89. Laurie E. Pearce, "Continuity and Normality in Sources Relating to the Judean Exile," *HeBAI* 3 (2014): 163–84.
90. See chapter 6.
91. Vanderhooft, "Ezekiel in and on Babylon," 107.
92. See ibid., 106–14; Winitzer, "Assyriology," 165–67; and Mankowski, *Akkadian*, ad loc.
93. Winitzer, "Assyriology," 114.
94. Christoph Uehlinger and Susanne Müller Trufaut, "Ezekiel 1, Babylonian Cosmological Scholarship and Iconography: Attempts at Further Refinement," *TZ* 57 (2001): 140–71, quote on 163.
95. Ibid.
96. Wilfred G. Lambert, *Babylonian Creation Myths* (Winona Lake, IN: Eisenbrauns, 2013), 227–32.
97. Stanley M. Burstein, *The Babyloniaca of Berossos* (Malibu, CA: Undena, 1978), 14.
98. Wayne Horowitz, *Mesopotamian Cosmic Geography* (Winona Lake, IN: Eisenbrauns, 1998), 3–19; Lambert, *Creation*, 197–99.
99. Translated (slightly adapted) from Horowitz, *Geography*, 4 (lines 31–32).
100. Winitzer, "Assyriology," 169.
101. See Johan Lust, "Major Divergences between LXX and MT in Ezekiel," in *The Earliest Text of the Hebrew Bible: The Relationship between the Masoretic Text and the Hebrew Base of the Septuagint Reconsidered*, ed. Adrian Schenker, SCS 52 (Atlanta: Society of Biblical Literature, 2003), 83–92; Timothy P. Mackie, *Expanding Ezekiel: The Hermeneutics of Scribal Addition in the Ancient Text Witnesses of the Book of Ezekiel* (Gottingen: Vandenhoeck & Ruprecht, 2015), 127–29.
102. *CAD* E, 108, which adds, "*Elmešu* may well be connected with Heb. חשמל which likewise appears only in similes referring to the extraordinary sheen of a quasi-mythical stone"; see, recently, Vanderhooft, "Ezekiel in and on Babylon," 112; Winitzer, "Assyriology," 179.
103. See chapter 7.
104. See recently Gary N. Knoppers, *I Chronicles 10–29*, AB 12A (New York: Doubleday, 2004), 946–47; H. G. M. Williamson, *Studies in Persian Period History and Historiography* (Tübingen: Mohr Siebeck, 2004), 169–70.
105. Knoppers, *Chronicles*, 964.
106. Ibid., 962–63.
107. Oded Lipschits, *The Fall and Rise of Jerusalem: Judah under Babylonian Rule* (Winona Lake, IN: Eisenbrauns, 2015), 218. See also Avraham Faust, *Judah in the Neo-Babylonian Period: The Archaeology of Desolation* (Atlanta: Society of Biblical Literature, 2012); Charles E. Carter, *The Emergence of Yehud in the Persian Period: A Social and Demographic Study* (Sheffield: Sheffield Academic Press, 1999).

108. Israel Finkelstein, "The Territorial Extent and Demography of Yehud/Judea in the Persian and Early Hellenistic Periods," *RB* 117 (2010): 44.
109. Schniedewind, *Social History*, 144–60, quote on 148.
110. Finkelstein, "Demography," 46.
111. Joachim Braun, *Music in Ancient Israel/Palestine: Archaeological, Written, and Comparative Sources* (Grand Rapids, MI: Eerdmans, 2002), 32–35.
112. On the impact of Hellenism on late biblical literature, see Erich S. Gruen, *Heritage and Hellenism: The Reinvention of Jewish Tradition* (Berkeley: University of California Press, 1998).
113. It is difficult to date any particular prose text to the tenth century, but the possibility cannot be precluded. Monumental Northwest Semitic inscriptions from the ninth century BCE (Mesha stele, Tel Dan stele) and Hebrew literary texts from the end of the ninth century (the plaster inscriptions at Kuntillet 'Ajrud) indicate that social and scribal requirements for major literary production were in place by this time. See Matthieu Richelle, "Elusive Scrolls: Could Any Hebrew Literature Be Written Prior to the Eighth Century B.C.E.?" *VT* 66 (2016): 556–94.
114. See David Talshir, "The Habitat and History of Hebrew during the Second Temple Period," in *Biblical Hebrew: Studies in Chronology and Typology*, ed. Ian Young (London: T&T Clark, 2003), 251–75; Talshir rightly emphasizes the era of the Second Return (mid-fifth century), with the influx of native Aramaic speakers, as crucial in this linguistic transition.
115. Whewell, *Novum*, 91.
116. Gabriel Barkay, Marilyn J. Lundberg, Andrew G. Vaughn, and Bruce Zuckerman, "The Amulets from Ketef Hinnom: A New Edition and Evaluation," *BASOR* 334 (2004): 41–71; see also Aḥituv, *Echoes from the Past*, 49–55; F. W. Dobbs-Allsopp, J. J. M. Roberts, C. L. Seow, and Richard E. Whitaker, *Hebrew Inscriptions: Texts from the Biblical Period of the Monarchy with Concordance* (New Haven, CT: Yale University Press, 2005), 263–75; and Jeremy D. Smoak, *The Priestly Blessing in Inscription and Scripture: The Early History of Numbers 6:24–26* (New York: Oxford University Press, 2016), 12–42.
117. This point is stressed in Barkay et al., "Amulets," 68.
118. See John Rogerson and Philip R. Davies, "Was the Siloam Tunnel Built by Hezekiah?" *BA* 59 (1996), 146. For a rebuttal of the late dating of the amulets on paleographical and archaeological grounds, see Barkay et al., "Amulets," 43–55. See also Nadav Na'aman, "A New Appraisal of the Silver Amulets from Ketef Hinnom," *IEJ* 61 (2011): 184–95, who dates the amulets to the late sixth or early fifth century BCE; and the rebuttal by Shmuel Aḥituv, "A Rejoinder to Nadav Na'aman's 'A New Appraisal of the Silver Amulets from Ketef Hinnom,'" *IEJ* 62 (2012): 223–32.
119. See chapter 7, and Davies, "Biblical Hebrew," 156: "Could CBH survive in Persian and Hellenistic Judah as a literary language? The crucial question is not

whether it *did*, but whether it *could have*." But this is precisely *not* the crucial question, as it elevates possibility above the standards of probability, evidential warrant, and consilience.

120. See, e.g., Andrew Teeter, *Scribal Laws: Exegetical Variation in the Textual Transmission of Biblical Law in the Late Second Temple Period*, FAT 92 (Tübingen: Mohr Siebeck, 2014).
121. Shimon Gesundheit, "Introduction: The Strengths and Weaknesses of Linguistic Dating," in Gertz et al., *Formation of the Pentateuch*, 299, quoting Eleanor Dickey, *Ancient Greek Scholarship* (New York: Oxford University Press, 2007), 9.
122. See further the extensive refutation of the parallel from Atticistic Greek by Frank H. Polak, "Storytelling and Redaction: Varieties of Language Usage in the Exodus Narrative," in Gertz et al., *Formation of the Pentateuch*, 449–54.
123. Jorge Luis Borges, "Pierre Menard, Author of the *Quixote*," in *Collected Fictions* (New York: Penguin, 1998), 88–95.
124. See *supra* note 4.
125. Lipton, *Inference*, 56.

Appendix 1. Historical Linguistics and the Books of the Hebrew Bible

1. The two volumes of Young and Rezetko, *Linguistic Dating*, contain much information, but because the authors reject all relevance of language to dating issues, they are unable to give an idea of what is more or less plausible. In their view, the Hebrew of Daniel can be assigned to a late date with no more assurance than that of Ruth or Jonah, or indeed Genesis or Judges. See appendix 2.
2. Samuel R. Driver, *Introduction to the Literature of the Old Testament*, 6th ed. (New York: Scribner's, 1897).
3. Richard M. Wright, *Linguistic Evidence for the Pre-Exilic Date of the Yahwistic Source*, LHBOTS 419 (London: T&T Clark, 2005).
4. Christoph Levin, review of *Linguistic Evidence for the Pre-Exilic Date of the Yahwistic Source*, by Richard M. Wright, *RBL* 1 (2006): http://www.bookreviews.org.
5. Driver, *Introduction*, 455.

Appendix 2. A Critique of the Revisionist Model

1. Young and Rezetko, *Linguistic Dating*; Robert Rezetko and Ian Young, *Historical Linguistics and Biblical Hebrew: Steps toward an Integrated Approach*, ANEM 9 (Atlanta: SBL Press, 2014).
2. Rezetko and Young, *Historical Linguistics*, 2.
3. Ibid.
4. Ibid., 242.

5. See Jan Joosten, review of *Linguistic Dating of Biblical Texts*, by Ian Young, Robert Rezetko, and Martin Ehrensvärd, *Babel und Bibel* 6 (2012): 535–42.
6. Young and Rezetko (*Linguistic Dating*, e.g., 1:59, 1:104, 2:85) refer to the conventional approach as the "chronological model," indicating that theirs is a nonchronological model.
7. See ibid., 1:24–31, and Hurvitz, *Lexicon*, 165–70. This historical development was noted by Gesenius (*Geschichte*, 29). The form *malkūt* is historically Aramaic (the construct of the abstract noun *malkū*), attested already in Old Aramaic (Sefire A.1.25, eighth century BCE).
8. B. Elan Dresher, "Methodological Issues in the Dating of Linguistic Forms: Considerations from the Perspective of Contemporary Linguistic Theory," in *Diachrony in Biblical Hebrew*, ed. Cynthia L. Miller-Naudé and Ziony Zevit (Winona Lake, IN: Eisenbrauns, 2012), 19.
9. Young and Rezetko, *Linguistic Dating*, 1.130 and *passim*.
10. Ibid., 1.104 and *passim*.
11. Ibid., 1.309.
12. Ibid., 1.304: "The answer to the question whether there are any Persian loanwords in EBH texts can, on the basis of Deut 33:2 alone, be answered with an unequivocal 'yes.'"
13. Num 24:7; 1 Sam 20:31; 1 Kgs 2:12; Jer 10:7; 49:34; 52:31.
14. Ibid., 1.86.
15. See chapter 4.
16. Steiner, "דָּת and עֵין: Two Verbs," 693–717. This reading has been adopted by Richard D. Nelson, *Deuteronomy: A Commentary*, OTL (Louisville, KY: Westminster John Knox, 2002), 383; and Theodore J. Lewis, "Divine Fire in Deuteronomy 33:2," *JBL* 132 (2013): 791–803.
17. Gary A. Rendsburg, "Linguistic Variation and the 'Foreign' Factor in the Hebrew Bible," in *Language and Culture in the Near East*, ed. Shlomo Izre'el and Rina Drory, IOS 15 (Leiden: Brill, 1995), 183–84; Rezetko and Young acknowledge this proposal (*Historical Linguistics*, 344).
18. Jer 10:4 and 49:34 are lacking in the LXX, indicating that they belong to the book's later edition; and Jer 52:31 is a doublet of 2 Kgs 25:27, which reads מָלְכוֹ ("his reign"), probably the earlier reading.
19. Young and Rezetko, *Linguistic Dating*, 1:104.
20. Avi Hurvitz, *The Transition Period in Biblical Hebrew: A Study in Post-Exilic Hebrew and its Implications for the Dating of Psalms* (Jerusalem: Bialik, 1972), 67–69 (Hebrew); and recently, Hurvitz, *Lexicon*, 10–11.
21. Robert D. Holmstedt, "Historical Linguistics and Biblical Hebrew," in *Diachrony in Biblical Hebrew*, ed. Cynthia L. Miller-Naudé and Ziony Zevit (Winona Lake, IN: Eisenbrauns, 2012), 98.
22. Mark Hale, *Historical Linguistics: Theory and Method* (Oxford: Blackwell, 2007), 25.

23. Ibid., 23. Hale aptly describes the critical dialectic of this procedure: "A comprehensive philological assessment of a text . . . moves back and forth . . . with additional linguistic evidence informing subsequent philological analysis, and new philological insights informing the relevant linguistic analysis" (23n6).
24. Rezetko and Young, *Historical Linguistics*, 210.
25. Ibid., 242.
26. Ibid., 114, 169 (repeated verbatim).
27. Ibid., 78.
28. Ibid., 143.
29. Ibid., 60.
30. Ibid., 466.
31. See further, Hendel, *Steps*, 127–47.
32. Young and Rezetko, *Linguistic Dating*, 1:56.
33. Ibid., 1:57.
34. Ibid., 1:199.
35. From Rezetko and Young, *Historical Linguistics*, 343. Reprinted with permission (with our thanks to Robert Rezetko).
36. Ibid., 344.
37. Ibid., 346.
38. Ibid., 599.
39. In a footnote they cite Nadav Na'aman's reading of Ḥorvat 'Uza ostracon no. 5 (7th cent. BCE), which, in their words, "attests מלכות in line 8. This could be interpreted to suggest that מלכות was more prominent in First Temple period Hebrew than the biblical writings conventionally dated to that period lead us to believe" (ibid., 349n50). However, Na'aman's proposed reading is מלכת?, which is obviously tentative; see Nadav Na'aman, "A New Look at Epigraphic Finds from Ḥorvat 'Uza," *TA* 39 (2012): 89–90. More important, the photograph does not bear out Na'aman's proposed reading. As Itzhak Beit-Arieh comments in his editio princeps, "Of this line only one letter, a *mem*, has survived"; see Itzhak Beit-Arieh, *Ḥorvat 'Uza and Ḥorvat Radum: Two Fortresses in the Biblical Negev* (Tel Aviv: Institute of Archaeology, 2007), 132. Our examination of the digital photograph clearly supports Beit-Arieh's reading (seconded by Ada Yardeni's drawing) of מ alone. Our thanks to Bruce Zuckerman and the West Semitic Research Project for making the digital photograph available to us.
40. Dresher, "Methodological Issues," 26.
41. Ibid.
42. Ibid.
43. Ian Young, "Ancient Hebrew without Authors," *JSem* 25 (2016): 999, referring to the fuller treatment in Rezetko and Young, *Historical Linguistics*, 393–94.
44. Ibid.
45. See chapter 5.

Bibliography

Ackerman, Susan. "Asherah, the West Semitic Goddess of Spinning and Weaving?" *JNES* 67 (2008): 1–29.

Aharoni, Yohanan. *The Land of the Bible: A Historical Geography.* Translated and edited by Anson F. Rainey. 2nd ed. Philadelphia: Westminster, 1979.

Aḥituv, Shmuel. *Echoes from the Past: Hebrew and Cognate Inscriptions from the Biblical Period.* Translated by Anson F. Rainey. Jerusalem: Carta, 2008.

———. "A Rejoinder to Nadav Na'aman's 'A New Appraisal of the Silver Amulets from Ketef Hinnom.'" *IEJ* 62 (2012): 223–32.

Aḥituv, Shmuel, and Ada Yardeni. "Silver, Pistachio and Wheat: Two Letters of the Seventh-Sixth Centuries BCE." Pages 15–28 in *Zaphenath-Paneah: Linguistic Studies Presented to Elisha Qimron on the Occasion of his Sixty-Fifth Birthday*. Edited by Daniel Sivan, David Talshir, and Chaim Cohen. Beer Sheva: Ben Gurion University Press, 2009.

Aḥituv, Shmuel, W. Randall Garr, and Steven E. Fassberg. "Epigraphic Hebrew." Pages 55–68 in *A Handbook of Biblical Hebrew*. Edited by Steven E. Fassberg and W. Randall Garr. Winona Lake, IN: Eisenbrauns, 2016.

Alram, Michael. "The Coinage of the Persian Empire." Pages 61–87 in *The Oxford Handbook of Greek and Roman Coinage.* Edited by William E. Metcalf. New York: Oxford University Press, 2012.

Avigad, Nahman. "Two Hebrew 'Fiscal' Bullae." *IEJ* 40 (1990): 262–65.

Baden, Joel S. *The Composition of the Pentateuch: Renewing the Documentary Hypothesis*. ABRL. New Haven, CT: Yale University Press, 2012.

Barbour, Jenny. *The Story of Israel in the Book of Qohelet: Ecclesiastes as Cultural Memory*. Oxford: Oxford University Press, 2012.

Barkay, Gabriel, Marilyn J. Lundberg, Andrew G. Vaughn, and Bruce Zuckerman. "The Amulets from Ketef Hinnom: A New Edition and Evaluation." *BASOR* 334 (2004): 41–71.

Barr, James. "Hebrew, Aramaic, and Greek in the Hellenistic Age." Pages 79–114 in *The Cambridge History of Judaism*. Edited by W. D. Davies and Louis Finkelstein. Cambridge: Cambridge University Press, 1990.

Barthélemy, Dominique. *Critique textuelle de l'Ancien Testament*. Vol. 1: *Josué, Juges, Ruth, Samuel, Rois, Chroniques, Esdras, Néhemie, Esther*. OBO

50, no. 1. Fribourg: Éditions Universitaires; Göttingen: Vandenhoeck & Ruprecht, 1982.

———. *Critique textuelle de l'Ancien Testament.* Vol. 2: *Isaïe, Jérémie, Lamentations.* OBO 50, no. 2. Fribourg: Éditions Universitaires; Göttingen: Vandenhoeck & Ruprecht, 1986.

Bauer, Hans, and Pontus Leander. *Historische Grammatik der hebräischen Sprache des Alten Testaments.* Halle: Niemeyer, 1922. Reprint, Hildesheim: Olms, 1962.

Becking, Bob. "The Identity of Nabu-sharrussu-ukin, the Chamberlain: An Epigraphic Note on Jeremiah 39,3, with an Appendix on the Nebusarsekim Tablet." *BN* 140 (2009): 35–46.

Beaulieu, Paul-Alain. "Arameans, Chaldeans, and Arabs in Cuneiform Sources from the Late Babylonian Period." Pages 31–55 in *Aramaeans, Chaldaeans, and Arabs in Babylonia and Palestine in the First Millennium B.C.* Edited by Angelika Berlejung and Michael P. Streck. Wiesbaden: Harrassowitz, 2013.

Beit-Arieh, Itzhak. *Ḥorvat 'Uza and Ḥorvat Radum: Two Fortresses in the Biblical Negev.* Tel Aviv: Institute of Archaeology, 2007.

Bekins, Peter. "The Difficulty with Diagnosing *Lamed Objecti.*" *JNSL* 42, no. 2 (2016): 1–22.

Ben-Ḥayyim, Ze'ev. *A Grammar of Samaritan Hebrew.* Jerusalem: Magnes Press, 2000.

———. *The Literary and Oral Tradition of Hebrew and Aramaic amongst the Samaritans.* Vol. 4: *The Words of the Pentateuch* [Hebrew]. Jerusalem: Academy of the Hebrew Language, 1977.

Berg, Sandra B. *The Book of Esther: Motifs, Themes and Structure.* Missoula, MT: Scholars Press, 1979.

Black, Jeremy, and Anthony Green. *Gods, Demons and Symbols of Ancient Mesopotamia: An Illustrated Dictionary.* London: British Museum; Austin: University of Texas Press, 1992.

Bloch, Alfred. *Vers und Sprache im Altarabischen.* Basel: Verlag für Recht und Gesellschaft, 1946.

Bloch, Marc. *The Historian's Craft.* Translated by Peter Putnam. New York: Vintage, 1953.

Bloch, Yigal. "On Some Alleged Developments of the Proto-Semitic Phoneme /ṯ/ in Iron Age Canaanite Dialects." *JSS* 53 (2008): 1–28.

Blum, Erhard. "The Linguistic Dating of Biblical Texts: An Approach with Methodological Limitations." Pages 303–25 in *The Formation of the Pentateuch: Bridging the Academic Cultures of Europe, Israel, and North America.* Edited by Jan C. Gertz, Bernard M. Levinson, Dalit Rom-Shiloni, and Konrad Schmid. FAT 111. Tübingen: Mohr Siebeck, 2016.

Bodi, Daniel. *The Book of Ezekiel and the Poem of Erra.* OBO 104. Fribourg: Universitätsverlag; Gottingen: Vandenhoeck & Ruprecht, 1991.

Borges, Jorge Luis. "Pierre Menard, Author of the *Quixote.*" Pages 88–95 in *Collected Fictions.* Translated by Andrew Hurley. New York: Penguin, 1998.

Bosker, Hans R. "Sibilant Consonants." Pages 557–61 in vol. 3 of *Encyclopedia of Hebrew Language and Linguistics*. Edited by Geoffrey Khan. 4 vols. Leiden: Brill, 2013.

Braun, Joachim. *Music in Ancient Israel/Palestine: Archaeological, Written, and Comparative Sources*. Grand Rapids, MI: Eerdmans, 2002.

Bridge, Edward J. "Female Slave vs. Female Slave: אָמָה and שִׁפְחָה in the Hebrew Bible." *JHS* 12 (2012): https://doi.org/5508/jhs.2012.v12.a2.

Burckhardt, Jacob. *The Greeks and Greek Civilization*. Edited by Oswyn Murray. Translated by Sheila Stern. New York: St. Martin's, 1998.

Burke, Peter. *What Is Cultural History?* 2nd ed. Cambridge: Polity, 2008.

Burstein, Stanley M. *The Babyloniaca of Berossos*. Malibu, CA: Undena, 1978.

Campbell, Lyle. *Historical Linguistics: An Introduction*. 2nd ed. Cambridge, MA: MIT Press, 2004.

Carmignac, Jean. "Précisions apportées au vocabulaire de l'Hébreu biblique par la guerre des fils de lumière contre les fils de ténèbres." *VT* 5 (1955): 345–65.

Carr, David M. *The Formation of the Hebrew Bible: A New Reconstruction*. New York: Oxford University Press, 2011.

Carter, Charles E. *The Emergence of Yehud in the Persian Period: A Social and Demographic Study*. Sheffield: Sheffield Academic Press, 1999.

Cogan, Mordechai, and Hayim Tadmor. *II Kings*. AB 11. New York: Doubleday, 1988.

Collingwood, R. G. *The Idea of History*. Revised ed. Oxford: Oxford University Press, 1994.

Cook, John A. "Detecting Development in Biblical Hebrew Using Diachronic Typology." Pages 83–95 in *Diachrony in Biblical Hebrew*. Edited by Cynthia L. Miller-Naudé and Ziony Zevit. Winona Lake, IN: Eisenbrauns, 2012.

Cooke, George A. *A Text-Book of North-Semitic Inscriptions: Moabite, Hebrew, Phoenician, Aramaic, Nabataean, Palmyrene, Jewish*. Oxford: Clarendon, 1903.

Corwin, Rebecca. *The Verb and the Sentence in Chronicles, Ezra and Nehemiah*. Borna: Noske, 1909.

Cross, Frank M. "Inscriptions in Phoenician and Other Scripts." Pages 333–72 in *Ashkelon I: Introduction and Overview (1985–2006)*. Edited by Lawrence E. Stager, J. David Schloen, and Daniel M. Master. Winona Lake, IN: Eisenbrauns, 2008.

Crouch, Carly L. *Israel and the Assyrians: Deuteronomy, the Succession Treaty of Esarhadon, and the Nature of Subversion*. ANEM 8. Atlanta: SBL Press, 2014.

Davies, Graham I. *Ancient Hebrew Inscriptions. Corpus and Concordance*. 2 vols. Cambridge: Cambridge University Press, 1991–2004.

Davies, Philip R. "Biblical Hebrew and the History of Ancient Judah: Typology, Chronology and Common Sense." Pages 150–63 in *Biblical Hebrew: Studies in Chronology and Typology*. Edited by Ian Young. JSOTSup 369. London: T&T Clark, 2003.

———. *In Search of "Ancient Israel."* JSOTSup 148. Sheffield: JSOT Press, 1992.

Dijkstra, Meindert. "'He Pours the Sweet Wine Off, Only the Dregs Are for the Wicked': An Epigraphic Note on *Mizzæh* in Psalm 75, 9." *ZAW* 107 (1995): 296–300.

Dion, Paul E. "Deuteronomy 13: The Suppression of Alien Religious Propaganda in Israel during the Late Monarchical Era." Pages 147–216 in *Law and Ideology in Monarchic Israel*. Edited by Baruch Halpern and Deborah W. Hobson. JSOTSup 124. Sheffield: JSOT Press, 1991.

Dobbs-Allsopp, F. W. "Late Linguistic Features in the Song of Songs." Pages 27–77 in *Perspectives on the Song of Songs / Perspektiven der Hoheliedauslegung*. Edited by Anselm C. Hagedorn. BZAW 346. Berlin: de Gruyter, 2005.

———. "Linguistic Evidence for the Date of Lamentations." *JANESCU* 26 (1998): 1–36.

Dobbs-Allsopp, F. W., J. J. M. Roberts, C. L. Seow, and R. E. Whitaker. *Hebrew Inscriptions: Texts from the Biblical Period of the Monarchy with Concordance*. New Haven, CT: Yale University Press, 2005.

Dresher, B. Elan. "Methodological Issues in the Dating of Linguistic Forms: Considerations from the Perspective of Contemporary Linguistic Theory." Pages 19–38 in *Diachrony in Biblical Hebrew*. Edited by Cynthia L. Miller-Naudé and Ziony Zevit. Winona Lake, IN: Eisenbrauns, 2012.

Driver, Samuel R. *Deuteronomy*. ICC. Edinburgh: T&T Clark, 1895.

———. *Introduction to the Literature of the Old Testament*. 6th ed. New York: Scribner's, 1897.

———. *Notes on the Hebrew Text of the Books of Samuel*. Oxford: Clarendon, 1890.

———. "On Some Alleged Affinities of the Elohist." *Journal of Philology* 11 (1882): 201–36.

Dykehouse, Jason C. "An Historical Reconstruction of Edomite Treaty Betrayal in the Sixth Century B.C.E. Based on Biblical, Epigraphic, and Archaeological Data." PhD diss., Baylor University, 2008.

Ehrensvärd, Martin. "Once Again: The Problem of Dating Biblical Hebrew." *SJOT* 11 (1997): 29–40.

Emerton, John A. "Some Comments on the Shibboleth Incident (Judges XII 6)." Pages 149–57 in *Mélanges bibliques et orientaux en l'honneur de M. Mathias Delcor*. Edited by André Caquot, Simon Légasse, and Michel Tardieu. AOAT 215. Neukirchen-Vluyn: Neukirchener, 1985.

Eshel, Esther. "A Late Iron Age Ostracon Featuring the Term לערכך." *IEJ* 53 (2003): 151–63.

Eskhult, Mats. "The Importance of Loanwords for Dating Biblical Hebrew Texts." Pages 8–23 in *Biblical Hebrew: Studies in Chronology and Typology*. Edited by Ian Young. JSOTSup 369. London: T&T Clark, 2003.

———. *Studies in Verbal Aspect and Narrative Technique in Biblical Hebrew Prose*. Uppsala: Almqvist & Wiksell, 1990.

———. "Verbal Syntax in Late Biblical Hebrew." Pages 84–93 in *Diggers at the Well: Proceedings of a Third International Symposium on the Hebrew of the Dead Sea*

Scrolls and Ben Sira. Edited by Takamitsu Muraoka and John F. Elwolde. Leiden: Brill, 2000.

Fassberg, Steven E. "The Lengthened Imperative קָטְלָה in Biblical Hebrew." *HS* 40 (1999): 7–13.

———. "The Movement from *Qal* to *Pi'el* in Hebrew and the Disappearance of the *Qal* Internal Passive." *HS* 42 (2001): 243–55.

———. *Studies in Biblical Syntax* [Hebrew]. Jerusalem: Magnes, 1994.

Faust, Avraham. "The Bible, Archaeology, and the Practice of Circumcision in Israelite and Philistine Societies." *JBL* 134 (2015): 273–90.

———. *Judah in the Neo-Babylonian Period: The Archaeology of Desolation*. Atlanta: Society of Biblical Literature, 2012.

Finkelstein, Israel. "The Philistine Countryside." *IEJ* 46 (1996): 225–42.

———. "The Philistines in the Bible: A Late-Monarchic Perspective." *JSOT* 27 (2002): 131–67.

———. "The Territorial Extent and Demography of Yehud/Judea in the Persian and Early Hellenistic Periods." *RB* 117 (2010): 39–54.

Fox, Michael V. *The Song of Songs and the Ancient Egyptian Love Songs*. Madison: University of Wisconsin Press, 1985.

Frankel, Zecharias. *Über den Einfluss der palästinensischen Exegese auf die alexandrinische Hermeneutik*. Leipzig: Barth, 1851.

Frankena, Rintje. "The Vassal-Treaties of Esarhaddon and the Dating of Deuteronomy." *OtSt* 14 (1965), 122–54.

Garr, W. Randall. *Dialect Geography of Syria-Palestine, 1000–586 B.C.E.* Philadelphia: University of Pennsylvania Press, 1985.

Garr, W. Randall, and Steven E. Fassberg, eds. *A Handbook of Biblical Hebrew*. 2 vols. Winona Lake, IN: Eisenbrauns, 2016.

Geertz, Clifford. "Thick Description: Toward an Interpretive Theory of Culture." Pages 3–30 in *The Interpretation of Cultures: Selected Essays*. New York: Basic Books, 1973.

Gesenius, Wilhelm. *Geschichte der hebräischen Sprache und Schrift*. Leipzig: Vogel, 1815.

Gesundheit, Shimon. "Introduction: The Strengths and Weaknesses of Linguistic Dating." Pages 295–302 in *The Formation of the Pentateuch: Bridging the Academic Cultures of Europe, Israel, and North America*. Edited by Jan C. Gertz, Bernard M. Levinson, Dalit Rom-Shiloni, and Konrad Schmid. FAT 111. Tübingen: Mohr Siebeck, 2016.

Ginsberg, H. L. "Behind the *Masoret*." *Tarbiz* 5 (1934–35): 208–23 (Hebrew).

———. "The Oldest Interpretation of the Suffering Servant." *VT* 3 (1953): 400–404.

———. "Studies on the Biblical Hebrew Verb: Masoretically Misconstrued Internal Passives." *AJSL* 46 (1929): 53–56.

Gitler, Haim, and Oren Tal, *The Coinage of Philistia of the Fifth and Fourth Centuries BC: A Study of the Earliest Coins of Palestine*. Milan: Ennere, 2006.

Giusfredi, Federico. "The Problem of the Luwian Title *Tarwanis*." *Altorientalische Forschungen* 36 (2009): 140–45.

Gogel, Sandra Landis. *A Grammar of Epigraphic Hebrew*. RBS 23. Atlanta: Scholars Press, 1998.

Goodman, Nelson. *Fact, Fiction, and Forecast*. Cambridge, MA: Harvard University Press, 1983.

Gould, Stephen J. *Wonderful Life: The Burgess Shale and the Nature of History*. New York: Norton, 1989.

Grayson, Alan K. *Assyrian Rulers of the Early First Millennium BC: II (858–754 BC)*. Toronto: University of Toronto Press, 1996.

Grayson, Alan K., and Jamie Novotny. *The Royal Inscriptions of Sennacherib, King of Assyria (704–681 BC), Part 1*. Winona Lake, IN: Eisenbrauns, 2012.

Greenberg, Moshe. "The Hebrew Oath Particle *ḥay/ḥē*." *JBL* 76 (1957): 34–39.

Greenfield, Jonas. "Aramaic Studies and the Bible." Pages 110–30 in *Congress Volume Vienna 1980*. Edited by John Emerton. VTSup 32. Leiden: Brill, 1980.

Grotius, Hugo. *Annotata ad Vetus Testamentum*. 3 vols. Paris: Cramoisy, 1644.

Gruen, Erich S. *Heritage and Hellenism: The Reinvention of Jewish Tradition*. Berkeley: University of California, 1998.

Guenther, A. R. "A Diachronic Study of Biblical Hebrew Prose Syntax: An Analysis of the Verbal Clause in Jeremiah 37–45 and Esther 1–10." PhD diss., University of Toronto, 1977.

Gunther, K. "אֲנִי." Pages 162–66 in *TLOT*.

Hale, Mark. *Historical Linguistics: Theory and Method*. Oxford: Blackwell, 2007.

Halpern, Baruch. "Erasing History: The Minimalist Assault on Ancient Israel." Pages 415–26 in *Israel's Past in Present Research: Essays on Ancient Israelite Historiography*. Edited by V. Philips Long. Winona Lake, IN: Eisenbrauns, 1999.

Hamilton, Gordon J. "Paleo-Hebrew Texts and Scripts of the Persian Period." Pages 253–90 in *"An Eye for Form": Epigraphic Essays in Honor of Frank Moore Cross*. Edited by Jo Ann Hackett and Walter E. Aufrecht. Winona Lake, IN: Eisenbrauns, 2014.

Haran, Menahem. "The Books of the Chronicles 'Of the Kings of Judah' and 'Of the Kings of Israel': What Sort of Books Were They?" *VT* 49 (1999): 156–64.

Harrington, Hannah K. "The Use of Leviticus in Ezra-Nehemiah." *JHS* 13 (2013): https://doi.org/10.5508/jhs.2013.v13.a3.

Hays, Christopher B. "The Date and Message of Isaiah 24–27 in Light of Hebrew Diachrony." Pages 7–24 in *Intertextuality and Formation of Isaiah 24–27: Ancient Israel and Its Literature*. Edited by J. Todd Hibbard and Paul Kim. AIL 17. Atlanta: Society of Biblical Literature, 2013.

Hendel, Ronald. "'Begetting' and 'Being Born' in the Pentateuch: Notes on Historical Linguistics and Source Criticism." *VT* 50 (2000): 38–46.

———. "Genesis 1–11 and Its Mesopotamian Problem." Pages 23–36 in *Cultural Borrowings and Ethnic Appropriations in Antiquity*. Edited by Erich S. Gruen. Stuttgart: Steiner, 2005.

———. *Remembering Abraham: Culture, Memory, and History in the Hebrew Bible.* New York: Oxford University Press, 2005.

———. "Sibilants and *šibbōlet* (Judges 12:6)." *BASOR* 301 (1996): 69–75.

———. *Steps to a New Edition of the Hebrew Bible.* TCS 10. Atlanta: SBL Press, 2016.

Hillers, Delbert. "Dust: Some Aspects of Old Testament Imagery." Pages 105–9 in *Love and Death in the Ancient Near East: Essays in Honor of Marvin H. Pope.* Edited by John H. Marks and Robert M. Good. Guilford, CT: Four Quarters, 1987.

Hoftijzer, Jacob, and Karel Jongeling. *Dictionary of the North-West Semitic Inscriptions.* HdO 1, no. 21. 2 vols. Leiden: Brill, 1995.

Holmstedt, Robert D. "Historical Linguistics and Biblical Hebrew." Pages 97–124 in *Diachrony in Biblical Hebrew.* Edited by Cynthia L. Miller-Naudé and Ziony Zevit. Winona Lake, IN: Eisenbrauns, 2012.

———. *The Relative Clause in Biblical Hebrew.* Winona Lake, IN: Eisenbrauns, 2016.

———. *Ruth: A Handbook on the Hebrew Text.* Waco, TX: Baylor University Press, 2010.

Hornkohl, Aaron. *Ancient Hebrew Periodization and the Language of the Book of Jeremiah: The Case for a Sixth-Century Date of Composition.* SSLL 74. Leiden: Brill, 2013.

Horowitz, Wayne. *Mesopotamian Cosmic Geography.* Winona Lake, IN: Eisenbrauns, 1998.

Housman, A. E. "The Application of Thought to Textual Criticism." Pages 131–50 in *Selected Prose.* Edited by John Carter. Cambridge: Cambridge University Press, 1961.

Huehnergard, John. "On the Etymology of the Hebrew Relative *šɛ*." Pages 103–25 in *Biblical Hebrew in Its Northwest Semitic Setting: Typological and Historical Perspectives.* Edited by Steven E. Fassberg and Avi Hurvitz. Winona Lake, IN: Eisenbrauns, 2006.

———. *An Introduction to Ugaritic.* Peabody, MA: Hendrickson, 2012.

Hurowitz, Victor A. "In Search of Resen (Genesis 10:12): Dūr-Šarrukīn?" Pages 511–24 in *Birkat Shalom: Studies in the Bible, Ancient Near Eastern Literature, and Postbiblical Judaism Presented to Shalom M. Paul.* Edited by Chaim Cohen et al. Winona Lake, IN: Eisenbrauns, 2008.

Hurvitz, Avi. *A Concise Lexicon of Late Biblical Hebrew: Linguistic Innovations in the Writings of the Second Temple Period.* VTSup 160. Brill: Leiden, 2014.

———. "The Date of the Prose-Tale of Job Linguistically Reconsidered." *HTR* 67 (1974): 17–34.

———. "The Historical Quest for 'Ancient Israel' and the Linguistic Evidence of the Hebrew Bible." *VT* 47 (1997): 301–15.

———. *A Linguistic Study of the Relationship between the Priestly Source and the Book of Ezekiel.* CahRB 20. Paris: Gabalda, 1982.

———. "The Origins and Development of the Expression מְגִלַּת־סֵפֶר: A Study in the History of Writing-Related Terminology in Biblical Times" [Hebrew]. Pages 37*–46* in *Texts, Temples, and Traditions: A Tribute to Menahem Haran*. Edited by Michael V. Fox et al. Winona Lake, IN: Eisenbrauns, 1996.

———. *The Transition Period in Biblical Hebrew: A Study in Post-Exilic Hebrew and its Implications for the Dating of Psalms* [Hebrew]. Jerusalem: Bialik, 1972.

Jakobson, Roman. *On Language*. Edited by Linda R. Waugh and Monique Monville-Burston. Cambridge, MA: Harvard University Press, 1990.

Janzen, J. Gerald. *Studies in the Text of Jeremiah*. HSM 6. Cambridge, MA: Harvard University Press, 1973.

Jenni, Ernst. "Miszellen zu Einzeltexten: Jer 3,17 'nach Jerusalem': Ein Aramaismus." *ZAH* 1 (1988): 107–11.

Joosten, Jan. "Diachronic Aspects of Narrative *Wayhi* in Biblical Hebrew." *JNSL* 35 (2009): 43–61.

———. "Diachronic Linguistics and the Date of the Pentateuch." Pages 327–44 in *The Formation of the Pentateuch: Bridging the Academic Cultures of Europe, Israel, and North America*. Edited by Jan C. Gertz, Bernard M. Levinson, Dalit Rom-Shiloni, and Konrad Schmid. FAT 111. Tübingen: Mohr Siebeck, 2016.

———. "The Disappearance of Iterative WEQATAL in the Biblical Hebrew Verbal System." Pages 135–47 in *Biblical Hebrew in Its Northwest Semitic Setting: Typological and Historical Perspectives*. Edited by Steven E. Fassberg and Avi Hurvitz. Winona Lake, IN: Eisenbrauns, 2006.

———. "The Distinction between Classical and Late Biblical Hebrew as Reflected in Syntax." *HS* 46 (2005): 327–39.

———. "L'excédent massorétique du livre de Jérémie et l'hébreu post-classique." Pages 93–108 in *Conservatism and Innovation in the Hebrew Language of the Hellenistic Period: Proceedings of a Fourth International Symposium on the Hebrew of the Dead Sea Scrolls and Ben Sira*. Edited by Jan Joosten and Jean-Sébastien Rey. STDJ 73. Leiden: Brill, 2008.

———. "The Knowledge and Use of Hebrew in the Hellenistic Period: Qumran and the Septuagint." Pages 115–30 in *Diggers at the Well: Proceedings of a Third International Symposium on the Hebrew of the Dead Sea Scrolls and Ben Sira*. Edited by Takamitsu Muraoka and John F. Elwolde. Leiden, Brill, 2000.

———. "The Lengthened Imperative with Accusative Suffix in Biblical Hebrew." *ZAW* 111 (1999): 423–26.

———. "Linguistic Clues as to the Date of the Book of Job: A Mediating Position." Pages 347–57 in *Interested Readers: Essays on the Hebrew Bible in Honor of David J. A. Clines*. Edited by James K. Aitken, Jeremy M. S. Clines, and Christl M. Maier. Atlanta: Society of Biblical Literature, 2013.

———. "The Operation of a Syntactic Rule in Classical Biblical Hebrew and in Hebrew Inscriptions of the Monarchic Period." Pages 493–505 in *On Stone and Scroll: Essays in Honour of Graham Ivor Davies*. Edited by James K. Aitken, Katherine J. Dell, and Brian A. Mastin. BZAW 420. Berlin: de Gruyter, 2011.

———. "Pseudo-Classicisms in Late Biblical Hebrew, in Ben Sira, and in Qumran Hebrew." Pages 146–59 in *Sirach, Scrolls and Sages: Proceedings of a Second International Symposium on the Hebrew of the Dead Sea Scrolls, Ben Sira, and the Mishnah, held at Leiden University, 15–17 December 1997*. Edited by Takamitsu Muraoka and John F. Elwolde. Leiden: Brill, 1999.

———. "Pseudo-Classicisms in Late Biblical Hebrew." *ZAW* 128 (2016): 16–29.

———. Review of *Linguistic Dating of Biblical Texts*, by Ian Young and Robert Rezetko, with the assistance of Martin Ehrensvärd. *Babel und Bibel* 6 (2012): 535–42.

———. "Sectarian Terminology and Biblical Interpretation: The Meaning of the Verb אות in the Qumran Scrolls" [Hebrew]. *Meghillot* 1 (2003): 219–26.

———. "Textual Developments and Historical Linguistics." Pages 21–31 in *After Qumran: Old and Modern Editions of the Biblical Texts—The Historical Books*. Edited by Hans Ausloos, Bénédicte Lemmelijn, and Julio Trebolle Barrera. BETL 246. Leuven: Peeters 2012.

———. "The Tiberian Vocalization and the Edition of the Hebrew Bible Text." Pages 19–32 in *Making the Biblical Text: Textual Studies in the Hebrew and Greek Bible*. Edited by Innocent Himbaza. OBO 275. Fribourg: Academic Press; Göttingen: Vandenhoeck & Ruprecht, 2015.

———. *The Verbal System of Biblical Hebrew: A New Synthesis Elaborated on the Basis of Classical Prose*. JBS 10. Jerusalem: Simor, 2012.

———. "Wilhelm Gesenius and the History of Hebrew in the Biblical Period." Pages 94–106 in *Biblische Exegese und hebräische Lexikographie: Das "Hebräisch-deutsch Handwörterbuch" von Wilhelm Gesenius als Spiegel und Quelle alttestamentlicher und hebräischer Forschung, 200 Jahre nach seiner ersten Auflage*. Edited by Stefan Schorch and Ernst-Joachim Waschke. BZAW 427. Berlin: de Gruyter, 2013.

Jursa, Michael. "Nabû-šarrūssu-ūkin, *rab ša-rēši*, und 'Nebusarsekim' (Jer. 39:3)." *NABU* 5 (2008): 9–10.

Keel, Othmar. *Jahwe-Visionen und Siegelkunst: Eine neue Deutung der Majestätsschilderungen in Jes 6, Ez 1 und 10 und Sach 4*. SBS 84/85. Stuttgart: Katholisches Bibelwerk, 1977.

Kilchör, Benjamin. *Mosetora und Jahwetora: Das Verhältnis von Deuteronomium 12–26 zu Exodus, Levitikus und Numeri*. BZABR 21. Wiesbaden: Harrassowitz, 2015.

Kim, Dong-Hyuk. *Early Biblical Hebrew, Late Biblical Hebrew and Linguistic Variability: A Sociolinguistic Evaluation of the Linguistic Dating of Biblical Texts*. VTSup 156. Leiden: Brill, 2013.

Kirk, Geoffrey S., John E. Raven, and Malcolm Schofield, *The Presocratic Philosophers*. 2nd ed. Cambridge: Cambridge University Press, 1983.

Kister, Menahem. "Some Lexical Features of the Writings from Qumran" [Hebrew]. Pages 561–69 in vol. 2 of *The Qumran Scrolls and Their World*. Edited by Menahem Kister. 2 vols. Jerusalem: Izhak Ben-Zvi, 2009.

Knauf, Ernst Axel. "War 'Biblisch-Hebräisch' eine Sprache? Empirische Gesichtspunkte zur linguistischen Annäherung an die Sprache der althebräischen Literatur." *ZAH* 3 (1990): 11–23.

Knohl, Israel. *The Sanctuary of Silence: The Priestly Torah and the Holiness School.* Minneapolis: Fortress, 1995.

Knoppers, Gary N. *I Chronicles 10–29*. AB 12A. New York: Doubleday, 2004.

Kogan, Leonid. "Proto-Semitic Phonetics and Phonology." Pages 54–151 in *The Semitic Languages: An International Handbook*. Edited by Stefan Weninger. Berlin: de Gruyter, 2011.

Kooij, Arie van der. "The City of Babel and Assyrian Imperialism: Genesis 11:1–9 Interpreted in the Light of Mesopotamian Sources." Pages 1–17 in *Congress Volume: Leiden 2004*. Edited by André Lemaire. VTSup 109. Leiden: Brill, 2006.

Kratz, Reinhard G. *The Composition of the Narrative Books of the Old Testament.* Translated by John Bowden. London: T&T Clark, 2005.

Kropat, Arno. *Die Syntax des Autor der Chronik*. BZAW 16. Giessen: Töpelman, 1909.

Kutscher, Eduard Yechezkel. "Hebrew Language: The Dead Sea Scrolls." Columns 1583–90 in vol. 16 of *Encyclopedia Judaica*. Edited by Cecil Roth. Jerusalem: Keter, 1972.

———. *The Language and Linguistic Background of the Isaiah Scroll (1QIsa[a])*. Leiden: Brill, 1974.

Lambert, Wilfred G. *Babylonian Creation Myths*. Winona Lake, IN: Eisenbrauns, 2013.

Lauinger, Jacob. "Esarhaddon's Succession Treaty at Tell Tayinat: Text and Commentary." *JCS* 64 (2012): 87–123.

Layton, Scott C. *Archaic Features of Canaanite Personal Names in the Hebrew Bible.* HSS 47. Atlanta: Scholars Press, 1990.

Lehmann, Reinhard G. "Wilhelm Gesenius and the Rise of Phoenician Philology." Pages 209–66 in *Biblische Exegese und hebräische Lexikographie: Das "Hebräisch-deutsche Handwörterbuch" von Wilhelm Gesenius als Spiegel und Quelle alttestamentlicher und hebräischer Forschung, 200 Jahre nach seiner ersten Auflage.* Edited by Stefan Schorch and Ernst-Joachim Waschke. BZAW 427. Berlin: de Gruyter, 2013.

Leichty, Erle. *The Royal Inscriptions of Esarhaddon, King of Assyria (680–669 BC).* Winona Lake, IN: Eisenbrauns, 2011.

Lemche, Niels Peter. *The Israelites in History and Tradition*. LAI. Louisville, KY: Westminster John Knox, 1998.

Lemaire, André. "Edom and the Edomites." Pages 225–43 in *The Book of Kings: Sources, Composition, Historiography, and Reception*. Edited by André Lemaire and Baruch Halpern. VTSup 129. Leiden: Brill, 2010.

———. "A History of Northwest Semitic Epigraphy." Pages 5–29 in *"An Eye for Form": Epigraphic Essays in Honor of Frank Moore Cross*. Edited by Jo Ann Hackett and Walter E. Aufrecht. Winona Lake, IN: Eisenbrauns, 2014.

Leuchter, Mark. "The Sociolinguistic and Rhetorical Implications of the Source Citations in Kings." Pages 119–34 in *Soundings in Kings: Perspectives and Methods in Contemporary Scholarship*. Edited by Mark Leuchter and Klaus-Peter Adam. Minneapolis: Fortress, 2010.

Levin, Christoph. Review of *Linguistic Evidence for the Pre-Exilic Date of the Yahwistic Source*, by Richard M. Wright, *RBL* 1 (2006): http://www.bookreviews.org.

Levinson, Bernard M. "Esarhaddon's Succession Treaty as the Source for the Canon Formula in Deuteronomy 13:1." *JAOS* 130 (2010): 337–47.

Levinson, Bernard M., and Jeffrey Stackert. "Between the Covenant Code and Esarhaddon's Succession Treaty: Deuteronomy 13 and the Composition of Deuteronomy." *JSJ* 3 (2012): 123–40.

Lewis, Theodore J. "Divine Fire in Deuteronomy 33:2." *JBL* 132 (2013): 791–803.

Lipschits, Oded. *The Fall and Rise of Jerusalem: Judah under Babylonian Rule*. Winona Lake, IN: Eisenbrauns, 2015.

Lipton, Peter. *Inference to the Best Explanation*. 2nd ed. London: Routledge, 2004.

Longacre, Drew. "Developmental Stage, Scribal Lapse, or Physical Defect? 1QIsa[a]'s Damaged Exemplar for Isaiah Chapters 34–66." *DSD* 20 (2013): 17–50.

Lust, Johan. "Major Divergences between LXX and MT in Ezekiel." Pages 83–92 in *The Earliest Text of the Hebrew Bible: The Relationship Between the Masoretic Text and the Hebrew Base of the Septuagint Reconsidered*. Edited by Adrian Schenker. SCS 52. Atlanta: Society of Biblical Literature, 2003.

Macdonald, John. "Some Distinctive Characteristics of Israelite Spoken Hebrew." *BO* 32 (1975): 162–75.

Mackie, Timothy P. *Expanding Ezekiel: The Hermeneutics of Scribal Addition in the Ancient Text Witnesses of the Book of Ezekiel*. Gottingen: Vandenhoeck & Ruprecht, 2015.

Maeir, Aren M. "Introduction, Overview and Synopsis of Results." Pages 1–83 in *Tell es-Safi/Gath I: The 1996–2005 Seasons*. Edited by Aren M. Maeir. Wiesbaden: Harrassowitz, 2012.

———. "The Historical Background and Dating of Amos VI 2: An Archaeological Perspective from Tell es-Safi/Gath." *VT* 54 (2004): 319–34.

Mankowski, Paul V. *Akkadian Loanwords in Hebrew*. HSS 47. Winona Lake, IN: Eisenbrauns, 2000.

McCarthy, Carmel. *Deuteronomy*. BHQ. Stuttgart: Deutsche Bibelgesellschaft, 2007.

Millard, Alan R. "Israelite and Aramean History in the Light of Inscriptions." Pages 129–40 in *Israel's Past in Present Research: Essays on Ancient Israelite Historiography*. Edited by V. Philips Long. Winona Lake, IN: Eisenbrauns, 1999.

Mizrahi, Noam. "The Linguistic History of מדהבה: From Textual Corruption to Lexical Innovation." *RevQ* 26 (2013): 93–116.

———. "A Matter of Choice: A Sociolinguistic Perspective on the Contact between Hebrew and Aramaic, with Special Attention to Jeremiah 10." Pages 107–24 in *Discourse, Dialogue and Debate in the Bible Essays in Honour of Frank H. Polak*. Edited by Athalya Brenner-Idan. Sheffield: Phoenix Press, 2014.

Müller, Reinhard, Juha Pakkala, and Bas ter Haar Romeny. *Evidence of Editing: Growth and Change of Texts in the Hebrew Bible*. RBS 75. Atlanta: Society of Biblical Literature, 2014.

Muraoka, Takamitsu. "An Approach to the Morphosyntax and Syntax of Qumran Hebrew." Pages 193–214 in *Diggers at the Well: Proceedings of a Third International Symposium on the Hebrew of the Dead Sea Scrolls and Ben Sira*. Edited by Takamitsu Muraoka and John F. Elwolde. Leiden: Brill, 2000.

Na'aman, Nadav. "A New Appraisal of the Silver Amulets from Ketef Hinnom." *IEJ* 61 (2011): 184–95.

———. "A New Look at Epigraphic Finds from Ḥorvat 'Uza." *TA* 39 (2012): 84–101.

———. "The Temple Library of Jerusalem and the Composition of the Book of Kings." Pages 129–52 in *Congress Volume: Leiden 2004*. Edited by André Lemaire. VTSup 109. Leiden: Brill, 2006.

Naveh, Joseph. *Early History of the Alphabet*. Jerusalem: Magnes, 1997.

Nelson, Richard D. *Deuteronomy: A Commentary*. OTL. Louisville, KY: Westminster John Knox, 2002.

Noegel, Scott B., and Gary A. Rendsburg, *Solomon's Vineyard: Literary and Linguistic Studies in the Song of Songs*. AIL 1. Atlanta: Society of Biblical Literature, 2009.

Notarius, Tania. "The Archaic System of Verbal Tenses in 'Archaic' Biblical Poetry." Pages 193–207 in *Diachrony in Biblical Hebrew*. Edited by Cynthia. L. Miller-Naudé and Ziony Zevit. Winona Lake, IN: Eisenbrauns, 2012.

———. *The Verb in Archaic Biblical Poetry: A Discursive, Typological, and Historical Investigation of the Tense System*. SSLL 68. Leiden: Brill, 2013.

Pakkala, Juha. *God's Word Omitted: Omissions in the Transmission of the Hebrew Bible*. FRLANT 251. Göttingen: Vandenhoeck & Ruprecht, 2013.

Parpola, Simo, and Kazuko Watanabe. *Neo-Assyrian Treaties and Loyalty Oaths*. Helsinki: Helsinki University Press, 1988.

Pat-El, Na'ama. "Traces of Aramaic Dialectal Variation in Late Biblical Hebrew." *VT* 58 (2008): 650–55.

———. "Syntactic Aramaisms as a Tool for the Internal Chronology of Biblical Hebrew." Pages 245–63 in *Diachrony in Biblical Hebrew*. Edited by Cynthia. L. Miller-Naudé and Ziony Zevit. Winona Lake, IN: Eisenbrauns, 2012.

———. "Israelian Hebrew: A Re-Evaluation." *VT* 67 (2017): 227–63.

Pat-El, Na'ama, and Aren Wilson-Wright. "Features of Archaic Biblical Hebrew and the Linguistic Dating Debate." *HS* 54 (2013): 387–410.

———. "The Features of Canaanite: A Reevaluation." *ZDMG* 166 (2016): 41–55.

Paul, Shalom. "Signs of Late Hebrew in Isaiah 40–66." Pages 293–300 in *Diachrony in Biblical Hebrew*. Edited by Cynthia L. Miller-Naudé and Ziony Zevit. Winona Lake, IN: Eisenbrauns, 2012.

Pearce, Laurie E. "Continuity and Normality in Sources Relating to the Judean Exile." *HeBAI* 3 (2014): 163–84.

Pintori, Franco. “Seren, Tarwanis, Turannos.” Pages 285–322 in *Studi orientalistici in ricordo di Franco Pintore*. Edited by Onofrio Carruba, Mario Liverani, and Carlo Zaccagnini. Pavia: GJES Edizione, 1983.

Polak, Frank H. “On Prose and Poetry in the Book of Job.” *JANESCU* 24 (1996): 61–97.

———. “Sociolinguistics: A Key to the Typology and the Social Background of Biblical Hebrew.” *HS* 47 (2006): 115–62.

———. “Sociolinguistics and the Judean Speech Community in the Achaemenid Empire.” Pages 589–628 in *Judah and Judeans in the Persian Period*. Edited by Oded Lipschits and Manfred Oeming. Winona Lake, IN: Eisenbrauns, 2006.

———. “Storytelling and Redaction: Varieties of Language Usage in the Exodus Narrative.” Pages 443–75 in *The Formation of the Pentateuch. Bridging the Academic Cultures of Europe, Israel, and North America*. Edited by Jan C. Gertz, Bernard M. Levinson, Dalit Rom-Shiloni, and Konrad Schmid. FAT 111. Tübingen: Mohr Siebeck, 2016.

———. “Syntactic-Stylistic Aspects of the So-Called ‘Priestly’ Work in the Torah.” Pages 345–82 in *Le-ma‘an Ziony: Essays in Honor of Ziony Zevit*. Edited by Frederick E. Greenspahn and Gary A. Rendsburg. Eugene, OR: Wipf and Stock, 2017.

Polzin, Robert. *Late Biblical Hebrew: Toward an Historical Typology of Biblical Hebrew Prose*. HSM 12. Missoula, MT: Scholars Press, 1976.

Porter, Stanley E., ed. *The Language of the New Testament: Classic Essays*. JSNTSup 60. Sheffield: Academic Press, 1991.

Qimron, Elisha. *The Hebrew of the Dead Sea Scrolls*. HSS 29. Atlanta: Scholars Press, 1986.

Quick, Laura. *Deuteronomy 28 and the Aramaic Curse Tradition*. Oxford: Oxford University Press, 2017.

Rainey, Anson F. Review of *A Grammar of Epigraphic Hebrew*, by Sandra Landis Gogel. *JQR* 91 (2001): 419–27.

Rendsburg, Gary A. “A Comprehensive Guide to Israelian Hebrew: Grammar and Lexicon.” *Orient* 38 (2003): 5–35.

———. *Diglossia in Ancient Hebrew*. AOS 72. New Haven, CT: American Oriental Society, 1990).

———. “Late Biblical Hebrew and the Date of ‘P.’” *JANESCU* 12 (1980): 65–80.

———. “Late Biblical Hebrew and the Qumran Pesher Habakkuk.” Pages 132–59 in *Hebrew of the Late Second Temple Period: Proceedings of a Sixth International Symposium on the Hebrew of the Dead Sea Scrolls and Ben Sira*. Edited by Eibert Tigchelaar and Pierre Van Hecke. STDJ 114. Leiden, Brill, 2015.

———. “Late Biblical Hebrew in the Book of Haggai.” Pages 329–44 in *Language and Nature: Papers Presented to John Huehnergard on the Occasion of His 60th Birthday*. Edited by Rebecca Hasselbach and Na’ama Pat-El. Chicago: Oriental Institute, 2012.

———. "Linguistic Variation and the 'Foreign' Factor in the Hebrew Bible." Pages 177–90 in *Language and Culture in the Near East*. Edited by Shlomo Izre'el and Rina Drory. IOS 15. Leiden: Brill, 1995.

———. "Some False Leads in the Identification of Late Biblical Hebrew Texts: The Cases of Genesis 24 and 1 Samuel 2:27–36." *JBL* 121 (2002): 23–46.

———. "The Strata of Biblical Hebrew." *JNSL* 17 (1991): 81–99.

———. "Style Switching." Pages 633–36 in volume 3 of *Encyclopedia of Hebrew Language and Linguistics*. Edited by Geoffrey Khan. 4 vols. Leiden: Brill, 2013.

Renz, Johannes, and Wolfgang Röllig. *Handbuch der althebraïschen Epigraphik*. 3 vols. Darmstadt: Wissenschaftliche Buchgesellschaft, 1995.

Revell, E. John. "Conditional Sentences in Biblical Hebrew Prose." Pages 1278–90 in *Semitic Studies in Honor of Wolf Leslau*. Edited by Alan S. Kaye. Wiesbaden: Harrassowitz, 1991.

———. "The Two Forms of First Person Singular Pronoun in Biblical Hebrew: Redundancy or Expressive Contrast?" *JSS* 40 (1995): 199–217.

Reymond, Eric D. "The Passive *Qal* in the Hebrew of the Second Temple Period, Especially as Found in the Wisdom of Ben Sira." Pages 1110–27 in *Sibyls, Scriptures, and Scrolls: John Collins at Seventy*. Edited by Joel Baden, Hindy Najman, and Eibert Tigchelaar. Leiden: Brill, 2017.

Rezetko, Robert. "The Qumran Scrolls of the Book of Judges: Literary Formation, Textual Criticism, and Historical Linguistics." *JHS* 13 (2013): https://doi.org/10.5508/jhs.2013.a2.

Rezetko, Robert, and Ian Young. *Historical Linguistics and Biblical Hebrew: Steps toward an Integrated Approach*. ANEM 9. Atlanta: SBL Press, 2014.

Richelle, Matthieu. "Elusive Scrolls: Could Any Hebrew Literature Be Written Prior to the Eighth Century B.C.E.?" *VT* 66 (2016): 556–94.

Rofé, Alexander. "An Enquiry into the Betrothal of Rebekah." Pages 27–39 in *Die Hebräische Bibel und ihre zweifache Nachgeschichte: Festschrift für Rolf Rendtorff zum 65. Geburtstag*. Edited by Erhard Blum, Christian Macholz, and Ekkehard W. Stegemann. Neukirchen: Neukirchener Verlag, 1990.

———. *Introduction to the Literature of the Hebrew Bible*. JBS 9. Jerusalem: Simor, 2009.

———. "Not by Language Alone: The Dating of Biblical Sources." Pages 656–65 in *Houses Full of All Good Things: Essays in Memory of Timo Veijola*. Edited by Juha Pakkala and Martti Nissinen. Helsinki: Finnish Exegetical Society; Göttingen: Vandenhoeck & Ruprecht, 2008.

———. "Studying the Biblical Text in the Light of Historico-Literary Criticism: The Reproach of the Prophet in Judg 6:7–10 and 4QJudg[a]." Pages 111–23 in *The Dead Sea Scrolls in Context: Integrating the Dead Sea Scrolls in the Study of Ancient Texts, Languages, and Cultures*. Edited by Armin Lange, Emanuel Tov, and Matthias Weigold. VTSup 140. Leiden: Brill, 2011.

Rogerson, John, and Philip R. Davies. "Was the Siloam Tunnel Built by Hezekiah?" *BA* 59 (1996): 138–49.

Römer, Thomas. "How to Date Pentateuchal Texts: Some Case Studies." Pages 357–70 in *The Formation of the Pentateuch: Bridging the Academic Cultures of Europe, Israel, and North America*. Edited by Jan C. Gertz, Bernard M. Levinson, Dalit Rom-Shiloni, and Konrad Schmid. FAT 111. Tübingen: Mohr Siebeck, 2016.

Rooker, Mark. *Biblical Hebrew in Transition: The Language of the Book of Ezekiel*. JSOTSup 90. Sheffield: Academic Press, 1990.

Rosenthal, Franz. *A Grammar of Biblical Aramaic*. PLO 5. Wiesbaden: Harrassowitz, 1974.

Rubin, Aaron D. "Egyptian Loanwords in Hebrew." Pages 793–94 in volume 1 of *Encyclopedia of Hebrew Language and Linguistics*. Edited by Geoffrey Khan. 4 vols. Leiden: Brill, 2013.

Sáenz-Badillos, Angel. *A History of the Hebrew Language*. Translated by John Elwolde. Cambridge: Cambridge University Press, 1993.

Sanders, Seth. *The Invention of Hebrew*. Urbana: University of Illinois Press, 2009.

Sappan, Raphael. *The Typical Features of the Syntax of Biblical Poetry in Its Classical Period* [Hebrew]. Jerusalem: Kiryat Sefer, 1981.

Sass, Benjamin. *The Alphabet at the Turn of the Millennium: The West Semitic Alphabet ca. 1150–850 BCE. The Antiquity of the Arabian, Greek and Phrygian Alphabets*. Tel Aviv: Institute of Archaeology, 2005.

Sasson, Jack M. *Judges 1–12*. AB 6D. New Haven, CT: Yale University Press, 2014.

Schechter, Solomon. *Fragments of a Zadokite Work*. Documents of Jewish Sectaries 2. Cambridge: Cambridge University Press, 1910.

Schloen, J. David. "Caravans, Kenites, and *Casus Belli*: Enmity and Alliance in the Song of Deborah." *CBQ* 55 (1993): 18–38.

Schmid, Konrad. *The Old Testament: A Literary History*. Translated by Linda M. Maloney. Minneapolis: Fortress, 2012.

Schneider, Edgar. "Shakespeare in the Coves and Hollows? Toward a History of Southern English." Pages 17–35 in *English in the Southern United States*. Edited by Stephen J Nagle and Sara L. Sanders. Cambridge: Cambridge University Press, 2003.

Schniedewind, William M. "The Geopolitical History of Philistine Gath." *BASOR* 309 (1998): 69–77.

———. *A Social History of Hebrew: Its Origins through the Rabbinic Period*. ABRL. New Haven, CT: Yale University Press, 2013.

———. "Sociological Reflections on the Letter of a "Literate" Soldier (Lachish 3)." *ZAH* 13 (2000): 157–67.

Schniedewind, William M., and Daniel Sivan. "The Dialect of the Elisha-Elijah Narratives: A Case Study in Northern Hebrew." *JQR* 87 (1997): 303–37.

Schorch, Stefan. "'Vielleicht wird der Herr doch gnädig sein!': Das Konzept der Unverfügbarkeit *Jhwhs* in der alttestamentlichen Prophetie." Pages 457–68 in *Ex oriente Lux: Studien zur Theologie des Alten Testaments: Festschrift für Rüdiger Lux zum 65. Geburtstag*. Edited by Angelika Berlejung and Raik Heckl. Leipzig: Evangelische Verlagsanstalt, 2012.

———. *Die Vokale des Gesetzes*. Vol. 1: *Genesis*. BZAW 339. Berlin: de Gruyter, 2004.

Schüle, Andreas. "Zur Bedeutung der Formel *wajjehi* in Übergang zum mittelhebräischen Tempussystem." Pages 115–25 in *Studien zur hebräischen Grammatik*. Edited by Andreas Wagner. OBO 156. Fribourg: Presses Universitaires; Göttingen: Vandenhoeck & Ruprecht, 1997.

———. *Die Syntax der althebräischen Inschriften: Ein Beitrag zur historischen Grammatik des Hebräischen*. AOAT 270. Münster: Ugarit-Verlag; 2000.

Shulman, Ahouva. "The Use of Modal Verb Forms in Biblical Hebrew Prose." PhD diss., University of Toronto, 1996.

Seow, Choon-Leong. "Linguistic Evidence and the Dating of Qohelet." *JBL* 115 (1996): 643–66.

———. *Job 1–21: Interpretation and Commentary*. Illuminations. Grand Rapids, MI: Eerdmans, 2013.

Smith, Mark S. *Poetic Heroes: Literary Commemorations of Warriors and Warrior Culture in the Early Biblical World*. Grand Rapids, MI: Eerdmans, 2014.

Smoak, Jeremy D. *The Priestly Blessing in Inscription and Scripture: The Early History of Numbers 6:24–26*. New York: Oxford University Press, 2016.

Snyder, Laura J. *Reforming Philosophy: A Victorian Debate on Science and Society*. Chicago: University of Chicago Press, 2006.

Sommer, Benjamin D. "Dating Pentateuchal Texts and the Perils of Pseudo-Historicism." Pages 85–108 in *The Pentateuch: International Perspectives on Current Research*. Edited by Thomas B. Dozeman, Konrad Schmid, and Baruch J. Schwartz. FAT 78. Tübingen: Mohr Siebeck, 2011.

Stager, Lawrence E. "Archaeology, Ecology, and Social History: Background Themes to the Song of Deborah." Pages 221–34 in *Congress Volume: Jerusalem 1986*. Edited by John A. Emerton. VTSup 40. Leiden: Brill, 1988.

———. "Biblical Philistines: A Hellenistic Literary Creation?" Pages 375–84 in *"I Will Speak the Riddles of Ancient Times": Archaeological and Historical Studies in Honor of Amihai Mazar*. Edited by Aren M. Maeir and Pierre de Miroschedji. Winona Lake, IN: Eisenbrauns, 2006.

Steiner, Richard C. *The Case for Fricative-Laterals in Proto-Semitic*. AOS 59. New Haven: American Oriental Society, 1977.

———. "דָּת and עֵין: Two Verbs Masquerading as Nouns in Moses' Blessing (Deuteronomy 33:2,28." *JBL* 115 (1996): 693–717.

Steymans, Hans Ulrich. *Deuteronomium 28 und die adê zur Thronfolgeregelung Asarhaddons: Segen und Fluch im Alten Orient und in Israel*. OBO 145. Freiburg: Universitätsverlag; Göttingen: Vandenhoeck & Ruprecht, 1995.

———. "Deuteronomy 28 and Tell Tayinat." *Verbum et Ecclesia* 34 (2013): https://doi.org/10.4102/ve.v34i2.870.

Syring, Wolf-Dieter. *Hiob und sein Anwalt: Die Prosatexte des Hiobbuches und ihre Rolle in seiner Redaktions- und Rezeptionsgchichte*. BZAW 336. Berlin: de Gruyter, 2003.

Tadmor, Hayim, and Shigeo Yamada. *The Royal Inscriptions of Tiglath-pileser III (744–727 BC) and Shalmaneser V (726–722 BC), Kings of Assyria.* Winona Lake, IN: Eisenbrauns, 2011.

Talmon, Shemeryahu. "The Paleo-Hebrew Alphabet and Biblical Text Criticism." Pages 125–70 in *Text and Canon in the Hebrew Bible: Collected Studies.* Winona Lake, IN: Eisenbrauns, 2010.

Talshir, David. "The Habitat and History of Hebrew during the Second Temple Period." Pages 251–75 in *Biblical Hebrew: Studies in Chronology and Typology.* Edited by Ian Young. JSOTSup 369. London: T&T Clark, 2003.

Tawil, Hayim ben Yosef. *An Akkadian Lexical Companion for Biblical Hebrew: Etymological-Semantic and Idiomatic Equivalents with Supplement on Biblical Aramaic.* Jersey City, NJ: KTAV, 2009.

Teeter, Andrew. *Scribal Laws: Exegetical Variation in the Textual Transmission of Biblical Law in the Late Second Temple Period.* FAT 92. Tübingen: Mohr Siebeck, 2014.

Thomason, Sarah G. *Language Contact: An Introduction.* Edinburgh: Edinburgh University Press, 2001.

Tov, Emanuel. *Textual Criticism of the Hebrew Bible.* 3rd ed. Minneapolis: Fortress, 2012.

Tsevat, Mattitiahu. *A Study of the Language of the Biblical Psalms.* Philadelphia: Society of Biblical Literature, 1955.

Tucker, Aviezer. *Our Knowledge of the Past: A Philosophy of Historiography.* Cambridge: Cambridge University Press, 2004.

Uehlinger, Christoph. "Nimrod." Pages 627–30 in *DDD.*

Uehlinger, Christoph, and Susanne Müller Trufaut. "Ezekiel 1, Babylonian Cosmological Scholarship and Iconography: Attempts at Further Refinement." *TZ* 57 (2001): 140–71.

Ulrich, Eugene. "The Developmental Composition of the Book of Isaiah: Light from 1QIsa[a] on Additions in the MT." *DSD* 8 (2001): 288–305.

Vanderhooft, David S. "Biblical Perspectives on Nineveh and Babylon: Views from the Endangered Periphery." *Canadian Society for Mesopotamian Studies Journal* 3 (2008): 83–92.

———. "Ezekiel in and on Babylon." *Transeuphratène* 46 (2014): 99–119.

———. *The Neo-Babylonian Empire and Babylon in the Latter Prophets.* HSM 59. Atlanta: Scholars Press, 1999.

———. "ʾel-mĕdînâ ûmĕdînâ kiktābāh: Scribes and Scripts in Yehud and in Achaemenid Transeuphratene." Pages 529–44 in *Judah and Judeans in the Achaemenid Period: Negotiating Identity in an International Context.* Edited by Oded Lipschits, Gary Knoppers, and Manfred Oeming. Winona Lake, IN: Eisenbrauns, 2011.

Wagner, Max. *Die lexikalischen und grammatikalischen Aramaismen im alttestamentlichen Hebräisch.* BZAW 96. Berlin: Töpelmann: 1966.

Weinfeld, Moshe. *Deuteronomy and the Deuteronomic School.* Oxford: Clarendon Press, 1972.

———. "Julius Wellhausen's Understanding of the Law of Ancient Israel and Its Fallacies." *Shnaton* 4 (1980): 62–93 (Hebrew).

———. "Sabbatical Year and Jubilee in the Pentateuchal Laws." Pages 39–62 in *The Law in the Bible and in Its Environment.* Edited by Timo Veijola. Göttingen: Vandenhoeck & Ruprecht, 1990.

———. "Traces of Assyrian Treaty Formulae in Deuteronomy." *Bib* 36 (1965): 417–47.

Weitzman, Steven. "Why Did the Qumran Community Write in Hebrew?" *JAOS* 119 (1999): 35–45.

Wellhausen, Julius. *Prolegomena to the History of Israel.* Translated by John S. Black and Allan Menzies. Edinburgh: Black, 1885.

———. *Der Text der Bücher Samuelis.* Göttingen: Vandenhoeck & Ruprecht, 1871.

Whewell, William. *Novum Organon renovatum: Being the Second Part of the Philosophy of the Inductive Sciences.* 3rd ed. London: Parker, 1858.

Williamson, H. G. M. "Eschatology in Chronicles." Pages 162–95 in *Studies in Persian Period History and Historiography.* FAT 38. Tübingen: Mohr Siebeck, 2004.

———. *Isaiah 1–5.* ICC. London: T&T Clark, 2006.

———. "Scribe and Scroll: Revisiting the Great Isaiah Scroll from Qumran." Pages 329–42 in *Making a Difference: Essays on the Bible and Judaism in Honor of Tamara Cohn Eskenazi.* Edited by David J. A. Clines, Kent Harold Richards, and Jacob L. Wright. Sheffield: Phoenix Press, 2012.

———. "The Setting of Deutero-Isaiah: Some Linguistic Considerations." Pages 253–67 in *Exile and Return: The Babylonian Context.* Edited by Jonathan Stökl and Caroline Waerzeggers. BZAW 478. Berlin: de Gruyter, 2015.

Wilson, Edward O. *Consilience: The Unity of Knowledge.* New York: Knopf, 1998.

Wise, Michael O. *Language and Literacy in Roman Judaea: A Study of the Bar Kokhba Documents.* ABRL. New Haven, CT: Yale University Press, 2015.

Wilson-Wright, Aren. "From Persepolis to Jerusalem: A Reevaluation of Old-Persian-Hebrew Contact in the Achaemenid Period." *VT* 65 (2015): 152–67.

———. "A Reevaluation of the Semitic Direct Object Markers." *HS* 57 (2016): 7–15.

Winitzer, Abraham. "Assyriology and Jewish Studies in Tel Aviv: Ezekiel among the Babylonian *Literati.*" Pages 163–216 in *Encounters by the Rivers of Babylon: Scholarly Conversations between Jews, Iranians, and Babylonians in Antiquity.* Edited by Uri Gabbay and Shai Secunda. Tübingen: Mohr Siebeck, 2014.

Woodhouse, Robert. "The Biblical Shibboleth Story in the Light of Late Egyptian Perceptions of Semitic Sibilants: Reconciling Divergent Views." *JAOS* 123 (2003): 271–89.

Wright, Jacob L. "Deborah's War Memorial: The Composition of Judges 4–5 and the Politics of War Commemoration." *ZAW* 123 (2011): 516–34.

Wright, Richard M. *Linguistic Evidence for the Pre-Exilic Date of the Yahwistic Source.* LHBOTS 419. London: T&T Clark, 2005.

Yasur-Landau, Assaf. *The Philistines and Aegean Migration at the End of the Late Bronze Age*. Cambridge: Cambridge University Press, 2010.

Young, Ian. "Ancient Hebrew without Authors." *JSem* 25 (2016): 972–1003.

———. *Diversity in Pre-Exilic Hebrew*. FAT 5. Tübingen: Mohr Siebeck, 1993.

———. "Late Biblical Hebrew and Hebrew Inscriptions." Pages 276–311 in *Biblical Hebrew: Studies in Chronology and Typology*. Edited by Ian Young. JSOTSup 369. London: T&T Clark, 2003.

———. "Late Biblical Hebrew and the Qumran Pesher Habakkuk." *JHS* 8 (2008): https://doi.org/10.5508/jhs.2008.v8.a25.

———. "Observations on the Third Person Masculine Singular Pronominal Suffix *-h* in Hebrew Biblical Texts." *HS* 42 (2001): 225–42.

Young, Ian, and Robert Rezetko, with the assistance of Martin Ehrensvärd. *Linguistic Dating of Biblical Texts*. 2 vols. London: Equinox 2008.

Zevit, Ziony. "Dating Ruth: Legal, Linguistic, and Historical Observations." *ZAW* 117 (2005): 574–600.

Zukerman, Alexander. "Titles of 7th Century BCE Philistine Rulers and Their Historical-Cultural Background." *BO* 68 (2011): 465–71.

Index of Scripture and Other Ancient Sources

Hebrew Bible

Index of Authors

Index of Subjects

Index of Words and Expressions

Hebrew